THE FROZEN FRONTIER

Polar Bound Through the Northwest Passage

JANE MAUFE

ADLARD COLES NAUTICAL

BLOOMSBURY

LONDON · OXFORD · NEW YORK · NEW DELHI · SYDNEY

Adlard Coles Nautical
An imprint of Bloomsbury Publishing Plc

50 Bedford Square
London
WC1B 3DP
UK

1385 Broadway
New York
NY 10018
USA

www.bloomsbury.com
www.adlardcoles.com

ADLARD COLES, ADLARD COLES NAUTICAL and the Buoy logo
are trademarks of Bloomsbury Publishing Plc

First published 2017

© Jane Maufe, 2017

British Library Cataloguing-in-Publication Data
A catalogue record for this book is available from the British Library.

Library of Congress Cataloguing-in-Publication data has been applied for.

ISBN: HB: 978-1-4729-3571-7
ePDF: 978-1-4729-3574-8
ePub: 978-1-4729-3573-1

2 4 6 8 10 9 7 5 3 1

Typeset in Minion Pro by Deanta Global Publishing Services, Chennai, India
Printed and bound in Great Britain by CPI Group (UK) Ltd,
Croydon CR0 4YY

To find out more about our authors and books visit www.bloomsbury.com.
Here you will find extracts, author interviews, details of forthcoming
events and the option to sign up for our newsletters.

To my parents, Commander and Mrs Conrad Franklin Rawnsley,
and to Rear-Admiral Sir John Franklin RN, my four-times
great-uncle, for giving us a lead in the right direction

CONTENTS

CONTENTS

MAPS

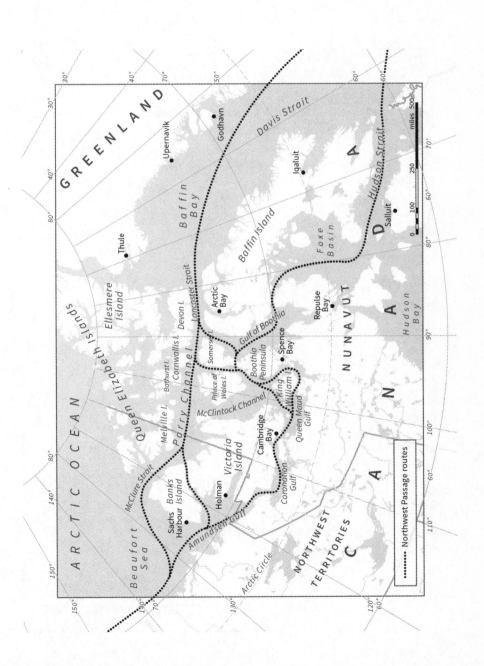

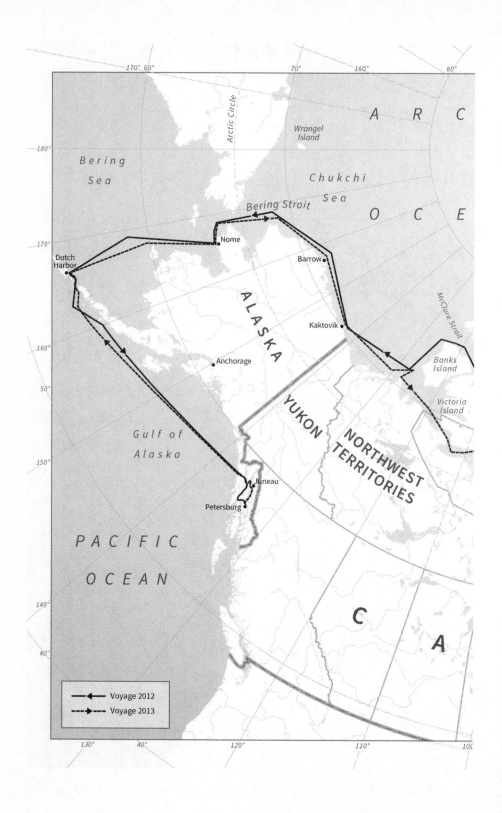

Voyage 2012

Voyage 2013

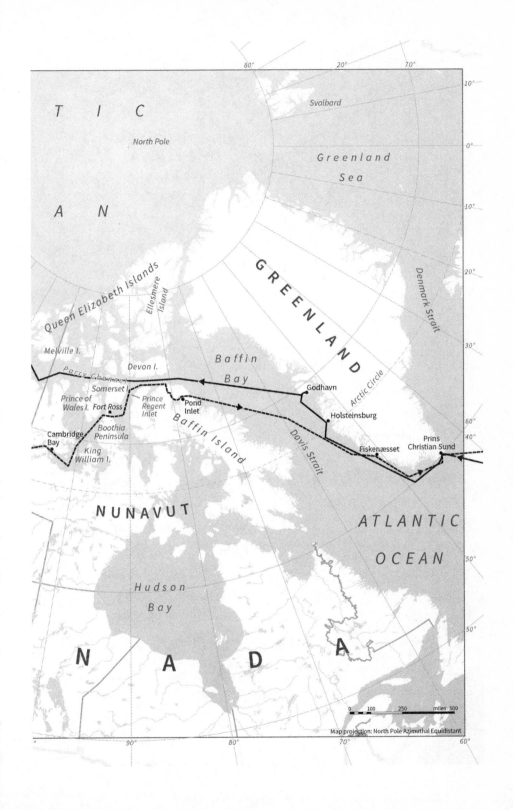

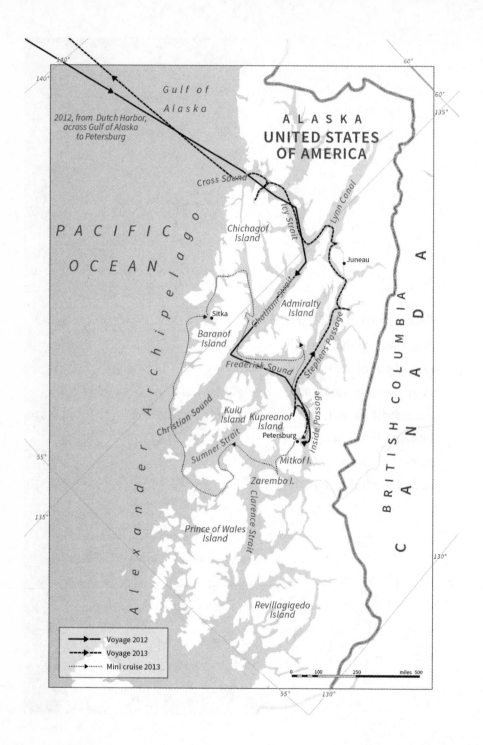

2012, from Dutch Harbor,
across Gulf of Alaska
to Petersburg

Gulf of
Alaska

ALASKA
UNITED STATES
OF AMERICA

PACIFIC

OCEAN

Cross Sound

Chichagof
Island

Icy Strait

Lynn Canal

Juneau

Admiralty
Island

Sitka

Chatham Strait

Baranof
Island

Stephens Passage

Frederick Sound

Christian Sound

Kuiu
Island

Kupreanof
Island

Inside Passage

Petersburg

Sumner Strait

Mitkof I.

Zarembo I.

Prince of Wales
Island

Clarence Strait

BRITISH COLUMBIA

CANADA

Revillagigedo
Island

Alexander Archipelago

Voyage 2012
Voyage 2013
Mini cruise 2013

0   100   250   miles 500

PREFACE

Please note that this is not intended to be a scientific treatise of Arctic conditions, global warming or the lack of it and such like. Nor is it a monologue of dreary course alterations, wind directions, sail changes, reefing points and compass bearings (True or Magnetic, Real or Imagined). In fact, the greatest magnetism around is that between the captain and his crew, and so it is a personal account of our experiences voyaging together through these frozen wastes in the hope that we and our hull would still be intact when we came out the other end.

PART ONE

DEPARTURE

ONE

THE CHRISTMAS CARD

I N DECEMBER 2011 I RECEIVED A Christmas card from David Scott Cowper, a man who had once kissed me over forty years earlier. In it, he asked me to accompany him on his next expedition to the High Arctic to transit the Northwest Passage, departing at the end of July 2012. His ambition was to attempt the most northerly route, via the frozen McClure Strait north of Banks Island, and, if successful, his would be the first private vessel ever to make the passage, a goal that had been eagerly sought for more than four hundred years.

I was hesitant. Did he really want his bachelor stronghold invaded by a woman? I had not been in touch with David since I was about twenty-nine, so there had been a lot of water under the bridge. He thought that since I am the four-times great-niece of Rear Admiral Sir John Franklin I might like to see the area in which, back in 1848, he and his two ships, the *Erebus* and the *Terror*, and their entire crew – a complement of 129 men – were engulfed by ice and perished from cold and from rotten tinned food. Had they survived being iced in during that winter, they were on track to unveil the secrets of the Northwest Passage the following summer.

3

My life had come to something of a standstill following the death of my husband from Alzheimer's after twelve years of deterioration. This would be a new challenge and a big adventure. I did not sit on the fence for long.

The full transit of the Northwest Passage is acknowledged by the Scott Polar Research Institute in Cambridge, England, who monitor all transits, to be from the Davis Strait in the east through to the Bering Strait in the west on the 66 and a half degree latitude of the Arctic Circle. Sometimes people say they have been through the Northwest Passage, and while they may indeed have journeyed through the myriad islands scattered throughout this area, most of them have not made the entire transit, as many have flown out to Greenland to avoid crossing the North Atlantic, and will have boarded their vessel north of the Arctic Circle.

David had a great desire to add another 'first' to his already impressive list of transits of the Northwest Passage. He had only two more to win to have completed all seven possible transits (see page 302), and to be the first to do so. All his earlier records had been made solo, and it didn't stop with the Arctic; he was the first to sail solo around the world in both directions, and the first to motor around the world alone. In all, he had completed six solo circumnavigations of the globe, two under sail and four under motor – no mean achievement.

This time the goal was to be the first vessel ever to pass through the Northwest Passage by the most northerly, most ice-bound route, the McClure Strait, and quite possibly we might even have been the first vessel of any description to have transited the entire Northwest Passage by this route. The ice in the strait makes the passage fickle and uncertain. For most of the year its dense layer of ice is ventured upon solely by polar bears and seals, and accessed only by the occasional icebreaker. In late summer, the grip of the ice might weaken enough for the passage to open up for a few hours. It did, so in 2011, but only for a matter of hours. We hoped for the same in 2012.

David's custom-built 30 ton aluminium, self-righting, all-weather vessel, *Polar Bound* (50 tons burthen with fuel & stores aboard) is twelve times the required Lloyd's specification and regarded as the strongest surface vessel for her size in the world. Based on the lines of a lifeboat with lower deck level at her waist midships, she has an upswept bow, and rounded stern with fixed centre ladder down to the water to facilitate boarding from a dinghy, and has knife edges at the bow and stern to protect her from ice impact. She has four watertight bulkheads, is double hulled in the engine room, and double bottomed in the for'rd section. She is very distinctive, with centre wheelhouse and coachroof being painted bright yellow with grey hull below, and is instantly recognised in the Arctic and Antarctic and many places around the globe.

David had planned our 2012 departure to coincide with a brief possible thaw by calculating the days required for the voyage from Cumbria, where *Polar Bound* was snugly berthed in the marina at Whitehaven. This was going to be non-stop, except for one night in Northern Ireland to take on fuel and a couple of topping-up stops in Greenland. *Polar Bound* has the capacity to take on 10 tons of fuel – sufficient for 5,000 miles if not pushed beyond an average of 6 knots.

Several emails and telephone calls were exchanged with David's friend and ice master Peter Semitouk, who, as an amateur and volunteer, monitors conditions from his home in Winnipeg. Peter has the advantage of having lived at a place called Cambridge Bay, halfway along the southerly transit route. Familiar with conditions in that region, and knowing where to do his research, he was best placed to report on the forecasts and expectations. At no time did he state which route to take – the decision and responsibility for that lay with David alone.

This was to be a major expedition. The boat had to be prepared for every eventuality as we had no idea whether this was going to be the year when a transit might be possible, the worst scenario being that we get frozen in with no escape until a thaw the following year. Even release a year later wouldn't be a certainty – sometimes the thaw is not sufficient to allow navigation. And as the summer in England drew on, we learnt of five or six other vessels that were already up in the Arctic and hoping to make the transit via the accepted southerly route. This gave rise to some unease in case someone had the same idea as David to try the most northerly route and might even make the attempt before we did. This would have been a terrible blow.

TWO

MY REUNION
WITH DAVID

I WAS INTRODUCED TO DAVID WHEN I was twenty-three or twenty-four by a mutual friend with whom he shared his digs in London. The friend thought that as we had a common interest it would be fun for us to meet. We were both working in London at the time, and in addition David was attending night school for three years to gain the Board of Trade Ship Master's Ticket. This was for merchant seamen, and far harder than a Yachtmaster's Certificate. Meanwhile I was doing the Captain OM Watts Postal Navigation Course, just for my own amusement; I had a full-time secretarial job in London.

I shall always remember that first encounter, early one evening. My flatmate Meg Dashwood answered the door – by prior arrangement with me as I was feeling nervous. I was in the basement at the kitchen table with my navigation course spread out. An exchange of voices floated down, a quick step on the stair and then David entered the room – a tall, slim, athletic figure with dark hair, wonderfully bright eyes and a warm smile, though I was somewhat put out to notice that at the age of twenty-five he appeared to have a thinning patch right on the top of his head. He was dressed in a pinstripe suit with waistcoat, collar and tie, all of which met with much approval. At that time men were still wearing bowler hats, and they nearly all wore suits.

As we shook hands I noticed his firm handshake and confident, enthusiastic manner. He took an immediate interest in the course I was doing. The chart I was reading focused on the area around the Wash, and we studied that together for a while with David explaining some of the symbols to me. We chattered about this and that and I said how difficult it was to remember the points of the compass. 'Oh, it's easy,' he said, 'you just have to remember that it is every twelve and half degrees between points, and if you are going from the north to the east, the names of the points are towards the next intermediate principal point – i.e. N, NE, E – so in between N and E is N, NxE, NNE, NExN, NE, NExE, ENE and ExN,' he chirped in triumph. I began to get even more confused, but he assured me that it was all 'easy-peasy'. I had to be content with his lesson number one, but I found him a lot more interesting than the course.

After that first encounter he began to ring me up at work several times a week. We had lengthy conversations, which sometimes held long pauses while he was trying to think of something else to say to keep me on the line, and I was beginning to wonder if he had rung off. I used to transfer the call to the boardroom of the company I was working for so my boss couldn't hear me through the wall. After about half an hour, I would have to sink down to the floor as the telephone cord was too short to stretch to the boardroom chairs. I was working for the Association of Land and Property Owners in Bressenden Place and I only used to be given about one letter a week to type, so I had the connivance of my boss, who was probably quite pleased I was being entertained. He had no objection to my studying my navigation course at work – he began to take an interest in it himself, and asked me about it sometimes, and what mark I got from my postal instructor. He was even apologetic if he had to interrupt my studies.

David's and my lives went different ways a year or so later. I was getting itchy feet and feeling bored with the superficiality of London life, or at least that was how I saw it then. I answered an advertisement in *The Times* and ended up with a crewing job in the Windward Islands. Before I left, David invited me to go to the Odeon in Kensington to see a film. Afterwards, being a true gentleman, he saw me home to my front door in Abingdon Villas where, to my enormous surprise, he made a move towards me and the next minute I was receiving a kiss like no other – I thought I would never be able to breathe again. After some minutes in the moonlight, and a moment of embarrassed silence, he said, 'Well, I better be on my way then.' That was the last time I saw David until many years later, after his marriage, when I spent ten days or so with him and his wife in his first commissioned sailing boat, *Airedale*. I was helping them to move her round from Scotland to the east coast through the Caledonian Canal, and I spent my twenty-ninth birthday aboard with them.

My strongest recollection of that passage was when David's wife was selecting something for supper from under one of the bunks. Her hand finally settled on a tin of Fray Bentos Steak and Kidney Pie.

'There,' she said, handing it to me.

'That won't be enough for *three* of us, surely?' I replied.

'Oh! I don't think he'd allow us to have two!'

Extravagance can only be permitted on the boat itself; it seems that nothing has changed as all these years later, he still does not have much idea of portion size – it's no wonder his trousers keep falling down.

A few months later I agreed to a last-minute crewing job, sailing across the Atlantic in a 43-foot ketch, *Tallulah*, with the owners, Plat and Philip Allen, members of the Royal Cruising Club. It proved to be a wonderfully fortunate and life-changing choice, as on that boat I met my husband-to-be, David Maufe.

And so a long time passed with both of us being married, and having our respective families to bring up, although a lot of the time David was away at sea. Occasionally I received a telephone call, and the odd postcard from some frozen quarter of the globe, but our paths were not to cross again until he made the first move following the death of my husband.

Just before leaving my home in Norfolk for a winter sojourn in Portugal, I decided to take down the Christmas cards I had received as I didn't want to return in the spring and find them curling at the edges and gathering dust. I went through them methodically; some went into the bin, others were made into tags for future presents, and some were put aside. I hesitated when it came to David's, and finally decided that I would take it with me and perhaps respond to him from sunnier climes. After some deliberation, once I was settled in my winter quarters, curiosity overcame me and I sent him a short email. This brought forth a swift request that any future correspondence should be addressed to his personal email and not his office. He is a methodical two-finger typist and even this brief reply must have taken some time to create, but it had sufficient worth to arouse my interest.

He asked me to let him know when I was back in England. I did so, and he told me he had to come south to Norfolk from his home in Newcastle to collect the windows for *Polar Bound*, which were being refurbished by a specialist firm. A date was fixed for a visit, and I seem to remember that it was a sunny spring day for I had just been cutting the grass in my garden and looked somewhat dishevelled when I answered his knock. (I have a magnificent front door which may well weigh more than half a ton – it is huge and very heavy;

the door bell is inaudible, and so most callers have to resort to the knocker, which makes an equally impressive reverberation around the house.)

We stood rather awkwardly in the hall, both speaking at once while we took stock of one another. David looked as tall and slim and upright as I last remembered him thirty-nine years earlier, but probably with even less hair. He had high cheekbones and somewhat sallow colouring and hazel eyes, but the eyes still had that wonderful enthusiasm and vibrancy, and his voice, well, that was another thing. A friend once told me his voice was 'to die for'. I wouldn't go that far, but it certainly made me go weak at the knees.

His bag was left forgotten in the car and he followed me into the kitchen for a cup of tea. Once we had satisfied protocol, he wanted to see my sailing dinghy, so we set off the mile and a half to the field above the slipway, where my boat lives in the summer. I felt rather embarrassed that he should express such enthusiasm for something I would have thought of little interest to a world-renowned lone ocean sailor of the seven seas, with a list of awards as long as your arm, and a member of the Royal Cruising Club to boot. I recall being most impressed by his courteous manners in holding the car door open for me, and also walking on the outside when we were in the road. These things were normal at one time, but now they are largely forgotten – perhaps I had met another Edwardian, like myself!

We parked nearby and then he wanted to see the cover taken off and proceeded to examine everything in the boat. My little dinghy is called *Sorceress*, named after my grandparents' Bristol Channel pilot cutter, which they owned before the war, and in which they voyaged to Biscay and beyond with a paid hand. She belongs to the Adventurer class, originally designed to train naval cadets; she has a Bermudan sloop rig, lifting centreboard and is comparable in performance to a Mirror. Honour satisfied – but not before David had spotted that my downhaul had been reeved incorrectly and wasn't achieving anything. It had been like that for about forty years and no one else had ever noticed. Now, however, my future attempts for supremacy on the waters of Burnham Overy Staithe looked certain to succeed and I would be able to outmanoeuvre the Mirrors when running – I usually just managed to beat them close-hauled. As we put the cover back on I became aware that David must have imagined he was securing a large vessel against Arctic storms. He lashed the three ties with so many complicated knots that she was safeguarded against a hurricane, and the next time I took her sailing it took me twenty minutes to untie everything.

Returning to the village, I offered David a drink and then learnt that he is a virtual teetotaller. I persuaded him to have a glass of wine, then immediately felt rather uncomfortable that I was downing a whisky, and quite likely to have a second one too – never mind the wine with dinner. I gave him moules marinières – it was a particularly good choice as he very much liked them and I learnt rather a good way of eating them by following his example and using the first one as tongs for the remainder. He also taught me how to peel an orange by cutting off its top and bottom and drawing the knife in longitudinal segments around its girth – why had I never done that before! We talked on into the evening, then I showed him to the spare room – a large blue room, which he seemed a bit lost in. We picked out a few sailing books for him to look at, and then, having offered to bring him a cup of tea in the morning, I firmly closed the door and retreated to my room.

The following morning I was knocking on his door at 7.30 with tea in hand and found him wide awake, reading. Ensconced in my dressing gown and slippers, I sat down in the old armchair across the room and we became lost in talk as the tea got cold. Time passed and I was conscious that he had a long drive ahead back up north. After a good breakfast, he was on his way, having extended a return invitation for me to visit him in Newcastle, and perhaps also to drive over to Whitehaven to have a look at *Polar Bound*. This I readily accepted, and said I would be in touch shortly.

During this brief visit, I was acutely aware of David's 'maleness'. Everything about him spoke 'man': his gestures, his stance, the way he held a newspaper, how he scrunched up his knuckles on the floor when he was examining a chart. He had no need of bad language to adopt masculinity, and not for him the pomades and potions of modern man. Indeed, he was totally without vanity and, as I came to learn, had frequently to be reminded to get his hair cut when it began to curl on his collar. I was very taken.

A date was fixed for a week or so later and I paid a return visit, spending a night with old friends in Harrogate en route. On arrival, I was somewhat put out. No sooner had he greeted me and opened the boot of my car to get out my luggage than a woman passer-by hailed him and they became immersed in conversation. I was left to fend for myself. The front door was open, and I carried my luggage inside and upstairs to his library, to which I had been appointed. Here a single bed from his student days was overlooked by an array of wonderful books on the Arctic and Antarctic and several magnificent oil paintings. I began to sort out my belongings, from time to time taking a surreptitious glance out of the window at the conversational scene below, to which there seemed to be no end. I felt somewhat annoyed, having just arrived after a five-hour drive specially to see him. When I asked him later who she was, he passed off the encounter in a very casual, offhand manner, and was noncommittal.

Later on I had a tour of his house. It started in the basement, where chaos reigned. Having pushed the door open, you had to step over several enormous rolls of carpet and around cardboard boxes, items of cast-out furniture and lampshades, only to come across leaning stacks of fly-blown dusty Venetian blinds, discarded aluminium saucepans, tins of unused, long-congealed paint, rubber dinghies, a giant Chinese painted fan, and, most intriguingly, the inside-out skin of a penguin, all soft and luxuriously furry inside so that you could slide your hand in and out as if it were a muff, with rough and horny dried skin on the outside; this had been retrieved from a beach in Antarctica. Whale vertebrae you could barely lift jostled for position with huge caribou horns that threatened to pierce your legs; among these were some ancient, yellow-stained teeth and claws. Far in the corner stood a forlorn, petulant-looking washing machine with mouldering packets of unused soapsuds perched on top, alongside a hopeful anticipatory washing basket with some oddments draped over its rim. It was no better in the room next door, which served as a workshop. Where you would unearth any required item, I do not know. It was most certainly a bachelor stronghold, and the dwelling of an adventurer and explorer, I decided.

The sitting room upstairs was more orderly, but even that had heaps of papers, magazines, charts, files and objects stacked against the walls and under the furniture. The grand piano, which I had taken in with an appreciative sweep of the eyes, was covered in loose change, keys, small marine instruments, files, parallel rules and tide tables, which rendered it unusable. (When I finally managed to clear the top sufficiently to try the piano out, I discovered that it had the most beautiful singing tone. And no wonder – it was a Blüthner.) Two comfortable armchairs beckoned and, on removing a few objects from one of them, I sank back while David made me a cup of tea and we took stock of the situation. I could see I was going to have my work cut out here. Kleptomania, I wondered? No, I didn't think so; just an inability to focus on any one thing to its conclusion. I began to realise that David might prove to be high maintenance. As time has gone on, this has turned out to be the case.

That evening he took me out to supper and we were not short of conversation – there was so much to catch up on. The following morning, it was his turn to bring me a cup of tea, and I had to give him an appreciative hug as no one had brought me tea in bed for years. As there was nowhere else to sit, he perched on the side of the bed while I sipped my tea with the sheets clutched modestly around me, and he asked me if I would like to use the bathroom first. In due course we both arrived downstairs, though he had had a head start and porridge awaited; so he did have some culinary skills, I observed.

When breakfast was over, we cleared the table together, and he seemed so hopeless at organising his kitchen storage cupboard of groceries and crockery that I became somewhat overwhelmed and, in an impulsive gesture, threw my arms around him. This had an electrifying effect. The unspoken desire of the intermediate years fell away around us in a split second, and I found I had invited rather more than I bargained for. After quite some time and in the moments that followed, we each regained our self-possession and David said quietly, eyeing me steadily, 'Well, I think that makes up for lost time.'

During the night that followed, in the small hours, David whispered, 'I should have married you years ago.' No doubt that has been said by lovers the world over many a time, but life doesn't always follow the obvious pattern – people are wayward and contrary, and we were both young, and for my part totally inexperienced. It was not until I was twenty-nine that I finally met the man I would marry in a sailing boat crossing the Atlantic – a wonderful test of compatibility – and we were very happily married for thirty-eight years.

The next morning David had to resume work at his office. He looked immaculate, with detachable stiff collar and tie, and I was put in mind of another era; one in which I, too, would like to have lived. It was later than normal for him as we walked briskly through the park and university environs of Newcastle, arm in arm.

'I am so happy,' he said spontaneously, out of the blue. It gave me a wonderful feeling of pleasure and contentment. I, too, was immeasurably happy for the first time in many years, and that feeling remains with me. 'In my eyes,' he continued, 'you are quite beautiful.' I had the nagging doubt that, perhaps, in someone's else's, this might not be the case – however, as we know, 'beauty is in the eye of the beholder', so I had to be content with that.

Some nights later, he said, 'Oh, I *do* love you *so much*!'

'What is it particularly you love?' I asked in an endeavour to find out how this attraction could be enhanced. 'Oh,' came the reply, as he crushed me in a huge bear hug. 'Everything – everything about you – your hair, your voice, your scarf, your smell, your pearls . . .' He tailed off, then somewhat incongruously added, 'Your car.'

'My car!' I said incredulously, thinking of my Skoda estate.

'Well, just the sight of you in it,' he said. 'You know,' he continued, 'I feel I could say absolutely anything to you, anything.'

'Well, I feel exactly the same way – that also applies to me.'

We were like two delighted children who had been given their heart's desire. It was a new world opening up; together we could conquer it and achieve whatever we liked.

As for smell, I knew what he meant. Everyone has a presence – something to do with their bearing and manner, and their aura – which sets them apart from the rest. I think it is a deep-rooted animal instinct that causes us, when passing people in the street, to single one person out and take a more in-depth appraisal. Most people are passed by with barely a glance but every now and again, on rare occasions, someone stands out and you feel an immediate, reciprocal interest in them.

David and I are very alike, thinking and acting the same way on many different things. We are also exactly the same when it comes to any big task – we are masters of prevarication. We put off the important issue, which we know we can deal with but would rather think about a bit more, while getting sidetracked on to little niggling things that need attention, aren't essential but are easy and enjoyable to undertake. The 'big issue' awaits application at some future date. Why do today what you can put off until tomorrow? Much better to have a mad scramble at the last minute. Working under pressure is so much more fulfilling and somehow you imagine that you will complete the task more efficiently.

I spent several days up north getting to know something of David's life and activities while he was busy in his office with dictation and telephone calls. He manages his own commercial property interests, which include running a boatyard in Scotland and a storage depot in Newcastle, and in between fulfils his sailing ambitions, planning his expeditions with great diligence. If I couldn't do anything useful, I took myself off for a bit of window shopping. Newcastle centre is full of magnificent Georgian buildings and shops, and hordes of people pushing their way around Northumberland Street bumping into each other. Then I discovered the wonderful Grainger Market where virtually anything could be bought. I would be lost in the midst of all this when my mobile telephone would ring; it was invariably David. 'Where are you?' he would bark. 'Do you want to come with me to so-and-so?' Or, rather more urgently, 'Are we having any lunch today?' Or, 'I'm in such and such a shop. I'll see you in five minutes.' Or, 'What are we having for supper?' He could even pursue me into the hairdresser's in this manner, while I was sitting under the drier. His internal dynamo could be quite exhausting, but it was great fun.

He always wanted to know where I was and what I was doing. I felt glad that somebody was there who was taking such an interest. I loved the excitement of it all. The only shop we couldn't go to together was a jeweller for a lovely little ring, as sadly David was long ago spoken for, but the irony of this was that he kept on saying, 'You're mine now, and I'm not going to let you go', and somehow, in this constant reaffirmation, he seemed to convince himself that this was so. But, of course, as we all know it is said that a sailor has a girl in every port, and it was no good speculating as to how many ports, or girls, which causes a certain disquiet. Instead we spent quite a bit of time buying dried fruit and nuts for David's hungry corners, and bird seed and maggots for the voracious flock that descended on David's garden every day. Later, since it gave him so much enjoyment, I commissioned a bird table identical to my own in Norfolk and gave it to him for his birthday.

One day I was accompanying him on a mission to a supplier for a part for *Polar Bound* and, as we converged at a roundabout into a long queue of traffic, a rather hostile 4x4 with a red-faced driver pushed in to our right and tried to gain supremacy in the queue, but he'd reckoned without David. The man flashed his lights and shouted out of the window, 'You b— f— . .'. His last words were thankfully snatched away. As we drew level again, David coolly dropped his own window, leant out and, as we passed the man's towering vehicle, shouted out, 'What did you call yourself?' Luckily at that moment the jam moved on and we escaped unscathed.

THREE

HOUSE RULES

DAVID WAS BUSY WITH THE PREPARATIONS for our departure. This included organising his vast library of charts, putting together his specially printed logbooks – which were enormously cumbersome and heavy – and gathering and sorting electronic equipment, tools and audio devices. He had earphones, though I had none, but occasionally, when we were squeezed up on our bunk in the boat, he would poke one of his earpieces into my ear and we would listen to some music above the thud of the Gardner engine. Also among his equipment was a rifle.

Meanwhile I had to get home again. I had my own agenda: closing my house, seeing to necessary paperwork, making a new will and notifying my relations of my plans. I also felt very vulnerable about the rifle. I did not have the slightest clue how to load it, how to cock it, and least of all how to fire it. And I didn't like the idea of facing up to a polar bear without one. I was not going to provide Brumas with dinner without at least an attempt at self-defence. So I went to what I thought was a shooting school to ask if they would give me lessons in handling a rifle. The place I had in mind turned out to be a rifle range, and they

19

were not able to help. All I could do was hope that David would be on hand to come to my rescue.

After a particularly long, tiring day I decided to have an early night and was in a deep sleep when at around 1.30am the telephone started ringing. It gave me a bit of a fright, and it must have rung for nearly half a minute before I came to my senses. It was David, wildly excited and thoroughly over stimulated having just returned home from watching a James Bond film. Full of the thrill and excitement and quite sure he was Bond himself, he had to give me a complete run-through of the film while I was still trying to gather my wits – I was not at all pleased.

Another morning, sitting at my desk and talking to a woman on the telephone from the Anglian Water Board about a possible allowance to which I might be entitled for surface water drainage (rather than contributing to their sewerage system), my mobile rang. It was David, shouting, 'I need to see you now.' His bellowing voice carried across to the lady from Anglian Water, who became somewhat prim.

'I'll call you back in a minute,' I said to David. 'I'm just speaking to someone on the other phone.'

I managed to conclude my conversation before the mobile rang again, moments later, with more impatient declarations from David. It never seems to occur to him that if my landline is busy, quite possibly I might be on the other end of it; instead he must at once, with not a minute to lose, get instantaneous connection with the mobile.

As time went on, preparations became more pressing. I had to drive up to Newcastle to join David and give him a hand with all the ferrying to and fro to Whitehaven where *Polar Bound* lay; a shell of aluminium that was to become my new world. My introduction was on a cold, rather bleak day. Her pretty lines were sullied by an enormous amount of plastic refuse bobbing all around in a soup of scummy water, which had been driven up into the backwater and had no escape short of being removed by the marina staff. She was in the first bay of the marina as we entered, and we were able to stop the car more or less alongside her. As we descended the six metal steps of the companionway down into the after-cabin and I stood surveying the somewhat bachelor function-ality of the saloon-cum-galley, David assured me of her superior strength for the task ahead.

The layout of the after-cabin was fairly conventional, except that against the hull on either side were two out-berths, which David chose to refer to as 'coffin berths'. These are specifically designed to embrace you snugly. Any attempt to turn over is not to be too readily undertaken as you are virtually packaged in a box. Should the whole ship be thrown over, you would quite likely remain in position, only inverted. The saloon area was otherwise fairly standard with settee berths in a semi-circular curve around a fixed, drop-flap saloon table with fiddles.

I took more of an interest in the cooking arrangements and the stowage of the galley essentials. There were two stoves, neither of them gimballed to remain horizontal when the boat is not, but they were athwartships, considered to be the steadiest place, and located as near to the midships position as space would allow. There were also four detachable curved stainless steel arms that could be screwed on to a surrounding rail to firmly embrace the pan you were using. The Dickinson cast-iron stove was to be the hub of our home, giving out heat around the clock, should it be needed, and fed by diesel; this had two hobs and an oven below, the door of which was warped. Adjacent was the Wallis, a paraffin stove with single ring. There was a double stainless-steel sink with cupboards below. The sink had pumped fresh water and a saltwater pump too. To one side was a stainless steel lifting worktop secured with a piece of shock cord on a nasty, sharp hook; below was our very small fridge. Softening the general feeling of masculinity was a carpeted cabin sole, which had seen heavy usage, and four small watercolours of old paddle steamers.

Opposite the galley were the 'heads' – a good reliable marine loo, and a stainless-steel sink with cupboard below and a shower hooked above. The shiny sink and shower looked promising, but this was illusory. The pressure system was never switched on during our voyages. We only carried 65 gallons of fresh water, and I washed in the galley in saltwater. As for the loo, it is always something of an embarrassment to retreat there on an important mission. (Some boats I have been in put on 'loo music', which is quite a good plan as reticence on this issue can lead to constipation.) However, we were soon to get used to one another, and the noise of the Gardner engine could be relied upon to drown out everything anyway.

My estate car proved quite useful in making the run over to White-haven. It was a 200-mile round trip and so no journey was undertaken lightly, or wasted. We stowed the car to the gills, relying on the wing mirrors entirely as there was never an inch of space free for visibility out of the back window. One of the first things to be loaded into it was a curious sort of framework David had been constructing – a long flat board, and three sturdy square wooden braces; besides this was the sudden arrival of an additional settee cushion, long and thick. I couldn't imagine what these were for, but David did not provide explanations for everything he did. The items got accommodated in the car, and on arrival at the boat were shipped aboard. The mattress was placed in my coffin bunk. Its use only become apparent when we were far from land; it turned out that this had been a priority for David almost from the first time we encountered one another again.

As the days went by, things became more fraught and we both got quite tired. David had the lion's share of responsibility and this was beginning to tell. One day when we were about 15 miles off arrival at Whitehaven, after a long, companionable silence he suddenly said,

'I've left the keys behind.' This was a real blow after our early start and good timing, but he decided to go on just in case the hatch was not fully secured and he might be able to get in there. Needless to say, it was firmly shut. David had to arrange for a friend to meet us halfway back at a garage; he would bring the keys from David's office. This was very kind, but it certainly was inconvenient all round. Notwithstanding this, and David's amazing reliability, I found it reassuring that he, too, was a human being with all the frailties that mortals are prone to.

The boat had to be lifted out on the travel lift and stored in a cradle on the shingle in the marina confines in order that she be given a coat of antifouling. Luckily there was help on hand for this horrible task, although David did quite a bit and I, too, donned my overalls and scrambled on my back underneath the hull, though honestly I can think of better things to do. I really do loathe the smell of that ghastly blue paint, which gets all over your hands and feet and is practically impossible to eradicate.

There is nothing quite so uncomfortable as living aboard a boat up on dry land with no facilities. Every visit to the loo had to be a long descent down the ladder alongside, being careful not to put one's feet into the securing ropes, and usually with hands full of buckets, and then a walk across the sharp stones of the yard to the washroom area, which the yard were kind enough to allow us to use. These sharp stones are what are laid on railway tracks, and are extremely uncomfortable to walk on.

Then it came time to check over the stores and work out what was still needed. I had no say in the layout. Quite a lot of the items were already in place from an earlier trip and, lacking experience for this kind of expedition, I decided to go along with how things were. One large and convenient locker under the saloon bench on one side, which I had mentally appropriated for handy everyday food storage, was taken up entirely with David's extensive wardrobe, all protected in dress bags and sail bags and labelled: Extra-warm Pull-overs, Woolly Hats, Shirts, Tops, Socks, Pants, Handkerchiefs. The tiny hanging locker was dominated by the Browning 270 rifle in its canvas sleeve, standing incongruously alongside a smart blazer awaiting an invitation from a cruise ship captain to go aboard. (Such an invitation could, apparently, lead to a hot shower and even some freebie hand-outs from their chefs, plus laundry facilities.) He found me a small area at one end of the saloon locker, and, although I found this quite sufficient, it was extremely awkward to access as the cushions on top were heavy, cumbersome and unyielding to heave about.

There was a plentiful supply of Christmas puddings which had made the journey around the world at least once, quite probably twice, and vast quantities of apple dumplings with custard in razor-sharp foil packs. These were apparently ex-army rations. David kept telling me that the British Army went to war on them, so they should be good enough for me. There were also a number of extremely heavy boxes full of Fru-grains, which resembled dried twigs and were packed in cellophane. These were to prove a real challenge; they were chewy and unpalatable, and impossible to surreptitiously stuff back into the aged packaging, which crackled and tore. David said how good they were and tucked in with gusto, though I noticed that even his enthusiasm waned as time went on. He reminded me that Sir John Franklin had eaten his own boots on a sledging expedition he had made in the early nineteenth century. For the sake of family honour, I would keep my feelings to myself about the Fru-grains, though I could easily imagine they were made of dried leather. Some of the stores had a 'best before' date of 2002, and David looked horrified when I suggested that perhaps these should be replaced.

It was nearing our planned departure date when it looked as if there was going to be a major drama regarding the stowage in the huge forward hold. David had been worrying for some time over this complex problem as the considerable number of fuel cans on the stern had to be balanced with an equal distribution of weight of the heavy boxes and bins of equipment and quantity of fuel cans in the forward hold. He had thought that he could manage this with ratchet straps, but it became apparent that this was not going to work. *Polar Bound* can apparently be thrown by a wave, so absolute security has to be ensured. He looked very glum and said the whole trip would have to be aborted as we were running out of time. It was unlike him to be defeated.

In desperation I suggested we should seek help from Robert Newton, on a neighbouring boat called *Mystique*, who had popped over from time to time to see if we needed anything. David was reluctant, so I volunteered, and in no time at all Bob came up with the solution. He accompanied us to a lumber yard where we purchased some shuttering and then, as soon as we got back to the boat, Bob's saw bench was brought around to the jetty. With his help, measurements were taken and the next day was spent sawing and fitting the shuttering to suit the tapering shape of the bows, with the stowage adjusted according to the position of the ribs (frames) so that the pieces could slide past each other to enable access. I was enrolled to allocate numbers according to whether they were to port or starboard, and according to shelf level. David then drilled holes at either end of the sawn boards, through which he threaded strong cable ties. These were attached to various fixing points. All the hollow spaces were jammed with folded cardboard, which is marvellous stuffing, and not a thing moved. We were enormously grateful to Bob, and to his friend Sally who later asked us both to a delicious dinner aboard *Mystique*. What had seemed an insuperable problem was simply and efficiently resolved. I was very impressed by David's thoroughness at lashing things down.

With this accomplished, the day arrived when we drove for the last time to Whitehaven, only this time in David's car. We went through the final checklist and paid one more visit to a large branch of Tesco's, conveniently located two minutes' walk away, where we did a major shop for fresh food. We met up with David's friend and helper, Tony, who had come over on the train and was going to drive the car back to Newcastle. It took quite a long time to stow everything away. Finally, the deep freeze was turned on and filled. David then took us out to supper at a small local hotel. I made the most of the luxury of being able to order something I had not had to think about myself, buy or prepare. We were to be off early in the morning, 29 July 2012, by arrangement with the lock-keeper overseeing the marina entrance. I tried to make the most, too, of my final night of undisturbed peace, but I don't think either of us slept very well with the impending departure.

We moved off at first light the following morning, a cold, grey day with incipient drizzle. I busied myself trying to coil up the vast ropes David uses. These are a far cry from the lovely smooth lines in a sailing boat; I was still a greenhorn and had a lot to learn about 'little ship' handling. We suddenly noticed the lonely figure of Tony, muffled up with scarf, woolly hat and jacket in the watery dawn light, walking briskly in the direction of the sea lock for a last photo opportunity. We were both touched that he had made such an effort to get up early as he is normally a late riser and not usually on parade until around 11.00am.

We entered the holding pool and approached the jetty to tie up alongside. The keeper closed the lock gate and flooded it with water to bring the level equal to that of the sea outside. All I had to do was to 'take a line ashore and tie up'. It sounded easy, but we had approached obliquely and there was a large gap between the shore and *Polar Bound*, and I was out of practice with pier-head leaps, particularly with large coils of hairy rope in my hands. David has large hands and I don't think he realised that I wasn't used to such great coils of rope. And although he was emphatic about detail, he hadn't explained whether it was to be the stern line or the bow line he wished to have tied up first, nor was there any particular indication inside the shelter of the lock where the wind was coming from. In my effort to please and get everything right, and with frantic gestures to him to get closer, I scrambled for the nearest bollard I could see. This involved diving down under a couple of railings, in the course of which I managed to tear some muscles around my ribcage. I was fairly sure I hadn't cracked a rib, but I could hardly breathe and I found it excessively painful. David looked impatient and shouted something, which was snatched away by the wind. However, my efforts were not in vain and we were eventually secured to David's satisfaction. Once the water levels were equalised, I then had to untie our lines and scramble back aboard.

As we passed the lock-keeper's lookout station, we waved to him, and at that moment noticed the rather touching sight of our farewell committee: Tony, balancing on the end of a brick wall to get a good shot of *Polar Bound*'s departure. We felt quite tearful, but there was a lot of deck tidying to do and David was already giving orders and telling me to be quicker. And then there were the fenders to think about. I was rather in the dark as to where to stow those away. Apparently they were to be lowered down into the forward hold. The huge, heavy hatch cover had to be lifted and lowered backwards – 'Gently!' (As if I would even think of dropping it, I thought crossly.) I then had to turn around and descend backwards into this large space where everything was so neatly stowed, and all the while the bows were beginning to plunge up and down over the waves. David came out and took over the final tidy-up. Knowing what we were about to encounter, he had been keen to get everything stowed away and secured before the plunging became paralytic. He had seemed unduly anxious about our departure, and in retrospect I think he was aware of how the conditions were going to be and wondering whether this would be make or break for his newfound crew.

With the lock gates opened remorselessly to the grey, uninviting Irish Sea, and with one last wave to Tony, we stood in the wheelhouse (as David calls the bridge deck) in contemplative silence and pulled away from the shore and out into the swell and white horses.

PART TWO

THE NORTHWEST
PASSAGE

FOUR

FROM PORTRUSH, NORTHERN IRELAND TO GREENLAND

'NOW, SAID DAVID, ADOPTING A STERN LOOK, standing tall and looking directly at me, 'there are three rules in this boat. Number one is no frying of anything in the galley; the second, no brown marks in the loo, and the third is to take ultimate care of everything in the boat.'

'You don't really mean no frying in the galley, do you? Because that eliminates sauté potatoes, and pretty well everything that has appeal – garlic, onions, olive oil...' My voice tailed off. I gave a wan smile as I studied his face. He relaxed slightly. He was evidently reminiscing about one or two itinerant visitors who had been let loose in his galley, 'and everything had got spattered in fat'. A compromise was reached, but on no account was I to *touch* the single-burner portable calor gas ring. I stared at him in amazement. I had been brought up on calor and mains gas and used them all my life. I had sailed all around the Mediterranean with my husband and baby son in our 40-foot sloop with nothing but calor gas, and also been in numerous other sailing boats, all with gas cylinders aboard.

But no, the intricacies of the calor gas ring were to be attempted only by himself, and generally its use was confined to making a huge bowl of popcorn, of which I was allowed a small portion if I was quick. He went on to explain that the hull was not wooden but aluminium and therefore had no escape route for unspent gas, which, if allowed to accumulate in the bilge, could be a time bomb. I knew about this too. A number of years ago on holiday in the British Virgin Islands, I was standing with my husband on a small beach in Virgin Gorda when we witnessed a large chartered sailing boat explode, bodies flung into the air and the hull burnt to the waterline. Remarkably, no one was injured.

However, having won the use of the frying pan, I kept quiet, deciding there would be no competition to be the first to struggle with the red cord around the gas cylinder lashed to the foot of the companionway. I was more than happy for David to attempt the contortion and the subsequent balancing act on his knees as he threw into the pan of hot oil a handful of hard pellets of corn, which then leapt and rattled around inside the hastily covered pan like castanets. As for the other rules – no brown marks in the loo and taking the greatest care of everything – he was already talking to the converted, but I suppose it is much easier to make these matters clear at the outset before you have to make an issue over them, which might be a cause of friction.

With the house rules sorted out, it was then time to put the kettle on and get used to my new world. Anticipation of a cup of tea must take place at least an hour before it is required as the Dickinson takes all of that to perform. I soon discovered where we had put the dry biscuits and pieces of crystallised ginger and secretly consumed a few pieces, and David wasn't far behind. This was to counteract seasickness. There had been some talk of its effectiveness before we embarked but, other than that, by an unspoken agreement absolutely no reference was made to *mal de mer*. In this we were resolute. If people bring up the subject, which they inevitably do, I always say, 'We don't think about it, talk about it, or make any reference to it at all – we don't even want to recognise it.' Somehow we found that this seemed to work. Quite possibly the nastiest sea for such misery was the notorious Irish Sea, and of course we were straight out into it right at the beginning of our voyage.

Neither of us slept on the passage to Portrush in Northern Ireland. We approached the coast in a murky dawn with thick mist swirling around, and decided to lie off until visibility improved. It was impossible to see the entrance, and there are a number of dangerous rocks when approaching from the southeast. While waiting for first light, we entertained each other by recounting tales of past *amours*, and I found huge comfort by stretching across David's lap, who was seated at the wheel, so that he could massage my back – it was wonderfully beneficial for my still painful ribcage.

After stooging up and down for a couple of hours, David decided to move off and begin his approach to the harbour entrance. I asked if I should be getting the warps out but he said, 'Not yet.' Obediently, I retreated into the wheelhouse. We called up the harbour master on the VHF to inform him of our arrival, then we rushed through the entrance with some verve; as David said, it was quite difficult to keep steerage way on since there was a strong cross wind blowing. As we were closing the quay at speed, I was ordered to go to the after-locker and get out the lines. It was all done in rather a rush. Left to myself I should have had them out half an hour earlier, all coiled up and ready to throw, but we were both out of practice, and it has to be remembered that David was unused to having crew aboard.

We spotted a very official-looking figure of a girl in a navy blue jumper with badges and epaulettes stuck all over her, standing by for our arrival. By this time we were being blown hard against the quay-side, and the girl proved rather ineffectual. David thrust a large buoy at her and ordered her to place it against the quay to stop us ramming it. I was detailed to stand midships with another buoy. There was a loud 'bang' and her buoy went off like a blown-up paper bag; of course, I got blamed. It was David's 'best' buoy.

'It cost well over £50, and now it's gone pop,' he said accusingly. Warming to his theme, he followed it up with, 'You should have been in position.' The growling went on for some time and I was annoyed as I had tentatively suggested getting out lines and buoys much earlier.

David was soon mollified by the arrival of the harbour master, who greeted him like a long-lost friend, and was followed by a couple of reporters from local newspapers who wanted photographs for the articles they were doing on his venture.

A bowser load of fuel was ordered and we tidied things away while we awaited its arrival. It was in attendance for quite a time as there were five tanks to fill, and the driver and his mate proved most helpful and obliging in filling up all the red five-gallon plastic fuel cans as well. I climbed down into the lazarette, and also into another very awkward small stowage area right up forward in the bows, to pass out the empty cans. These were all arranged in serried rows waiting for the nozzle to come along. Then they had to be wiped over, the seals in their lids checked and properly secured, and finally hauled aboard again. David was nothing if not thorough. He did a most impressive stow of two lines of them on the afterdeck, lashed with strong rope to ensure they went nowhere. The remainder had to be lugged to the cavernous forward hold, where they were lowered down to me and I shoved them, one by one, up on to the four shelves, where David was to come and tie them down. We stuffed cardboard into all the crevices and the new shuttering came into its own. By the time we had finished, not another thing could possibly be stored up in the bows. But there was still plenty of room to stand, and right forward was an enormous drum full of coils of very thick hawser, to which the main bower anchor was attached. The drum was secured with two wooden wedges.

I really do wonder how on earth David could have managed all these procedures alone. Obviously having automatic pilot is a big help, but coming alongside in adverse conditions and with high, flared bows is not the easiest, and you would have to do a lot of forward thinking, getting out the fenders and making a decision as to whether you were going to go port or starboard to (i.e. which side was to be pressed against the quay), so that you could secure the fenders on the cap rail on the correct side. There is an outside steering position as well, which gives better line of sight but is not much fun in the rain.

That evening I thought it would be nice to take David out to dinner. I found a restaurant about to open for the first time and booked a table. It was not particularly memorable, as I recall, but it was a great relief not having to think what to make for supper. I wonder whether men ever realise what a bore it can be having to conjure up something different every night – having to introduce variety, ensure a healthy diet, work out what time to turn the oven on so that everything comes together at the same time, never mind catering for fussy eaters. It can be a relief when you can just cook for yourself and have what you like – hence the joy of being taken out for a meal.

The next day we set off with quite a farewell party, including a couple of journalists, assembled on the quayside. After we got well away from land out into the North Atlantic for our passage to Greenland, David produced a gantry, which he had invented for the sole purpose of bringing inboard his main bower anchor. This weighs about 50 kilos and could become a liability if left dangling over the fairlead, clanking about. To retrieve the anchor, a line had to be passed through the ring coupling the chain to the anchor stock, which was done by reaching at arm's length forward over the nose of the boat. This line had then to be hauled around the cross member of the gantry. Once secured, we pulled the gantry vertical, bringing the anchor aloft from the fairlead. This enabled us to hoist her inboard, where she could be uncoupled and made fast with chains on a special block to one side of the forward deck.

We had 1,200 miles to go before reaching the southern tip of Greenland at Cape Farewell. In David's opinion it is the roughest cape in the world, but because few venture into these waters it is not notorious in the same way that Cape Horn is. The North Atlantic is an incredibly lonely sea, and in the early hours of the morning on the fourth day out, the only vessel we encountered was a gigantic oil tanker in ballast about five miles off, passing at some speed on a reciprocal course.

Our little floating world seemed snug and secure, and it might be appropriate at this point to give a brief description of the layout. Once aboard the waist of the vessel, you mount the raised area of the coach roof and pass through an immensely strong aluminium door with six swivel 'dogs' (huge turnbuckles) to secure it firmly – 'dogged down' is the term. You are then in an airlock, and this area has a small bench seat and hanging locker for oilskins. There is a further door to access the bridge deck (alias wheelhouse), where the console is mounted with the steering wheel and all navigation instruments, plus a full-sized chart table with storage drawers below. Unlike most modern seafarers, David relies primarily on his charts, of which he has a library of thousands. Only recently has he begun to consult electronic aids, which he concedes have their uses on occasions. When it comes to the minutiae of close-quarter work, however, he prefers his charts, finding electronic aids unreliable.

It is quite a long way across the wheelhouse when *Polar Bound* is pitching and bucking, and you could easily break a limb unless taking great care. Another house rule is not to grasp hold of the captain's chair, although it is a convenient central anchoring point. Apparently its arm could easily break off. I had a surreptitious wobble one day, and David was quite right; very definitely so. It was also quite evident that he himself had made a wild grab for the forbidden arm on innumerable occasions, which was why it was like that in the first place.

From the bridge deck, you can raise a large and heavy, insulated hatch cover and descend a vertical ladder – so long as you turn your knees sideways and go down like a caterpillar – into the engine room, where unfortunately you cannot stand full height but must creep around bent over like a hunchback. Here stands, centre stage, the great big Gardner engine, which gleams, with not a trace of oil in sight. Two of five huge bulging fuel tanks are here too, and there is a workbench with a massive vice and an air-cooled Yanmar generator. The hatch cover is left open quite a bit of the time (at the expense of one's ears) as the engine must be kept nice and cool. In fact, she is fussier than a woman, and receives infinitely more caressing and attention; every working part of her comes in for the same treatment. David is a great one for putting grease on absolutely anything that moves, and he is of course perfectly right for the good functioning of moving parts. However, most of us are used to objects that are seized up and require several squirts of WD40 before they will relinquish their rusty grip. He even managed to discover that the valve on top of my pressure cooker at home was a bit stiff and, the next time I used it, I found it covered in thick grease.

Back up again in the wheelhouse is a quarter, or settee, berth, with bookcase, barometer and inclinometer nearby. I can never see the need for an inclinometer, as it is quite evident when trying to keep your balance how much the boat is tilting. In a sailing boat it might be another matter to achieve the optimum angle of the hull according to the conditions, but we were not in a sailing boat.

At the side of the quarter berth are the aluminium steps (or companionway) down to the living quarters with the saloon/galley and the heads. As I was soon to discover, the quarter berth was not elevated enough to see out of the wheelhouse windows, and there was nowhere else to sit as David was normally firmly ensconced in the captain's chair; I had to take my opportunities when he was busy at the chart table.

The passage to Greenland took some adjustment. It was very rough with constant gale-force winds on the nose and heaving, white-crested 'grey-beards' that tossed *Polar Bound*'s 52 tons (fully laden, with stores, fuel, water and expedition equipment) around like a plastic duck in a bath. At one point the kettle shot out of its moorings despite the metal arms that are supposed to hold it in place. As we gradually got our sea legs we both found out about muscles we hadn't realised we had. My ribcage was still agony, but there was nothing to be done other than rub in some salve, which gave a comforting glow at least, and David was very willing to undertake this.

I found my coffin berth incredibly difficult to get into, and even harder to get out of. David seemed to have no problems. He had developed a technique of approaching face forwards and swinging one leg over, and in one smooth movement he was ensconced – somewhat reminiscent of a well-practised blackbird alighting at the entrance to its nest, then a split second later it is inside looking serene as if nothing has happened. The technique reminded me of a Punch and Judy show, with Punch beaming with delight at his evident skill and dexterity, while I was still trying to work out which leg to put in first.

However, it wasn't long before the mysterious carpentry work made its reappearance. David was very busy below in the saloon and I peered down from time to time to see what he was up to. Some weeks before he had contrived a most ingenious fillet, the underside of which had locating lugs that locked into the three vertical braces, each one slightly higher than the other to compensate for the curve of the hull. Down on his knees, he was contorting himself to see the underside of the board in order to get the lugs to slot into the three braces, like a jigsaw. With a triumphant, 'There – that's done it!' he looked round for approval, at the same time reaching for the fat rubber cushion he had had made in Newcastle. It all went together beautifully and turned the settee berth next to the saloon table into a double berth, though the occupants had to be like two pencils as the width was barely more than 3 feet. Never mind; it was a huge improvement on my coffin berth, which I had already abandoned anyway for the saloon berth, in its normal arrangement. I made full use of it immediately and found it a huge improvement.

In view of the performance of setting this edifice up, it was evident that it was going to remain in situ while at sea, so I arranged a couple of sleeping bags, a rug and pillows on top, and I must say it looked most inviting. It was ideal for one, but a squeeze for two, particularly in view of the fact that David was adamant that the four-inch-thick backrest of the curving saloon seat was on no account to be pulled off. In such a small space, that four inches would have made a surprising difference, but house rules came to the fore and it had to remain. I was never quite sure why, though being packed in like sardines did have its advantages when *Polar Bound* was rolling or being tossed around. When one of us turned, the other had to as well, and if I was on the outside, I found my nose jammed into the cushion. David, on the other hand, found his knees rammed up against the flap of the saloon table. Nevertheless, snuggled together, our mutual warmth was wonderfully soporific, and once our timetables were adjusted to the watch-keeping arrangement we often had a couple of hours' siesta in the afternoon.

However, when the going got tough we had to be extra vigilant, and then David preferred his coffin berth. He was extremely adept at springing out of it, swinging his leg over the back rest of the saloon seat, and somehow managing to avoid stepping on my feet as he landed on the cabin sole. In the early mornings, sometimes his face would appear over the top of the back rest to see if I was awake, and similarly I could peer over to see what state he was in. Once in his bunk, he would switch on a small light above his head and attempt to read, but within half a page, the book had fallen forward and he was sound asleep. Many a time I had to turn off his light. In rough weather, when David was in his cramped bunk, I on the other hand had the 'double' bed to luxuriate in, but had to wedge cushions and pillows behind my back to stop from rolling in the heaving seas.

David had put in a comforting night light before leaving, and it was very useful for getting up in the darkness. Throwing out a warm red glow, it gave enough illumination to enable us to make our way about. Once up on the bridge deck, we had the subdued lights of the instruments to go by.

Having now adopted the new sleeping provisions, it became my duty to put the kettle on, because I was the nearest. This necessitated lighting the Dickinson, which was an adventure in itself. First you lifted off the cooking-plate cover and removed the flame-dispersal unit from the bowels of the stove, then popped a button in, which started a menacing flow of oil that 'pooled' in the well. Next you tore off a small wisp of paper towel fashioned into a sacrificial taper and, with a positive strike of the match, you gingerly poked (or in my case, dropped) this down, with scorching fingers, on to the oil until an incandescent flare announced 'take off'. After quickly replacing the dispersal unit and covering plate, you turned the switch on to start a fan going. After five minutes or so you would then authoritatively and ceremoniously tap the stainless-steel chimney-stack pipe to establish that it was heating up, and you could then switch off the fan and wait for an hour while the kettle came to the boil. The interim could be spent by having a wash, which I did every morning, absolutely starkers and freezing with cold, as it was generally done using cold sea water. When you wanted to turn the stove off, you only had to pop the diesel button out again.

Quite a number of mornings later, it was a red letter day for me: around 10 miles off the Greenland coast we began to spot icebergs dotted about. This was my first ever sighting, having only seen them in photographs before. In addition, there were some menacing small lumps. At first glance one of these could be mistaken for a breaking wave, while of course what you saw on the surface was only the treacherous tip – they are ten times as large below the water and, being frozen fresh water, are very hard if hit at 6.5 knots. As we neared land, the persistent fog became a real hazard. Icebergs and 'growlers' were all around us, and it was just as we were discussing the intricacies of the diesel stove that we were brought up short by a terrific thump. There was a tremendous report and we both dashed outside and ran forward to inspect the bow. No harm done as the ship is extremely strong, but the specially reinforced knife on the bow had blue ice cleaving to it – a stark reminder of the *Titanic*.

FIVE

CAPE FAREWELL, GREENLAND

ENCOURAGED BY APPROACHING LANDFALL, I decided to experiment with baking some stone-ground wholemeal bread, but my first attempt was literally a flop. Nevertheless, David made a valiant attempt at appreciation; perhaps not wishing to discourage me from trying again, I thought somewhat cynically. As I was busy at the galley making my preparations, David, who was lying back like some Eastern potentate on the saloon berth, propped up by cushions and eyeing my activities the while, quite out of the blue asked, 'Was your mother tall?' I was rather startled. This was the first question he had ever asked me about myself. Well... it was a start anyway.

As we closed Cape Farewell, David had decided to take the 60-mile passage inland up through the Prins Christian Sund. This cuts off the worst of the bad weather and, besides this advantage, is incredibly beautiful as well. It could be said to be the most beautiful sound in the world, surpassing even Milford Sound in New Zealand. The sea altered its characteristics and became much easier, and the fog and murk we had encountered most of the way across began to clear. At this moment we passed a really big iceberg about 150 feet in height with fractures and wind carving all over its face. We were able to get out on deck and take photographs, David with his incredibly sophisticated camera and complex lens arrangement, and I with my 'point and press' self-focusing one, given to me by my daughter, Jessica. This was my first close encounter of a berg and therefore especially memorable. The soft greys and shadowy forms of the mountainous coastline to both sides of this inlet were mysterious and full of a strange and remote beauty. A great glacier lay on the starboard bow, from which these local bergs would have carved.

Later that morning, 12 August 2012 – my mother's birthday; she had died two years earlier – we entered the sound and emerged out of the gloom into wonderful sunlight, motoring along at about 6.5 knots in virtually windless water with a high escarpment of smooth moulded rocks and stony scree to either side. Miniature glaciers appeared at intervals from the narrow crevasses where they discharged themselves into the sea; we passed a stand of floating, broken shards of ice. David said that thirty years ago, when he had first come through this sound, these rounded escarpments of ancient stone, now visible with moraines of scree running between them, had been covered by snow, creating glaciers. Many had now receded and the meltwater disappeared; all you could see were the tortured shale channels created by the action of the glaciers from past millennia. Every once in a while we saw a tumbling waterfall cascading from the summit. It was incredibly peaceful after the tumult of the open sea, the silence broken only by the timeless dancing and splashing of the silver-threaded cascades leaping from jutting rocks.

The sun made such a difference. Life began to take on a cheery aspect. Despite the cold, we had our first lunch sitting outside on the raised roof of the saloon. I hastily assembled the remnants of an iceberg lettuce, some smoked mackerel and a respectable tomato, together with hot horseradish sauce and a glass of water. It would have been rather nice to have had a glass of wine, but I didn't like to suggest it as David might have thought he'd got a wino on board. Looking around at those towering summits in the peaceful silence, I wondered whether any adventurous mountaineer had ever attempted to scale them. They looked formidable.

Another ethereal, viscous, white curtain of fog of ever-changing density began to close down on us again after our brief spell of sunshine, and suddenly David said, 'I think I can see a sailing boat ahead.' This was so unlikely that I thought it was a figment of his imagination, and that he was overtired because we had had only small snatches of sleep during the last week or so, but straining through my binoculars I spotted her too. We were amazed. This was only the second vessel we had seen in 1,200 miles, the first having been the oil tanker. She was tacking downwind ahead of us and making long boards across the sound. Eventually we caught up with her, but she was too far away to make contact or even to wave to. We could just read her name, *Astrid*, painted on a dark green hull, and she appeared to have three men aboard who were sailing with great competence and gusto; we couldn't imagine where on earth they had come from, nor where they were going.

David began to get a bit anxious at this stage and kept saying, 'I'm sure it is here – somewhere around here, just behind this huge boulder.' He went on, 'I've been in here a couple of times before but not for several years.'

'What is here?' I asked.

'A small settlement,' came the reply. Anything less likely in such a remote setting would be hard to imagine, beneath towering lofty peaks with not a trace of life or habitation to be seen anywhere. However, he was convinced he was in the right spot and started heading directly towards the cliffs. You could be forgiven for thinking he had lost control of his senses but, as we nudged in closer, things began to take shape. The huge rounded boulder, like a giant hill, became silhouetted against the soft hues of a rocky escarpment that lay behind. As we approached, the opening between widened, and now it seemed there was a passage appearing. At that moment a very small welcoming light twinkled like a lost star from the top of a post, and the enchantment grew in the shadowy evening light as we proceeded. A little way ahead was a concealed basin, to one side of which was the landing stage. Grouped around the water's edge a few small fishing boats were in evidence, and behind them on the shore wooden matchbox houses were dotted about.

We were approaching the small settlement of Augpilagtoq, about six hours from the easterly entrance to the sound. (There are Inuit names and given names by explorers, so on other charts, it might be different, but Augpilagtoq was what was on ours.) I marvelled at David having come to a place like this thirty years earlier, entirely alone. What if he'd got it wrong? One false move and his boat would have foundered hundreds of miles from anywhere. This turned out to be the only refuge with habitation throughout the sound's 60-mile length, completely hidden from the outside world and tucked behind a large bulging rock with dizzying heights above. However, the enjoyment and pleasure of our arrival was somewhat marred at the sight of the staging against which we would have to lie, and the thought of tying up with not a soul around to help.

We crept through the narrow, hidden entrance and, despite all preparations and briefings as to how nimble I needed to be in order to spring gazelle-like up on to what turned out to be an unpromising heap of pilings with concrete top and high slippery wooden bulwarks, as always the wind followed us in and my leap was halted before it began by a yawning gap. 'Jump!' shouted David, going astern and thus increasing the distance from the safety of the shore, and then without further ado he sprang like a tiger on to the boards, grabbing the line from my hand in passing. We were soon secure and David back on the boat, but I felt rather foolish and inadequate, and I was also quite annoyed with him, and said crossly, 'Don't shout at me like that – I'm not a dog!' I have heard stories of people doing pier-head leaps and getting crushed between the hull and the palings, and pointed this out to him, asking if he wanted to lose his crew so early in the voyage. The baulk of slippery wet timber was shoulder height, and I hadn't been able to see any way of negotiating it – particularly with the boat sliding away from me below.

David busied himself at the chart table and I started supper preparations, but presently he came down the companionway and gave me a very generous apology and a big hug, so all was forgiven. I had also been rather put out because my husband and I, when first married, had bought a 40-foot sloop and sailed it all around the Mediterranean, visiting over seventy ports en route. Having always been the one responsible for throwing warps and seeing to fenders, I felt I was quite up to doing what was required, but I hadn't reckoned on making the manoeuvre from a small 'ship' with high bulwarks on to hazardous, primitive jetties way above head height.

We found ourselves in this little community of perhaps a hundred people, if that, with painted, boarded wooden houses built, seemingly at random, on platforms on rock – not all of them level. Paths lay between, marking generations of well-trodden, familiar tracks, mainly to the simple wooden church, the little school, the cemetery and, to my surprise, a supermarket, then down to the jetty to unload probably a weekly or fortnightly visit from a supply ship. Absolutely everything had to be brought by water, and no doubt the community relied on a visit from doctor and dentist in this manner too.

The small sailing boat, *Astrid*, appeared in the distance, rounding the vast boulder. David, having anticipated this, had been busy laying on extra warps and fenders so they could lie alongside us, since there was nowhere else for them to go. They swept in with some panache, whirled round in a circle of their own length to size up the situation, had a quick consultation with David, then made a second pass at us and came to rest, each man throwing us a line to secure. The three men were extremely friendly, and amazingly were flying the Union flag. They also flew a rather spare-looking yellow duster; otherwise known as the 'Q' flag, it is obligatory to fly it on arrival in a foreign port in order to notify the authorities that you require clearance, both from Immigration and Customs, in exchange for which they extract revenue from you. No such formalities were on offer in this remote haven and the yellow flag hung limp and unnoticed.

David invited them aboard for a cup of tea and they did not seem in a hurry to leave. My supper preparations were well under way and it was far too late to stretch a meal for two to suit five, particularly as we were having stuffed peppers, but it was all put on the back burner anyway because it was so much more exciting to talk to the new arrivals. They too were from Newcastle (Sunderland), where *Polar Bound* was registered, and had noticed that we had this painted on our stern – such a coincidence in this remote spot.

The three men seemed very competent and well prepared, and were dressed rather like mercenaries (minus the weapons): dark, heavy-duty cold-weather gear and good strong harnesses. The owner was a very handsome, 6-foot 4-inch man of about fifty with blue eyes; a second man was of a similar age, and the third man, older and white-haired, I think was the support crew – namely cook and bottle-washer, like me. The boat had a sensible bridging traveller for the main sheet and seemed immensely strongly built. She drew two metres below the water, which no doubt contributed to her ability to go to windward so well, her sails setting perfectly.

We greatly enjoyed our encounter with them and were amazed at their adventurous nature. It transpired that we were the first boat they'd met since leaving Sunderland, and that they had left there the same day we had departed Whitehaven in Cumbria. In the intervening time they had been to the Faroes, Iceland, and 250 miles up the east Greenland coast, which is not normally visited. They were planning the following day to go to Nanortalik to the northwest of us, at the western end of Prins Christian Sund, to visit a large supermarket before departing for warmer climes in the Azores, and then on finally to the Mediterranean.

Two of the three turned out to be company directors – Nigel, managing director of a precision engineering firm, and Anders, who owned *Astrid,* managing director of a firm making heat exchangers. Tom, who was retired, had his own sailing boat, which he kept on Lake Windermere, where his wife felt more comfortable accompanying him. All three of them had taken a sabbatical and were certainly making the most of it; not for them a 'basking on the beach' holiday.

We were all too tired for any further jollifications and so, as our supper was wilting by the minute, they went back to their boat, with an invitation to us to visit them the following morning before they departed. Supper turned out be better than expected, with a rare glass of wine to chase it down. At night, as the village slept, the total silence was pure and peaceful, and we had a really good, uninterrupted sleep, the first since leaving Whitehaven.

The following morning we paid a quick visit aboard *Astrid* and noted the somewhat spartan cockpit with two little tip-up perching seats either side of the tiller and no attempt at softness of any sort – not a cushion in sight. The interior, with its two bunks, was crammed with belongings. As someone was always steering and keeping watch, they probably operated a 'hot bunking' system. They were anxious to get off so we didn't stay too long. We helped them untie their warps and they were away, swiftly heading for their supermarket. We felt rather forlorn after their departure, and decided to go ashore and inspect the settlement in more detail.

Despite it being August, the children were still at school. We learnt later that some of the residents spent their entire life there, never having left their tiny world from birth to death. We started off by visiting the Augpilagtoq supermarket, all of 30 seconds' walk away. The selection was really surprising for such a tiny community. No queues – just us and the Inuit who took David's credit card for all the world like Morrisons. There was also a beaming post-lady at her own kiosk who probably knew the finances of everyone in the village. We bought a delicious, still warm wholemeal loaf flavoured with malt, and two plums, one green pepper and a bottle of paraffin, which is the fuel used for the other stove, the single-ringed Wallis. The total cost was about £9 or £10, I think.

Then we walked around the habitations, which seemed almost deserted. Afterwards we visited the little church and admired the pure whiteness of the décor, adorned by the glitter and sparkle of the Byzantine-looking chandeliers, and the simple, well-maintained and polished wooden pews. Outside, neat rows of graves were each marked by an identical cross. Further on, we straddled the ridge, sitting on a thoughtfully provided wooden bench set in endless contemplation of what has to be one of the most spectacularly beautiful vistas of creation – the incredible scale of soaring mountains on either side, and the intense ice-cold sparkle of dark water with the odd grounded mini iceberg. I took a photograph of David, carefully placing his head in line with a tossed plastic bucket and polythene bag to hide them before capturing the scene.

While we were lost in thought, I reflected on my own position, and discovered I was very happy, if somewhat tired. While longing inwardly for the sailing life, I realised that a voyage such as we were undertaking, of 10,000 miles through what were going to be hostile, ice-strewn waters, would not be viable in a flimsy sailing boat. None the less, we heard that some hopefuls were gathering at Resolute in just such vessels, also hoping to be the first through the Northwest Passage, either west to east or east to west. Resolute is an untidy, straggly settlement on the south side of Cornwallis Island in the Barrow Strait, and being the principal township it has the only airport, so is useful for crews coming and going.

Arctic waters are no place for a conventional sailing boat, which can be crushed to pieces in a moment by pack ice. And whereas there may be the occasional short stretch that can be put in under sail, the engine is needed practically all the time, as we were to see later on.

One particular boat gave us concern. We heard by email from David's office that a sailing boat called *Belzebub II*, a 31-foot Hallberg-Rassy, also wanted to be the first to make the passage via the McClure Strait to the north of Banks Island. We were naturally rather put out. We heard that the *Belzebub* had already been in Resolute for many weeks awaiting a change in the weather and for the ice to melt, as the sea was still frozen solid in that quarter. She had an itinerant crew of six Swedes, and was very heavily sponsored with quite a lot of razzmatazz. It looked as if the race was on. David was nothing if not determined.

It was now Wednesday, 15 August, and time was passing quickly. We were very conscious of the fact that the brief summer up here would soon be over, and we still had a good way to go.

Later that morning we cast off our lines and got under way, leaving Augpilagtoq with some regret. The peacefulness and beauty of the surroundings were manifest in the crystal-clear, ice-cold air. The towering mountains were reflected serenely in the mirror-calm sea and water tinkled as it cascaded from the dizzy heights. The sun shone and we felt as if we were in paradise, but we did not lose sight of our objective – our rendezvous with the McClure Strait was paramount.

We marvelled at the sheer beauty of the place as the sound twisted and turned, opening up a new vista at every bend. As the day went on, a little wind sprang up. Ahead out in the open sea we noticed a blanket of fog just in the region of Nanortalik, where Anders and his crew were heading to stock up at the supermarket they told us about. A chill wind descended, and at that moment we spotted *Astrid* making up to windward exceedingly efficiently. As the gap slowly closed we aimed to get a good photograph of them steaming along. We all waved to each other, but by now the wind was quite fresh and they were well heeled over and concentrating on making the most of each tack.

As we left the shelter of Prins Christian Sund and entered the open sea, we became exposed to the elements once more. We resigned ourselves to losing that extreme clarity of air and once more being shrouded in fog. *Polar Bound* started her bucking motion again. I imagine it is like riding in a howdah on the back of an elephant – just as you get into one sway, you are brought up short by the ponderous gait from the other side. Watching David in the wheelhouse, seated grandly in the Captain's Chair with its bouncy, pneumatic springs, I was reminded of the rear view of a London bus driver as they negotiate the complexities of the capital's traffic system.

SIX

GREENLAND TO HOLSTEINBORG ACROSS THE ARCTIC CIRCLE

W E WERE MOTORING ALONG AT ABOUT 5 KNOTS, entering the area known as the Davis Strait and about to start a week-long section up the west coast of Greenland. There were a lot of icebergs about and we were in thick fog; this is where the radar comes into its own, especially at night. However, it is disconcerting charging on into the dark in swirling fog, and although we had confidence in the radar, some growlers did escape its net. You do get terribly sleepy and sometimes I had to prod David quite hard to get him to surface. One night I hadn't had the heart to wake him. Each time I went down to his bunk, I felt unable to disturb him – after all, he had all the responsibility – and returned to the bridge deck, drinking the cup of tea I had made him. I stayed on watch from 10pm until 5am. This is *not* good practice.

After that we kept proper two-hour watches. The fog rolled away and the sun came out, although the sea was somewhat turbulent as we were passing over a shallow bank. It was about 9 degrees outside. On the night of my foolish, self-imposed long watch, it had been below freezing, but on average it was about 2 degrees. By now, we were in the Arctic Circle proper, having crossed the 66-and-a-half-degrees latitude, and thus we could consider ourselves at the officially recognised commencement of the Northwest Passage, the Bering Strait at the western end being the termination. We would eventually attain about 75 degrees latitude north. Sleek, elegant seabirds flew in lovely swoops alongside us and then rose up to clear the pulpit and hover overhead on a thermal, scrutinising us with a friendly, beady eye.

It is difficult to keep your balance when *Polar Bound* goes over a particularly uneven wave, especially out of rolling sequence, and on one occasion I misjudged the timing badly. I came up from below in the saloon and, lunging against the quarter berth, gave the back of my head an almighty crack on a stainless-steel grab handle as I collapsed back on to the seat next to David, who was sitting reading a book. The resulting pigeon's egg took days to dissipate.

Way in the distance were high mountainous peaks with snowy tops, hazy and alluring, somewhat like the old blue dust-cover of the first edition of John Hunt's *Ascent of Everest*, which David had bought in the second-hand book shop in Portrush before we left and become immersed in. I could never focus on a book for long. I was always conscious of something else I should be doing: preparations for the next meal, sorting out a locker, making a foray to the forward hold there always seemed to be something.

I acted as David's secretary, trying to send emails to his office in Newcastle, keeping his staff on their toes by firing off demands for them to do this and that. I found it quite fun sitting at the saloon table with his computer on a non-skid mat, perched on two cushions swaying about, occasionally becoming airborne whenever a particularly large wave picked us up. I had to strain to hear what David was dictating as his voice is quite soft, and while he was experimenting with his flow of words, and possibly countermanding what he had just said, he would be wandering about in the cabin, sometimes with his back to me or, worse, disappearing up the companionway in mid-flow.

In due course, probably the following day, back would come a reply, occasionally rather terse if the recipient felt David was stepping out of line. He is quite circuitous in his dictation, and very solicitous to his two helpers in the office, one a secretary, and the other a book-keeper. His other assistant, of course, is Tony, who saw us off on our trip. He is an electrical technician, friend and odd-job man, and very clever. However, David gets irritated because he doesn't come into work until after 11am and needs copious cups of coffee before he can get going, and even then doesn't attend with alacrity to David's demands, which seem to involve chasing about the countryside following up bits of equipment that were 'borrowed' from his boat-yard in Scotland and have necessitated repair work as a result of the damage sustained before being returned to where the manager, Alan, anxiously awaited them.

David continued to receive ice reports by email from Peter Semi-touk in Winnipeg. Peter is, like David, a ham radio operator, and is in touch with all the aspiring adventurers who come for the challenge of the Northwest Passage. As well as filling them in on the ice conditions, he also keeps the authorities abreast of who is still in the surrounding waters before the icebreakers depart at the end of the season.

We had been gradually using up the boat-load of diesel we started off with in Portrush, Northern Ireland, held in five storage tanks: three smaller ones and two principal ones. Besides these were the red five-gallon plastic cans, all seventy-five of them, for use in emergency, most stored in the forward hold, with those that could not be accommodated inside lashed down on the stern deck and the bridge head.

We now needed more and, to cap it all, I had used up all the fresh drinking water (apparently) – 65 gallons of it! It was true that I had been washing in it and I suppose I had been a bit extravagant too when doing the washing-up. I measured the amount I used on a daily basis and it was 500ml, or just about a pint. It was very stupid of me to use it for washing but as David had never said anything, I assumed that he was planning to refuel and that the water tank could be replenished at the same time, so there was no need to be economical.

My water extravagance was discovered when there was a hollow 'glug' and explosive noises from the tap as it gulped at air – another black mark. David said, 'Surely you are the one who said they always washed in salt water – I thought you knew about it,' and continued, 'We are going to a desert, you know. How is it that I went right round the world and never filled up once?' I speculated on this 65 gallons for a moment or two, wondering if he had washed in salt water, and somewhat doubting he had washed at all, and that it was perhaps just as well his previous voyages had been solo. I also felt rather like a novice as of course I did know, but somehow only half my mind was properly focusing, perhaps because of the shortage of sleep. One had to climb out of one's sleeping bag several times during the night to check conditions, mainly on the *qui vive* for icebergs.

The need for diesel and fresh water necessitated a stop at Holsteinborg, or Sisimiut, as the Inuit call it. This is just north of the Arctic Circle and is Greenland's second largest town with a population of 5,000. We had reached the first settlement where sled-dogs are kept. Approaching via a few rocky archipelagos, we entered past the airport strip, custom-built to nestle into the stony mountain behind. From a distance there appeared to be a blue and white portaloo perched incongruously on the rocks with a leading mark nearby. As we drew closer, this turned out to be the airport's control tower. Outside the harbour was a rather elegant small cruise ship named the *Albatros*. Small lighters were dashing to and from the shore, taking passengers who wanted to explore and spend money on gaudy souvenirs.

The *Albatros* was anchored outside in the deeper water, but we continued past her and went into a tiny harbour jammed with fishing boats of every size. David was, outwardly at any rate, immensely calm about a scene that alarmed me somewhat – these big wooden fishing boats are quite formidable to go alongside. They often have sharp projections on them and their decks are not easily accessible. The populace looked on impassively – no cheery shouts and a wave of the arm to take a rope. David pointed out a boat to me.

'Number 290 looks the most likely choice.'

I looked around wildly and finally saw it. It was pandemonium in the tiny harbour with everyone pushing everyone else out of the way, and huge commercial fishing boats dwarfing all the individual opera-tors in their tiny dories.

'You had better get some fenders out,' he continued.

You need to be an Amazon to do this. They are nearly half my height, bulbous and awkward – some of them are vast fishing buoys found washed up on remote beaches. It is a bit like trying to wrestle with a fat Tesco shopper, then finding there isn't room to exit from the hatch together with your trophy: it's either you, or it, otherwise there is a logjam.

First, heave back the heavy lid over the fore hatch – 'Gently!' came a barked command – then enter down an aluminium ladder into the cavernous, cathedral-like gloom of the forward hold. Struggle to untie the lanyards and haul them up the hole, one at a time, out on to the deck, while David is saying peevishly, 'Hurry up – you need some lines out on deck.' Scurry back to the after-locker at the other end of the boat, where the warps lie. They too are huge; you can just get your hand round one to haul it out, and usually three warps are needed for this particular operation. Lower each fender over the side and keep tight hold while attempting to thread the lanyard through a narrow slit (freeing port) on the capping rail. (Why are there no convenient large cleats placed to port and starboard midships for this purpose, I wondered.)

Flustered by doing this, head down and struggling with clove hitches, anxious not to lose a fender in the process, I was then ordered to leap on to the fishing boat and secure to anything I could find. The gap was too great and I was not prepared to sacrifice myself, so for the second time David gave another shunt on the throttle and at one and the same time seemed to be over the side and on to this vast fishing boat to secure us. He was very impatient with me.

'You've got to *jump*! It's no good namby-pambying and standing on one leg like a ballerina. I mean, Jane, you really will have to be a bit quicker. Some of these places it has to be split-second timing' – and more in the same vein.

It was all very well for him, I thought angrily, with great long legs and apparently having excelled at high jump and long jump at school. I vowed that from then on I wasn't going to get caught out again. I was going to make my own decisions as to when to get out the necessary equipment for tying up. I also concluded that David just wasn't used to having anyone else to help him, and consequently never thought to give timely requests.

There then followed a short intermission while he went ashore to find the fuel man and I recovered my wits. Back he came.

'We must move over to the fuelling pontoon,' he said.

Inwardly I groaned at the thought of another monumental struggle to gain supremacy with the natives, who were also vying for the attentions of the fuel attendant. The fuelling pontoon was a very small floating raft, which was being nuzzled and bumped into by the tiny fishermen's boats with their pointed flared bows and shiny frail chrome rails with vast outboard motors perched on their sterns.

We untied all the ropes again and moved across to join the skirmish. David kept nudging rather menacingly into the throng, while they were all barging in under his bows. There was no polite 'after you'; it was every man for himself. I began to feel crosser and crosser and rather aggressive. We could shove and push too. David seemed to be in agreement and motored slowly on towards the pontoon as the fishermen swarmed around, trying to get in first. The little boats knew that *Polar Bound* was going to be hitched up to the pontoon for perhaps a couple of hours and they were in a hurry to organise their next fishing trip.

Eventually David got his turn, having kept remarkably calm. There was no shouting peevishly at *them*, I noticed. Luckily the wind was absent; it would have caused chaos. The fuel was delivered from a hosepipe like a filling station has, and it foamed and frothed into the fuel ports – you had to be very vigilant that it didn't go all over the place and splash on the deck. There's nothing quite so deadly as diesel on your topsides. If water gets added to this, you have a skating rink.

During this exercise an Inuit came over to say hello to David, having recognised his oh-so-unmistakable voice from the previous time David had visited Holsteinborg. David's voice was still making me go weak at the knees, so I could quite understand that other people might find it equally memorable. None the less it was amazing to have this friendly greeting in this remote spot, and all because the man remembered David's voice. He was most kind and helpful, too, and arranged for us to take on some water from the fish factory that dominated the quay nearby, and he commandeered a friend with a big pick-up to take us up into town to the supermarket. It was a long uphill journey with much swaying around the corners. We also took the opportunity of visiting a chandler, where David bought some expensive paraffin for the Wallis cooking ring. We made our way back downhill on foot with our fresh food supplies, and I decided I must make another attempt at a wholemeal loaf.

When we got back to *Polar Bound*, we found someone had made a very cursory attempt at tying up their boat on the outer side and then gone away and left the thing. We would have to move it for ourselves before we could go for water. This took a bit of forethought, shifting and pulling her straggly little lines, judiciously manoeuvring her around our bow, with her antennae and pulpit bending alarmingly. Then we motored over to the fish factory. The water was delivered by a man clad in white factory gear with a flimsy hygiene net over his hair, and bearing a fireman's hose with a huge nozzle. We were informed that there was an outbreak of disease in the town from the local water supply because it was contaminated. It must be boiled to 100 degrees to kill the bacteria before we ventured to drink it. However, we decided to press on and fill up, as it may have been no better whenever next available. An ambulance whizzed past at speed – no doubt one of the fallen.

As we drew away from the shore, the evening sunshine casting its slanting beams over the hillside, we watched a small, twelve-seater high-wing red aeroplane fly in to land on the nearby runway. Distance lent enchantment to the colourful wooden houses rising up the valley through which we had driven earlier. The last of the weary travellers from the *Albatros* had returned down the hill looking dazed and lost, seemingly not quite sure what they were meant to be photographing or even why they had gone ashore.

Holsteinborg would not be a must-visit on my agenda another time. A tiny, crowded, smelly harbour overrun with mosquitoes, jammed with locals in their fishing boats and desultory tourists from the cruise ship, who gathered in groups to be lectured on local culture before being released to wander the steep hill, avoiding the careering pick-ups that tore up and down with little regard for the rules of the road. A huge, yellow JCB was dipping its vast bucket deep down into the sea on the harbour wall and, after rummaging around on the sea bed, rising up like a dinosaur with dripping fangs and tipping the contents to one side. No doubt the harbour is scheduled for expansion and things may improve. At present it is a place lacking heart, with straggly blocks of cheap wooden housing like tenements, each festooned with washing and, incongruously, carved wooden balconies, and the nearby Sisimiut Hotel rising from its uncompromising surroundings, overlooking a vast cemetery filled with identical wooden crosses.

SEVEN

DISKO ISLAND TO LANCASTER SOUND

ABOUT 130 MILES LATER WE WERE approaching Disko Island. Numerous icebergs were in sight all around us – not surprisingly, as this area of the Vaigat is the main calving ground for the west coast of Greenland. The icebergs come from the glacier in Jakobshavn at the northern end of Disko, from where around 3,000 icebergs calve a year, and the island of Disko creates a choke point at which they congregate before passing through the narrow passage down the Vaigat.

We had decided to call in at Godhavn, on the southeast corner of Disko. David had been in there before, but it is a tricky place to enter and you must keep strictly to the leading marks. We arrived at about 8.30pm and had some difficulty in the evening light identifying the marker posts. We dodged about five or six fishing trawlers and icebergs of incredible shapes and sizes. Some may have been four or five years old, and some had reduced to dangerous 'bergy bits', which only show their tips of perhaps two or three feet, and in a swell are almost impossible to spot. The low evening sun here had a quality we had not seen before, a glowing luminosity, perhaps created by the presence of so many icebergs. At any rate, we had to concentrate on our approach before we could spot the triangles mounted on posts in prominent places. These had to be lined up, one behind the other, to guide us past dangerous underwater rocks. We noted one called Parry's Rock, which no doubt tells a story about this famous explorer's close encounter. Then we entered through a natural rock channel into an open harbour, which gave us sufficient depth to go alongside an invitingly empty wooden jetty.

A delightful, spontaneous couple of Greenlanders (who speak Greenlandic) were sitting on the jetty guarding their grandchild. With innate good manners and tact, they waited without impatience until we were ready and had sorted ourselves out, then took our mooring lines. It turned out that he was the manager of the water supply to Godhavn, which came from several springs up on the ice cap. He puts a tiny fraction of chlorine into the water to ensure it is uncontaminated, and says that it is the purest in Disko Island. How we wished we hadn't filled up in the crowded harbour of Holsteinborg the day before.

Uninvited and quite unselfconsciously, they decided to come aboard, complete with two-year-old grandchild, to look over our floating home, and pointed out to us their own house on the shore, issuing an invitation to visit them tomorrow. We were struck by the cleanliness and charm of the place. There seemed to be nobody about and all was calm and peaceful.

After a simple spaghetti supper, we went ashore to make a reconnaissance. Although it was late in the evening, being so far north there was still almost full daylight, with an evening slant that gave a wonderful atmospheric feel to the air. We walked to the fuel pontoon, where a rather complicated arrangement required paying for fuel in advance at a machine, then filling up before going back to get your receipt – all done automatically. We looked at all the wooden houses and were told that as Greenland is owned by the Danes the wood for all the houses is imported from Denmark. We wondered about how their economy works. There was a fish factory and it appeared that this must generate the pennies.

We were delighted by the serenity of our new surroundings, and by the thought of having an uninterrupted night's sleep. It had been a long day, and a short night before, so we were ready for a good sleep. We went to bed and I asked David why he always got into his bunk fully dressed (minus his shoes).

'Ready for an emergency,' came the reply.

I said, 'We're hardly likely to have one here.'

Next thing I knew was the sound of *Polar Bound*'s engine being fired up and the sight of David springing about in his socks in the dusky night. Alongside us was an enormous, menacing Portuguese fishing trawler and two crewmen who had untied our warps and were endeavouring to move our boat out of the way so they could lie alongside the jetty instead. I hastily grabbed some clothes and went out on deck to find a scene of total confusion, and a lot of shouting. Her bulwarks were high up above us, and there seemed to be a terrible noise of engines and generator, and a glare of lights along the ship's sides. David said afterwards that she was probably about 3,000 tons and *Polar Bound* would have sat very comfortably on her foredeck. Apparently they had come in to unload giant king crab that weigh several kilos each. In semi-gloom – it never seems to be entirely dark – we moved over to lie alongside a fishing boat near the fuel pontoon, rubbing the sleep from our eyes and feeling somewhat hostile towards 'our oldest allies'. David said, 'You don't argue with size.' I thought, considering how exhausted we both were, he was remarkably philosophical.

Later that morning, after we resurfaced, we went ashore and called on the helpful couple, Anni and Ludvig, who had taken our lines. As we neared their house, we saw that the outlook from their frontage was of enormous icebergs – somewhat different to looking out on to your own veggie patch or manicured green sward. Presumably the view can alter overnight as the bergs move. Some of them ground themselves, while those that diminish in size presumably drift off with the current. Their house was small and warm, their front-door mat covered with boots and shoes. We added ours and sat in their living room with an unrivalled view, both towards the harbour and out over the open sea to the west. Delicious black tea and homemade blueberry cakes, newly baked, were produced.

As we talked, we marvelled at their excellent English – both of them spoke with the right tenses and inflections. It is their second language, and is taught at school. Anni's father and mother (both now dead) lived at the research station, where she was brought up from the age of one. Botanists and biologists there monitor all the flora on Disko Island. Anni asked me if I was going to accompany David right the way through the Northwest Passage, and how we were getting back, and was I coming back with him, to which I replied, 'Well – that may be a possibility.'

'What do you mean?' said David, quick to pick me up on this casual remark. 'You can't come all this way out and not come back with me!'

I felt a warm glow when he said that, but I didn't want him to take me for granted. Anni, addressing David, said sagely, 'I don't think you'll be going anywhere without her' – showing great perception.

A thoroughly sweet, warm-hearted couple; we talked with them for some time. In the background sat their rather overweight, mature daughter with a streaming cold, curled up on a sofa and clad in a sleeveless black top, with her enquiring two-year-old son, who had investigated our boat the day before, clambering all over her, still breastfeeding. A huge television was showing a football match in full swing, to which no one seemed to be paying much attention.

Down by the fuel pontoon, we met the local doctor and his wife, both in their sixties. He was a locum, who spends several summer months a year on the island looking after the needs of the population, and lives in a house next to the hospital. They were Danish and spoke little Greenlandic. She was friendly and rather elegant, with mid-length iron-grey hair held in a tortoiseshell clip on the back of her head, and fairly plump and prosperous-looking. He was thin and lined, his face full of character. Being a Sunday, they were going off on a short fishing trip. We noted a large cool box at her feet awaiting the catch. Their Inuit crew helped David with the fuel pump, then they were on their way. The doctor had to be back by 6pm, when a helicopter was expected to airlift an elderly woman in need of a serious operation, flying her to the bigger hospital at Holsteinborg. The doctor's wife told me that Disko had a very good climate in the winter, with little wind and lots of sunshine.

Later in the day we were driven around by Ludvig and his wife, to be shown the research station where she had grown up. On the way we passed a whole lot of sled dogs, looking rather thin, chained to various fixing points on the hill outside their owner's house. They are fed only every other day, on fish and seal meat.

Just before we left, Anni gave us a small bag of leaves that she had gathered higher up near the ice cap. We were to make an infusion of them, and she assured me it was very good for the health if feeling low. As we motored out of the harbour, now more familiar with the leading marks, we adhered carefully to the course; we had no wish to fall victim to Parry's Rock.

We motored all that night through intermittent fog which blanketed down, without any discernible pattern or warning, obliterating all contact with our surroundings. This was especially alarming when we had just spotted an iceberg on the horizon. We went to our bunks and took turns to pop up from the saloon area on to the bridge deck to monitor the horizon with the aid of the radar. It was a horrible night, with a big cruise ship slowly overhauling us on a parallel course, and two or three icebergs passing the other way.

By way of diversion, I had been helping David revive his chess skills. Of course in no time at all he beat me three games in a row, but he takes his time to move (as I do), so it is quite a protracted affair, and the motion of the boat can cause total disruption. I wonder why it is in so many games that both players manage to lose their queens in consecutive moves? It is great fun to play, and we used an old guidebook written by Nigel Short (Britain's greatest player in 1993) for reference. In the course of studying this, we learned that in some circles it is not considered etiquette to announce 'Check!', since, should this be your misfortune, to a skilled player it should be apparent. However, on occasion it may have a psychological effect which can be put to good purpose.

A day or two later we had another game of chess. I won the toss to start, and I was determined to beat David, despite all his bravado. I had worked out a strategy, which I was able to put to the test, and I concentrated on getting out a couple of pawns followed by a bishop and a knight, and then I castled (as advised in Nigel's book). My preparations paid off handsomely. In due course David was rounded up into the corner and found himself checked by four or five pieces whichever way he moved – my morale was much restored.

David had been telling me all about Gino Watkins, an old Etonian still in his twenties who took an expedition to Greenland in 1930/31 to research weather patterns. He had had the idea that an air mail route from England to the Pacific coast of America via Iceland, Greenland, Baffin Land, Hudson Bay, Winnipeg, Edmonton and Vancouver would save a huge amount of time and would have the added safety advantage of fewer long sea crossings. Having presented his plans to the Royal Geographical Society, he hoped interested bodies might finance the exploration of the route. Pan American Airways, then in its infancy, showed considerable interest, and private members of the community also subscribed to their funds, including the Courtauld family.

Gino gave thought to the naming of this expedition; it had to have initials that would be easy to remember. He came up with British Arctic Air Route Expedition, BAARE. They would need sledges, dog teams, two light aircraft, motorboats and a suitable vessel in which to transport men and equipment to the east coast of Greenland. Watkins chartered the *Quest*, a schooner-rigged steamship formerly owned by Sir Ernest Shackleton, and in which he had died in 1922 in South Georgia. The idea was to make a year-long study of weather patterns. The *Quest* would drop them off, then return for them a year later.

They sailed from St Katharine Docks in London, calling at the Faroe Islands to take on board the dogs, and finally found a suitable landing spot 30 miles west of Angmagssalik on the east coast of Greenland. Here five of the crew were put ashore to journey with their dog team 250 miles inland and set up a base from which to make their respective expeditions. No one had dared to cross the icecap until 1888, and since then few traverses had been made. There was much to find out. The remaining party in the *Quest* sailed slowly northwards, putting ashore the Moth seaplanes where feasible so that Watkins and his crew could take survey photographs from 10,000 feet to supplement the work of the land party. They came upon a small fjord with a freshwater lake at its head, which they could use as a good flying base for their sorties.

Among Gino's party of undergraduates was a young man called Augustine Courtauld, later to become head of the Courtauld industrial empire. Courtauld was allocated the task of monitoring the instruments to study the weather over the Greenland plateau, where wind speeds reach 100mph. These instruments recorded temperature, wind speed and direction, barometric pressure, etc. They picked an area where the base could be made and set up a line of tall flagposts to remain visible after expected heavy snowfall during the course of the winter. Between themselves, they set up relief crews to monitor the weather-recording instruments on the plateau. This ended up with Courtauld volunteering after a particularly heavy fall of snow to remain alone with sufficient stores for five months. By being the only one, more food could then be allocated to the base camp.

On 5 December 1930, after a celebratory advance Christmas dinner, the others returned to base camp. Courtauld was left to monitor the weather instruments every four hours. His home was a dome-shaped tent, eight feet in diameter, with a snow house built over the top, and inside a reindeer-skin sleeping bag, a Primus stove and an Aladdin lamp. After a short while, Courtauld noticed a lot of itching on his arms and discovered lice. He had lent his bag to an Inuit girl a short while before and he had to put his clothes outside for two weeks in 50 degrees below zero to kill all the lice.

Harsh winter set in. Both the Moth seaplanes were blown upside down and badly damaged. Conditions relented sufficiently to allow one search party to be sent out to see if Courtauld was all right, but it failed to find him. Gino decided to search for himself, and set off with three sledges, taking two of his crew, surveying instruments and five weeks' food. The expedition navigated over the ice cap as carefully as a ship is navigated in mid ocean, and every now and again they checked their course with a compass sight, and confirmed their position by astronomical observation. They spotted a dark speck on the horizon which revealed itself to be a tattered Union Jack. Then, as they climbed the drift they spotted an inch or two of the brass ventilating tube projecting above the snow. Gino shouted down the hole, not knowing whether there would be any response. To his enormous relief a shout came back – five months to the day, and Gino was just in time as the food had run out.

The story had a sad ending. On a subsequent kayaking expedition Gino became separated from the rest of his party. When he didn't return, the others went to search for him. They found only his upturned kayak and some heavy clothing; his body was never recovered.

The likelihood of meeting any other vessel in these lonely waters was so remote that we could afford to operate an alarm-clock system for watch-keeping. After supper most evenings – we had supper quite late so as to shorten the night – I was ready for instant sleep, while David would write up the log sitting at the saloon table, finally checking that all was well before setting the alarm to go off after two or three hours and retiring. When the alarm went off, I would climb out and go straight up the companionway to check the horizon for hazards. Once my eyes had adjusted for night vision, I would have a good look around, then reset the alarm and go back to bed. We did not leave the radar on all night because it uses a tremendous amount of battery. If, on going up to the wheelhouse for a lookout, you found a lot of mist or fog, then it would be necessary to turn on the radar and scan the screen for yellow blobs, the tell-tale sign of an object on the horizon – almost always an iceberg. Allowing for the drift of an iceberg on the current and wind, and our advancing speed, it was more or less possible to judge how long it would be before evasive action – if needed at all – would be necessary. The icebergs as often as not would pass to either side of us; just occasionally they would be on a convergence course.

One morning in the small hours there was a drama. David had, as usual, taken the first watch. When he'd finished writing up the log, he retired, setting the alarm for three hours ahead. Twenty minutes or so before it went off, I woke up on my own. I felt uneasy. I stayed put for a few minutes, then decided I'd better get up and have a look. Absolutely dead ahead, and very close indeed, was a huge and menacing iceberg with growlers on both sides of it, and scattered debris of small lumps of ice in all directions. My heart beating wildly, I took off the autopilot and started hand-steering, but when I realised the extent of the lumps that had fallen off the berg, my nerve failed me. I had to go and shake David awake, who was in a deep sleep after being on the go all day. He was instantly out of his bunk and took over the hand steering. His tall frame silhouetted against the massive, glittering, iceberg towering above us was immensely reassuring, and after twenty minutes concentrated manoeuvring, he found safe passage for *Polar Bound* through the myriad stark ice scatter, and we left the monster berg to float away from us as we gathered momentum once more.

We had a narrow squeak that time, and normally we only leave it for two hours before going up to check. When I put the radar on, there was no trace of the berg – nor of another one on the beam later on, although, after we had passed it, it showed up on the radar as a small white blob dead astern of us. The radar doesn't seem to work well up in these latitudes.

No amount of short sleeps compensates for a good long night. Lack of sleep coupled with the rolling motion of *Polar Bound* is quite soporific-making. *Polar Bound* has several different gaits – the Irish Sea was not kindly and is the only time so far on this trip that we both felt ill-at-ease. The gales in the North Atlantic after leaving Portrush were awkward and uncomfortable, and I found I had to hang on really tightly. Also, everything seemed to take twice as long to do; I particularly didn't like standing on my nose to get a saucepan out of the galley cupboard with the door wildly swinging to and fro trying to chop off my fingers.

Another activity that is particularly trying is when something must be retrieved from under one of the bunks in the saloon. You have to haul the upholstered cushions off the settee berths and lift out the wooden covering board to reveal the locker space below. This will contain an assortment of items from clothing to parts for the boat, first aid, spare bilge pumps and the EPIRB (Emergency Position Indicating Radio Beacon, which you chuck over the side if all else fails and you want to rally a search and rescue party – although I am not sure if it would work out in this wilderness). Whichever hole you excavate, you can be sure that what you want is in a different one. It is very physical and quite tiring heaving the cushions about. At some point we could have done with a re-stow, but we would have needed time to spare and to be in port, not subject *to Polar Bound's* gaits. One gait she draws out of the hat when bored is her hobby horse mode. This is very uncomfortable. You start to plunge and are then brought up short. This is in contrast to the big swells, which, with her rounded hull and virtually no keel, she rides over like a rubber duck.

By 22 August we had clocked up at least 1,000 miles from Cape Farewell and were approaching Lancaster Sound from Baffin Bay.

The entrance at Lancaster Sound is about 20 miles wide and then it begins to narrow. We were approaching the Sound obliquely and we caught the occasional dim glimpse of the mountains that dominate the shoreline for a long period of time. It needs to be remembered that we were still in fog and also swirling mist that came and went in banks. The mountains being so high, they were still a long way away so it did take time to come up to the area where the Sound narrows somewhat. We proceeded like this for the next twenty-four hours or so, then, meeting on the bridge deck, David announced, 'Happy Birthday!' It was five minutes past midnight on the morning of 24 August, and I was quite suddenly sixty-nine. I don't like birthdays. I find that I rue the wasted years, and think of all the unfulfilled ambitions and the watersheds when life could have taken a new turn. Rather than a cause for celebration, for me a birthday is rather depressing.

Polar Bound put on a special 'birthday' gait for me. This is the one she adopts when the wind is behind us, coming from the east and chasing us along at a merry speed all day, all night and all the next day. This gives you an ear-popping feeling as you are lifted up from astern and sent surging forwards, only to sink back down again because the momentum cannot be sustained; then she has to scurry along under her own power at 5.5 to 6.5 knots, only to find herself, once again, sent chasing forward, willy-nilly, with the wonderful Gardner engine appearing to falter slightly as the surge takes charge, before releasing her into a welter of frothing water.

We had a birthday supper of a small joint of rolled shoulder of lamb – the first red meat since leaving Newcastle. I had marinated it for forty-eight hours in Dijon mustard, olive oil, black pepper, crushed garlic and dried thyme. We had baked potatoes and a tin of ratatouille to accompany it, and a special bottle of red Portuguese wine, which I had brought for the occasion, named Point West, as it seemed quite appropriate. I made gravy in the roasting tin, to which was added wine and cranberry sauce. We ate nearly all of it, and the rest went into a risotto for another time. A birthday card was rather deftly produced by David, which was very thoughtful of him considering how many more far important matters he had to deal with before our departure.

I felt rather strange around this time. My heart seemed to have a life of its own and I became short of breath. I spent a day doing up and undoing my bra, which I thought was perhaps too tight. Then I thought maybe it was caused through being so far north, and I quizzed David about altitude sickness. Or did the proximity to the North Pole account for it? Probably I was just overtired.

We were then at 74 degrees 20 minutes north, and the sun set at 11pm local time in a golden blaze. The sombre escarpment of Devon Island finally rose out of the shroud of gloom that had engulfed us all day throughout the approaches to Lancaster Sound, but only momentarily. It had been disconcerting charging along through a blanket of swirling fog and, despite anxious peering, seeing nothing – it was also disappointing to have a tantalising glimpse just when things were beginning to get interesting. The radar revealed nothing either, although earlier we had seen quite a few icebergs, which David said must have drifted up from Greenland because they are not normally in evidence here.

The magnetic variation in this part of the world is very great; almost as much as 40 degrees, so it is important to remember whether you should *add* or *subtract* the variation (which is only available on the relevant chart) as it makes a great difference to the true compass course being steered. Setting the course was luckily not my responsibility; I merely followed instructions, and made use of the binnacle to keep a steady course.

During the night we kept up visits to the bridge deck every hour and a half. When David's alarm woke me from a deep sleep, I went up and looked out on to an alien moonscape of black waves. On the starboard beam lay what appeared to be an outlying rocky archipelago, and nearby was an astonishing silhouette of what seemed to be a foundered super-tanker. A quick look at the chart dispelled these illusions, and I realised I was looking at floating slabs of multi-year pack ice against a faint, ethereally pink sky, and at the long shape of Devon Island terminating in Beachy Island, an isthmus at the westerly end where lie the graves of three of Franklin's men. What a terribly lonely place to die. Devon Island must be of fascination to geologists – how did it come by these three distinct horizontal sections, interspersed with a kind of rocky puckering not unlike elastic?

We awoke to more fog with what appeared to be 'ice blink' in the distance. This is a curious line of dazzling white which appears to be low in the sky, and is in fact a kind of reflected light cast up by impending pack ice. That day David got on to the satellite telephone to his contact in Winnipeg – Peter Semitouk – to consider the best tactics. The winds appeared to be easterly then going southerly, and David had concerns for the ice flow: whether we would be hemmed in, allowed free transit, or some other outcome. The next three days were critical for his ambition. We were nearing our goal.

We had been given intermittent reports about the progress of the other contender for the trophy of being the first private boat ever to transit east to west through the Northwest Passage via the McClure Strait and into the Bering Sea. Swedish *Belzebub II* with her crew of six, a 31-foot Hallberg-Rassy sailing yacht with engine, had been stooging for over a month, awaiting improved conditions. Then they had a setback – damaged their steering – and had to wait for a part to be flown into Resolute. Now, however, they were on their way once more: they left the previous night at 22.00 hours. They were ahead of us, but only just, and conditions like these were most unsuitable for a fragile, plastic hull like theirs, which could be crushed in minutes if pack ice chose to close in.

EIGHT

BARROW STRAIT AND VISCOUNT MELVILLE SOUND TO THE MCCLURE STRAIT

IT WAS NOW SUNDAY, 26 AUGUST 2012, and we had had a fairly sleepless night peering into the diaphanous gloom of intermittent blanket fog. We also had our first sighting of pack ice – shelf-like shapes of soft ice, some looking like wrecked ships, others slabs tipped on their sides. Enormous concentration was needed to weave *Polar Bound* between these floating hazards. Her rudder weighs half a ton, but even so she is finely balanced and only needs a touch on the wheel to correct her course – or so I was told. Most of the time since leaving Whitehaven, Cumbria on 29 July, she had been on autopilot, and so I had had little practice at steering her. As a result, when I did, I tended to over-steer, which meant turning the wheel excessively, first in one direction, then the other to counteract the first, resulting in a wild swing, which in turn put a big load on the rudder.

We reached Barrow Strait, and David decided not to waste time going into Resolute. Not only would it have meant delay, we should also have had to inflate the rubber dinghy, which would have been quite a palaver just when we were wanting to press on. The pack ice came in rafts and there were myriad leads, areas of clear water that opened up as the ice pulled apart then constantly changed formation, like the endless patterns of a kaleidoscope. You could easily get led astray by following a lead only to find yourself in a cul-de-sac and be forced to retrace your steps. I saw my first Arctic seal – a Ringed Seal, David told me; in fact, there were two of them and they both lumbered off their ice shelves and dropped easily into the sea. Some delightful little black and white birds, like bobbing coots, fluttered around in groups – I wondered if they were Sea Petrels. There were also Arctic Terns, and a large, pure white, swooping bird that soared effortlessly in front of the boat before making a banking glide.

David rang Peter Semitouk for a further ice report as our circumstances were becoming critical. We were now just off Steffanson Island and heading into Viscount Melville Sound, and hoping against hope that we could avoid being engulfed by the pack ice, which was on the move. We had had a brief encounter with an ice floe at lunch time, when we jolted poor *Polar Bound* forward and back in an effort to turn her round and extricate her, all most undignified. A sailing boat, on the other hand, would have been crunched to pieces.

What a night that Sunday turned out to be! To start with there was not even the ghost of a breeze, but gradually the open areas of sea took on a ruffled appearance, and before long wavelets gave way to bigger seas. As we scrutinised the pack ice with binoculars for open leads to pass through, David reconsidered his strategy. Instead of going due west and maybe getting stuck in Viscount Melville Sound surrounded by blocks of pack ice, he decided to take a southwest by west course, obliquely traversing the sound so as to be one jump ahead of the ice, and head for the corner of Banks Island in the Parry Channel. Here a little refuge offers a space in which to hide should that be necessary.

There we could await the right wind, which would chase the ice out of the final hurdle, the McClure Strait, or so we hoped, into the Arctic Sea, which becomes the Beaufort Sea.

Meanwhile, or so we heard from Peter Semitouk, *Belzebub II* had headed into the central area of Melville Sound and might well be hemmed in with ice. However, it was possible that this news, as relayed to Peter, might have been deliberately leaked in an effort to throw us off the scent. They were, according to Peter, 'hell bent on beating that "Cooper" man' to be the first private vessel to make this transit. In David, with his wonderful sense of timing and equal determination to achieve yet another record, they had formidable opposition. It was getting late in the season now and if we did not get favourable conditions for this challenge he decided that, having waited a few days, we would proceed down the Prince of Wales Strait, and exit the narrow section of the passage via the traditional southerly route.

I seasoned and scored some Bressingham duck breasts and made an apple sauce, but the conditions were deemed unsuitable for such a meal. David perhaps should have warned me, but he was far too preoccupied with the avoidance of ice packs. We ended up eating spaghetti. The ice pack was moving with a strong southeasterly, which was not the direction we wanted it from. I went below to my bunk and had a couple of hours' uneasy sleep, but felt as if I could have done with at least another six – my ankles and legs were quite swollen and felt heavy. All this bracing of unfamiliar muscles to keep on balance, and the constant sorties up and down the companionway, all took their toll. David said he felt wakeful too – I am sure he was. He now had the bit firmly between his teeth and was giving it everything he had. With just two of us aboard, we had no extra reserves to call up so we could not get proper rest.

When I re-emerged from my bunk, the scene was like Dante's *Inferno*. A full gale was blowing on the ship's beam and the entire frozen sea appeared to be on the march. Great rafts of pack ice proceeded with remorseless power on their individual trajectories. Some looked like huge, delicate lotus flowers in full sail, others like stacked-up railway sleepers; then there were the fantasies of the funfair: giant gondolas and rocking ducks, carnival floats, even a double pedalo with circular viewing hole through the centre like an old-fashioned plate camera. Grimms' Fairy Tales and the World of Oz all intertwined. Henry Moore, Barbara Hepworth and Elizabeth Frink creations everywhere you looked. Every conceivable resemblance to something or other imaginable was there.

After giving me a short time to acclimatise, David went below to get some sleep, entrusting me with our safety. I hoped I could justify his trust. I could hardly keep my balance; even the seat behind the wheel felt unsafe. After a few minutes to orientate myself, I realised that the only rogue pieces of pack ice that needed evasive action were the ones directly in our path. The rest were travelling in chaotic fashion on a parallel course, some appearing to gain, and others to collide with their brethren. To avoid these hazards necessitated the disconnection of the self-steering mechanism and then wrestling with *Polar Bound*'s big wheel, which seemed to have a mind of its own and tended to go into a wild swing when I was behind it.

I had never seen such an amazing sight. I wouldn't have believed it possible that so many square miles of thick pack ice could be broken up and moved so quickly by the combined action of wind and waves. The effect of this heaving mass was like walking briskly along the travelator at Heathrow where, disconcertingly, you can see walkers to either side of you who keep pace and occasionally go even faster. Dawn came, revealing a heaving grey sea with a few of the more cumbersome outriders still marching resolutely on their chosen track in pursuit of their long dissolved or relocated companions, with smaller debris scattered across the ocean, like the aftermath of a storm in the mountains.

In the next notification we had from Peter, we heard that the Swedish contender in this two-man race had liberated himself from the pack ice (if, indeed, he had ever been stuck), and arrived a few hours earlier at the entrance of the Prince of Wales Strait. Following advice, he was heading up a narrow lead of clear water up the coast of Banks Island in the Parry Channel. We were disconcerted by this news. David had been convinced that the Hallberg-Rassy boat would have been, by now, firmly stuck to the northeast of us. We were right to have doubted the story that they had headed into the central area of the Melville Sound.

All along we had thought the Hallberg-Rassy boat, after leaving Resolute following repairs to her steering, had become caught in pack ice somewhere well to the north east of us out in the Parry Channel. It seems now that, following advice, they were instead heading up a narrow lead of clear water close to the shore of Banks Island. The question now was whether they were ahead of us, or behind.

Originally David was taking a middle of the road route through Viscount Melville Sound, until we were confronted by this huge quantity of redistributed ice which had been broken up and then blown by the wind, piling up on top of itself. This was when we consulted Peter Semitouk, our ice adviser, as to where he thought we might find a lead. He suggested that we would find several channels if we headed more to the south west and crept round the back of the ice pack, close in up against the northeast side of Banks Island, in the vicinity of Russell Point. All this time we were shrouded in intermittent fog which was most hazardous at this particular juncture.

At this moment, another pall of blanket fog settled over the whole area. The difficulties to making forward progress seemed endless, and doubly hard through exhaustion from lack of sleep. I cannot imagine how David managed on his own on earlier voyages. He certainly has no shortage of courage – some would say foolhardiness. He has told me how a few people he has met over the years professed a willingness to accompany him, but when it came to the point, there always seemed to be a good reason why they were unable to. It crossed my mind that the characteristics of *Polar Bound* must have proved daunting. With her rounded shape, and only drawing 5 feet 6 inches, she does roll; it is, of course, this shape that makes her eminently suitable for this kind of expedition.

We crept along the Parry Channel heading towards Banks Island with an endless sea of frozen ice shapes stretching beyond the horizon. We strained our eyes trying to catch fleeting glimpses of the shoreline we knew was there if only the fog would lift. At one moment it did thin and we saw the low, black shoreline of Banks Island. It had an icing of smoky katabatic mist drifting in diaphanous pockets over it. We felt very uneasy, even frightened. We couldn't trust our eyes anymore; we couldn't be certain whether we were looking at landscape or cloud.

In the midst of all this, David turned on the radar and, after silent contemplation for quite some time, announced he had spotted a tiny yellow blob on the screen, keeping its distance behind us – in other words, travelling at the same speed. Whereas we had been convinced the Hallberg-Rassy had stolen a march on us of many hours, there was no doubting that what he was looking at in these hundreds of miles of empty wilderness could only be one thing: the Swedish contender, and, more importantly, not ahead of us, but behind.

This was wildly exciting. Exhaustion fell away; we were galvanised. You'd have thought it was the race between Scott and Amundsen! Tired, aching limbs were forgotten. We chuffed on, as indeed *Belzebub II* was doing, with David steering and me peering through the glasses in search of leads and helping him to locate them. We crawled up the remote and uninhabited coastline of Banks Island in the Parry Channel that gave way to the McClure Strait. Captain McClure was the nineteenth-century explorer who discovered this channel; he witnessed the frozen waste from the shore after his ship had foundered and, sledging across it, recognised it as the missing link in the shortest passage between the Atlantic and Pacific oceans. This most northerly route we transited turned out to be only a few miles different to the more conventional southerly route via the Amundsen and Coronation Gulfs, which had been the accepted route hitherto.

As global warming proceeds, one day, in a few years to come, you probably will be able to sail through. Where a sail could help is to give a little steadiness to the boat and stop her from rolling; and of course on open water, if the wind is favourable, you could then take advantage of a long stretch and sail with a free wind. This is the reason why David, eighteen years earlier, had built an immensely strong, wooden prototype for *Polar Bound*, 2 feet shorter in length, and had made provision for a gaff-rigged mainsail. However, he then set his heart on having a Gardner engine, the complexities of which he thought he could manage, should it break down thousands of miles from land. He discovered that the Gardner would not fit into the engine room of his prototype and so, reluctantly, he had to abandon the plan and start again. Potential adventurers reading this account should take note that his lovely prototype, looking as sturdy as Noah's Ark, two-thirds completed and lying under wraps in Scotland, is now available to a suitable buyer and on completion would make a marvellous, strong vessel...

Finally we emerged from the blanket fog and for the first time had clear sight of the waterways we had been groping our way down, scattered

▲ Writing my narrative in the aft cabin of *Polar Bound*.

▼ David Scott Cowper after a haircut in the Unimak Pass.

▲ My four-greats uncle, Sir John Franklin (1786–1847), an experienced and indomitable man who led two previous expeditions.

▲ Following seas in the North Atlantic.

▼ The chart table in the wheelhouse of *Polar Bound*.

▲ David's party trick – not bad for a 71 year old!

▼ Impressive icebergs carved near Disko Island, making their way down the Vaigat in the current.

▲ Spectacular scenery through Prins Christian Sund.

▼ A good example of how much ice is under the water compared with above, which reinforces the 9/10ths rule.

▲ A glacier in Navy Board Inlet.

▼ *Polar Bound* transiting Prins Christian Sund.

▲ *Polar Bound* leaving the sheltered harbour of Augpilagtoq, Prins Christian Sund.

▼ This iceberg has most probably turned turtle. The shiny side would originally have been underwater.

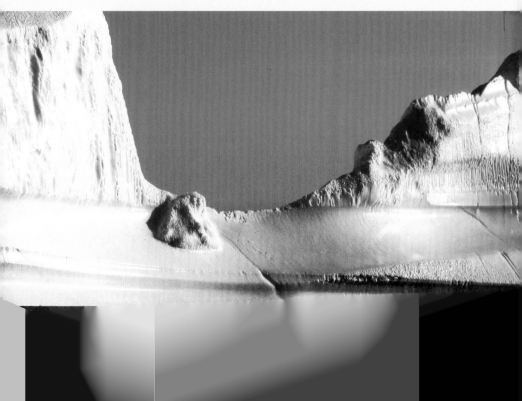

▲ *Polar Bound* threading her way through leads in the pack ice in Prince Regent Inlet.

▼ An iceberg drifting in the Davis Strait as it gradually reduces with the passage of time.

▲ Looking down from the mountain heights of Dutch Harbour in the Aleutians.

▼ Another view looking down from the mountain into the inner harbour of Dutch Harbour.

▲ Impressive cliffs at the entrance to Beechey Island, off Lancaster Sound.

▼ American gun emplacements at the top of the mountain above Dutch Harbour, built to guard the approaches during the Second World War.

▲ *Polar Bound* passing the well-known landmark of the Russian Orthodox church as she departs Dutch Harbour.

▼ A bald eagle with attitude – it is quite common for fishermen who need to repair their nets to lay them out on a hard surface where the eagles will clean them of fish pickings.

▲ David manoeuvring the 50-kilo Delta main anchor back into its retaining brackets on the foredeck.

▼ A peaceful anchorage in Alaska's inside highway.

▲ Refuelling *Polar Bound* at Dutch Harbour.

▲ Seals taking advantage of a resting place on a buoy, where they will not be disturbed, at the entrance to Petersburg, Alaska's inside highway.

▼ David about to throw a large fender for buffering against a pontoon in Petersburg.

▲ Build up of freezing spray as *Polar Bound* makes her way up Prince Regent Inlet.

▼ Pilot's house and pontoon at Elfin Cove, Icy Strait.

▲ Passing Mount Shishaldin, a still-active volcano on Unimak Island – apparently the most symmetrical cone-shaped mountain on earth.

▼ A lengthy inspection by a huge whale near the Unimak Pass.

with floating rafts of pack ice. The sea was mirror calm, reflecting the clouds and the dramatic 1400-foot-high escarpment about two-thirds of a mile off to port, a prominent peak named Cape Vesey Hamilton. We both went out on deck to take photographs, David snapping shots in quick succession with two different cameras – one huge, multiple-lens Canon and a handier Lumix with a zoom lens – while I persisted with my humbler 'point and press'. This was the most northerly point of our voyage at 74 degrees, 32 minutes north.

Cape Vesey confronted us like the forbidding headquarters of mountain trolls. Its convoluted rocky face has four distinct, horizontal seams of rock, the whole crossed by great striations as though made by giant griffin claws. The seams perhaps mark different ice ages, successive glacial flow wearing away the softer material. These are the guardian rocks to the western end of the McClure Strait. The eastern end, on Devon Island, shows similar strata. We re-emerged from putting on warmer clothing and continued to take pictures of this towering, defiant façade, soaring in silent majesty as if it were the last bastion of an extinct world, long to remain when mankind has been vanquished by its own greed.

The sky of soft pinks, greys and blues was exactly mirrored in the calm waters of the strait, in between floating lumps of ice. The solitude was immense, immeasurably powerful and all-embracing. *Belzebub II* had disappeared off our radar screen, probably because she had altered her position and there was no longer her angled beam from which to glance off – end to end with *Polar Bound* she would not show up on the radar. David calculated that she was about 26 miles behind us.

This, for us, was the historic moment. We had succeeded in making a passage that had been sought after for the last four centuries, and we had beaten a close contender too. In the short window of weather, with David's charts and navigational aids and, most importantly, his knowledge and determination, and with the help of our ice captain, we had done it. I like to think that my four-greats uncle Rear Admiral Sir John Franklin was celebrating in the firmament of the Great Beyond.

Three or four hours later we encountered yet another seemingly impenetrable wall of multi-year pack ice. We had to scour the face of it with glasses as we motored along, keeping our distance off, heading to the far horizon where David had a hunch we could find our way around. Sure enough, after quite an anxious time, we entered clear water and came out into a glorious, golden red sky, having lost all track of time. Finally we had quite a good supper of the long-awaited Bressingham roast duck breast with all the trimmings – this had to be eaten in relay as we could not relax our vigilance. We were both exhausted, and David went to his self-termed coffin berth for a good sleep. I remained on watch, but I am ashamed to say that for the first time ever I fell asleep sitting bolt upright on the quarter berth near the wheel.

We passed out of the McClure Strait, leaving Cape Crozier, Cape McClure, Cape Wrottesley and Cape Prince Alfred to port, and finally entered the Arctic Sea – more accurately the Beaufort Sea – on Wednesday 29 August 2012.

NINE

ACROSS THE BEAUFORT SEA TO THE CHUKCHI SEA

I N TRUTH, OUR ACHIEVEMENT WAS not quite yet in the
bag. We still had to transit the Bering Strait on the 66 and a half
degree parallel to have truly completed the Northwest Passage.
This is an international waterway divided between the Russians and
the Americans in Alaska, and our transit would only be complete on
arrival there in about ten days' time. However, congratulations were
already coming in to David's office, including from *Belzebub II*, as
well as from my sister and brother-in-law who had been following
our progress on a tracker.

Previously we had a head wind and now it had gone round 180
degrees. We were tearing along through the empty wilderness of the
Arctic Sea, devoid of any other shipping. Every now and again, a
particularly big wave slammed into our quarter and the boat gave a
lurch and rolled even more wildly.

David had been diligently keeping his log, in which he writes
a couple of morning entries, several in the afternoon if there is
a change of conditions, and a closing entry at the end of each day.

This recorded the number of days into the passage from when we left Whitehaven, where we'd just come from, and the point towards which we were heading. He included the time of each entry, the true course being steered, the magnetic compass course (in this latitude there was a 30-degree difference between the two), the speed at which we were travelling, the wind direction and strength, the state of the sea, the reading from the barometer (which was 986 on the day after our triumph), the temperature both externally and internally, and the latitude and longitude satellite position, giving us our exact position (a 'fix'). The most northerly position we reached was 74 degrees 32 minutes north, and out here in the Arctic Sea we were currently at 125 degrees 57 minutes west.

Occasionally I would take a surreptitious look at his log. I was surprised that nowhere was my name mentioned as even being aboard. Did he wish people to think he was travelling alone, or was it an oversight? 'We' means *Polar Bound* and himself; not me. Hitherto he had always travelled alone. What if the boat foundered – would any rescuer know to look for two people?

When we were at our most northerly position, off Banks Island, I had the curious sensation of finding that the horizon to the north, in the golden evening light, appeared to have an uphill tilt – in other words, it wasn't level; as if we were on a slant. Could this really be happening? Is it something to do with the fact that the degrees of longitude are only 16 miles in length in this area, whereas on the equator one degree equals 60 miles? Or could it be something to do with being not too far from the Magnetic North Pole? This strange illusion lasted about three days or so, while were in the McClure Strait, but David didn't seem to notice it at all.

The wind moved round on the starboard quarter, and the motion of *Polar Bound* began to reveal her more unpleasant characteristics; she corkscrewed and wallowed, and gave me cause to reflect on the virtue of participating in future voyages. The vertical position could not be sustained for more than a second and you had to brace your legs like a newly born giraffe struggling to its feet. You needed both hands to hang on and so it was difficult to do anything else. Everything in the small galley, despite non-skid mats, found its own level eventually, which was either on the floor or in the sink. I had strong memories of the stories I heard so often from my sailing husband, also called David, who had recounted his Royal Ocean Racing Club days to me. He had frequently skippered the Club boat, *Griffin II*, when on most occasions everything, crew included, ended up on the cabin sole – if they hadn't arrived there by accident, they had placed themselves there deliberately as being the lowest point in the boat and the safest place to be. My newly poured tea went straight over, undrunk, thankfully on to a tea towel that had obligingly slid off the rail in front of the solid fuel stove. The Dickinson gave out wonderful warmth similar to an Aga, and provided the hub of our waterborne home. It remained aloof to the vagaries of the tumult without and gave us a sense of security within.

Conditions can change hour by hour. Earlier that morning I had made another batch of bread, and David had run the boat off about 80 degrees so as to give a more manageable angle, both for the comfort of the ride and to facilitate the breadmaking. We also emerged once or twice from the cocooned world of the saloon and bridge deck, out through the massive aluminium door secured with its six vast turnbuckles, and up to the bows of the boat and the forward hold. This in turn is secured by an equally huge and heavy aluminium hinged hatch, into which you have to insert a massive key, which operates another big inner wheel. It's the sort of thing you see in cross-channel ferries and submarines. All this effort quite possibly only to bring back some potatoes or something for supper from the deep freeze.

On 30 and 31 August, out in the Beaufort Sea with the McClure Strait behind us, David decided to take a more direct route towards Point Barrow from Cape Prince Albert on the extreme north west corner of Banks Island. However, this proved impossible; we spotted ice blink on the horizon and soon encountered solid ice pack in front of us. We had to alter course, keeping closer towards Banks Island heading due south. Once in the clear, exhausted after over 48 hours of continuous vigilance in what had proved a very foggy and cloudy voyage so far, we both went to bed. After a few hours, on impulse, I decided to go up on to the bridge deck to take a look round. To my amazement there were two quite large islands, one of which we had already steamed past, and the second of which was just coming up. (Later on, when we consulted the chart, it turned out to be called Terror Island.) I went down to wake David, and said, 'We're going past a couple of islands,' knowing that this would electrify him, which it did.

'OK – ready,' he said. Dashing up to look, he was evidently relieved that we were safely past one and well clear of the other. He turned on the depth meter and identified where we were, and later admitted he hadn't allowed for this deviation, as he had laid off the course too close. There by the grace of God sail many adventurers, who are forced to take chances from time to time due to fatigue. Nevertheless, it was quite sobering. I asked him whether it would have damaged the boat if we'd hit, but he said not, although we would have had to get out all the ground tackle, blowing up the dinghy and spending a lot of time and effort hauling anchors around.

A couple of days later we progressed from the Beaufort Sea into the Chukchi Sea, still within the Arctic Ocean. For the last five or six days, since emerging from the corridor of the Northwest Passage and travelling south, we had been on a roller-coaster ride. A fresh northerly wind, gradually increasing to a force 8/9 gale with foaming white crests, had been chasing us along. The big seas had been cork-screwing us round, lifting the stern and causing cavitation around the propeller, before sinking us down and swinging onward in a welter of foam, occasionally leaving a great millpond of suds whirling around before the onslaught of the next. Cavitation happened when the wave sent a mixture of air and water around the propeller, causing it to spin in a vacuum like an enormous cement mixer, making an extraordinary gurgling sound.

It was now 3 September and we saw our first ship, the only one since the tanker we spotted back in the North Atlantic at the beginning of August. David saw it first, and said, 'I think there is an oil rig ahead of us.'

I snatched up my glasses with some excitement and identified it as a military or naval ship. It turned out to be an American patrol boat, No. 705. It was quite an excitement to see another vessel. As we got nearer, so it grew in stature. It appeared to be more or less marking time, placed centrally in our path, standing guard – a bastion of American might. And having spotted us, it was perfectly clear from their intentions that they wished to interrogate us.

Polar Bound has a somewhat official-looking stature of her own, and no doubt the Americans, with their sometimes trigger-happy attitude, were slightly alarmed by our appearance and thought the Yellow Peril had come to invade. We noticed that they had an Interceptor ready to launch over the side should we prove to be unfriendly. I said to David, 'Hadn't we better turn on the radio?'

I think he was about to do this anyway as we drew level with them. There was a bit of crackling, then the voice came over quite crisply. Americans never realise what a shock to the English system it is when you first hear an American voice, and depending on what part of America they come from, the accent and manner of speaking can sometimes be quite difficult to follow.

There then followed quite an exchange. They wanted to know our ship's name, boat registration number, David's date of birth, number of companions on board, my name and date of birth – at least my presence was recognised! – what was the purpose of our journey, to which he replied, 'Pleasure,' last port of call, next port of call, approximate ETA, and so on. When all this information had crossed the airwaves via the internationally recognised alphabet – Alpha, Bravo, Charlie etc. – David said, in a conversational sort of way, what a nice surprise it was to see someone in this ocean wilderness, and there then followed nearly an hour's conversation about ice conditions, past experience of ice conditions, the melting of the ice cap, the story of David's rescue of an American satellite beacon prototype near Hawaii a few years earlier (of which more later), and so on. We learned later that the entire complement of the ship's crew, some 120 men and women, were either riveted to their radio relays listening in to this conversation, or looking David up on Wikipedia and Google and marvelling at his voyages.

The conversation became very friendly and we were both invited to visit them when we reached Dutch Harbour in the Aleutian Islands. They were a United States Coastguard cutter, the *Bertholf*. They said they would look out for us, as they were heading there soon for supplies and a change of crew. With David's usual modesty, he merely told them he had just completed the Northwest Passage, and the route he had taken, never mentioning that he was the first ever to transit this most northerly route. His interlocutor, who turned out to have been the captain, was most respectful, interjecting 'sir' frequently into the conversation. Eventually, after more of the same, we parted company, but not before we had both stepped outside the wheelhouse and photographed and waved at them. They didn't wave back from their bridge, but they did call us a few minutes later to add a warning that the Inuit had shot a 30-foot whale off Point Barrow, which had died from its wounds and was floating in the water, just where we were heading. We never saw it.

We had another tumultuous night with a heavy sea running behind us. I had to resort to the small calor gas ring to finish off the supper preparations as both the stoves were failing, one through cold wind in the chimney, the other from the low level of fuel.

On 5 September we heard through David's office that there was a very good *Telegraph* article with photographs about *Polar Bound*'s achievement by Neil Tweedie. His office also reported that *Belzebub II*'s public relations people – they had twelve sponsors and a terrific back-up admin team – had produced a somewhat flowery account of their adventure. There was quite a bit about an aeroplane fluttering out of the mist in a patch of sunshine during a break in the clouds to photograph them. We couldn't imagine where it had taken off from and we never saw it, but as we were probably about five or six hours ahead of them that would have accounted for it. They also claimed to be the first *sailing* boat through the Northwest Passage. That, of course, was true – except that they weren't actually sailing, but proceeding steadily with their motor. It is absurd to consider that a small sailing boat could make the passage through other than by engine. They did apparently set their sail eventually, when they drew level with Cape Crozier, to sail out into the Beaufort Sea, once clear of ice. But other than that their journey was really no different to David making the passage in *Polar Bound*.

Belzebub also admitted they had picked us up on their radar when we were about 27 miles ahead of them as we both progressed through thick fog. They said they had caught a glimpse ahead of 'what could only have been the legendary Mr Cowper before his vessel was swallowed up in swirling mist'.

The next morning we woke to easier conditions after the last few days and nights of continuous gales through the Chukchi Sea. It was incredible to think that we were now halfway around the world and shortly to pass through the 46-mile-wide Bering Straits, with Siberia on our starboard hand, and Alaska, USA to port. The barometer had been abnormally low at 970 millibars, despite the fact that the gale-force following wind had gradually abated, but then the pressure started to rise, so it looked as if we were in for a quieter time.

TEN

THROUGH THE BERING STRAIT TO LANDFALL IN NOME, ALASKA

I N THE CHUKCHI SEA I BEGAN TO NOTICE a few birds again and wondered what they were. Perhaps it was the proximity of the Siberian coastline, but we saw pairs of ducks and more of the little bobbing coots, as well as a larger, totally black bird with scimitar wings – these were swooping about over the big seas we had had two or three days ago. This part of Siberia is home to the nomadic Laplanders, who herd huge numbers of caribou and whose way of life has largely gone unmolested by the Russian government. It was astonishing to think that this vast tract of water through which we were proceeding would shortly be completely frozen over for the winter; more sobering perhaps was the thought that the Beaufort Sea to the north used to be frozen over all year round, leaving only a narrow waterway close in near the coast. Now it is clear water half the year round.

On Friday, 7 September 2012, we finally passed through the 66 and a half degree parallel of latitude, marking the true culmination of the Northwest Passage, just to the north of the Bering Strait, a total of

93

nineteen and three-quarter days since crossing the Davis Strait. And so we had completed the passage, and if we had had a bottle of champagne, I would have had to drink it all as David doesn't like it. In fact, I had brought one, but it was buried deep in a locker and would have to wait for another occasion. The long-sought-after passage had been accomplished, but was only possible because of the melt of the ice cap, which will have its effect on mammals, marine life and mankind.

Peter Semitouk forwarded us a wonderful accolade he had received by satellite email from an admirer and follower of David's. I wrote him a response in which I asked the sender to support my application for a senior nomination for David, which he richly deserves after all his achievements and the records he has won for the United Kingdom. Unless I push this modest, retiring recipient to send it off, we'll get nowhere. He should have been recognised years ago, but it seems that only those who make a big noise and create a razzmatazz around them get noticed.

Our next destination, where we would take on fuel and stores, was to be Nome, Alaska. The night before, I happened to wake before the alarm went off and decided to go on deck and take a look outside. Not far away, though impossible to tell the distance, lay an enormous ship covered in lights. Some distance from its stern a green light indicated that it was showing its starboard side. Once again, I had to disturb David; this was an unusual equipage and I had no idea what it was. He identified three vertical white lights, which indicated it was towing something. It was hard to see clearly. Apart from a big swell, which made it difficult to view through the glasses, it was also murky and our bridge windows were covered in salt. David called them up on the VHF radio, channel 16, but there was no response – they were all asleep. Facing into the wind, they were lying ahead, the towing vessel possibly anchored as it was relatively shallow. David said that in a situation like that, if one is concerned, it can be good idea to fire off a flare gun. This illuminates the whole area and then you can see what's what. However, he didn't feel sufficiently concerned to take such measures.

We finally reached Nome on Sunday, 9 September, our first port of call since leaving Godhavn in Greenland; here we entered the United States of America. The harbour master contacted Customs on our behalf and later that day an Inuit officer made his way to our boat, where we were tied up alongside the jetty. Considerably over-weight, he decided, quite wisely, not to step on board; we were glad, having been fearful that he might get jammed in the entrance door. Instead, we climbed into his smart white 4X4 station wagon to shelter from the biting wind while he remained standing at the open back and duly stamped our passports, checked the ship's papers, which he photocopied, and helpfully issued us with a cruising permit without making any charge.

Nome is famous for the Great Gold Rush back in the 1900s when 40,000 people, having heard that gold nuggets were to be found on the beach, descended en masse to try their luck. The small township still houses prospectors, most of whom are scruffy and dishevelled drop-outs who are drunk quite a lot of the time – an expensive pastime. The prospectors have all manner of vessels; many look home-made and Heath Robinson. More successful participants have well-found aluminium vessels with a lot of equipment aboard to sift the bottom of the ocean, riddle it and dredge it, discarding it back on the seabed. Presumably when the sea has redistributed it in a gale, another hopeful will try his hand. Men in diving suits walk along the seabed, which is quite shallow – maybe 20 foot or so deep – in search of the metal; others lack the will to put the necessary effort in. Cast-iron buckets, from elevators on the dredgers that formerly carried the spoil, now lie on every street corner, or adorn houses filled with flowers or herbs. The town sports the longest saloon bar in Alaska with two vast, curving counters to accommodate all the drinkers, and a mahogany rail stretching to infinity in both directions. The eccentric landlord, with a free and easy manner, unkempt curly hair and a bloodshot eye, is very good at his public relations, and welcomed us – though we had only gone in to take photographs – with unbounded enthusiasm. In the midst of this vast long counter, punctuated by eight television screens mounted above the bartenders' heads, was only one other guest. The noise near midnight must be deafening, however, and we had no doubt that the wooden floorboards had had their share of pugilists; the spartan furniture certainly showed signs of punishment. We heard through the grapevine that there had been a few problems when *Belzebub II* arrived on the scene, and allegedly an embarrassed policeman had to be called to sort out a punch-up.

Nome's other claim to fame is the Iditarod dog sled race. This is an annual event, a race of 1,000 miles from Anchorage to Nome, and those wishing to compete with a team of huskies must first prove their worth by participating in four earlier events. This is to make sure the owners know how to look after their animals and are up to the responsibility that accompanies placing such taxing demands on the dogs. Welfare is all important. The dogs have to wear little leather bootees to protect their paws; after all, they must carry all their own food and the tented accommodation for their owners, who stop at night to rest.

Out of the blue a tall, young, friendly American by the name of Rolland Trowbridge came down to the quayside and called out to us with an invitation to join him and his wife for supper. He said they were vegans and would be very pleased if we would join them for a meal of vegetable lasagne in their house on the main street, and that they had asked the crews of four other boats too – without, it seems, knowing any of them.

We went along at 7.30 armed with a bottle of wine. The flat was accessed through an outer communal door and up a wooden staircase that tilted drunkenly to one side, on which one felt, even stone cold sober, somewhat insecure. The staircase opened into a room filled with a couple of desks and about six or seven computers, laptops and radio equipment. Few of the houses in Nome appear to be on the level. They are mostly small clapboard houses on wooden supports, clear of the ground, and leaning one way or the other.

We had a delightful evening in their lopsided flat. Rolland is a man of many parts, intelligent and capable with an entrepreneurial attitude, juggling four or five different jobs. He is an electronics engineer, computer boffin and technician, and a diver too. He is certainly making a place for himself in Nome, where he plans to invest in a second-hand crane to lift boats out of the water when their owners wish to overwinter. He is a semi-paramedic and a fire officer. His wife, Debbie, makes sail repairs on a large industrial sewing machine. She will even cut you a new sail; she borrows the church floor to lay out the cloth. They have two teenage daughters, and for a short time had two Inuit foster children. They also have sixteen husky dogs, housed along with twenty others in Dog Village, separated from human habitation for obvious reasons; these dogs, unlike the ones we saw chained on the rough terrain outside the houses in Godhavn, which got fed every other day, are fed on caribou and seal meat twice a day. Rolland told us he was planning to enter the Iditarod in 2014.

The other guests were an Australian couple with a young crew man, who undertook the washing-up after supper, an Austrian diver and an English woman who lives in Newfoundland, and two young teachers of photography, wielding very expensive, telescopic multi-lens cameras, who had arrived in Nome in a junk rig with a

single horsepower engine, and who were sailing in company with a
Frenchman in his sixties named Luc. Luc was sailing his own boat;
they kept in touch by VHF radio and discussed what they were going
to eat for supper, for which they rafted up each evening. On their
menu was duck, lamb or goose supplied by Luc, and pasta or potatoes provided by the other two. Luc was most entertaining. As for
his two young companions, David seemed already to have met them
on an earlier expedition. There were others, too, but I don't think we
got around to talking to everyone. Rolland and Debbie were certainly
wonderful ambassadors for their community. They would be very
worthy joint sheriffs of the neighbourhood.

The next day we spent walking about in Nome, David taking
photos and visiting gift shops. We decided the ivory walrus carvings
were overpriced: $800 to $1,200 for a four-inch-long representation
of a seal, and $2,000 for an Inuit in a kayak. I bought two or three
books for my grandchildren, and a pashmina for $16, which turned
out to have been imported.

Nome is the true Wild West like you see in cowboy films, with
square clapboard facades and, at the rear, nothing but untidy squalor,
rubbish and cast-out household items and car tyres. A pretty white
wooden church with an elegant spire sits on a bit of open ground with
a children's play area and a gigantic bronze monument of a vast gold
panning dish, along with the larger than life-sized figures of three
hatchet-featured prospectors. Elsewhere is a bronze of Amundsen
with his back to the sea, gazing fixedly into the main street of the
town, where festoons of wiring hang in ungainly lumps from drunken
telegraph poles. A hexagonal wooden visitor centre offers tea and
coffee and internet access, and any number of leaflets on what to do
in Nome. Quite a few visitors take an expensive cab ride out to a hot
spring, apparently slightly grubby with vertical wooden paling sides –
you have to be a real enthusiast to participate in one of these.

A very kind chap, son of a local fisherman, took us around in his pick-up in search of a herd of musk ox, said to be roaming on the fringe of the settlement. In due course, he located them and parked nearby, while David took his big camera and walked over as near as he dared to photograph them. They circled round and stamped the ground, dipping their heads in a menacing way. About twenty of them, shaggy and horned, stood together, sheltering two or three calves. Their legs seemed incredibly short and stumpy but they are surprisingly swift and should be given a wide berth. When shorn of their matted, long hair, they are quite small animals. They are said to be the oldest mammal on Earth, since the mammoth died out. A village elder told me that musk ox and grizzly bears are equal adversaries and do not like to take each other on. Out hunting one day many years ago, he had witnessed a musk ox with its horns deeply embedded in the ribs of a grizzly – both animals dead. The musk ox had been unable to withdraw its horns under the weight of the bear, which it had gored to death.

After a couple of days in Nome, we got under way again, heading down through the Bering Sea towards the Aleutian Islands and Dutch Harbour. We proceeded on a southerly course with Siberia to starboard. Increasing waves and wind on the port side gave us a heavy roll and made everything in the galley clatter and bang. Nothing could be put down for a minute or it would go straight over. We paid several visits to the bridge deck to monitor the radar during the night, and saw only one rather sinister-looking warship at dusk.

It was time to do a bit of office work again. David received some emails which had to be replied to. What it is to have staff! He had been receiving quite a few messages of congratulation, and naturally everyone thought he had been solo, as he always has before. Peter Semitouk still didn't know I was aboard. I felt David should be making capital out of the fact that he had as crew the four-greats niece of Sir John Franklin. No one had ever been right through before, and it was Captain McClure who discovered the missing link in 1853 in the *Investigator*, which he lost in Mercy Bay on Bank's Island. He sledged his men over to Winter Harbour on Melville Island, from where they were rescued. One hundred and sixty-one years later, David Scott Cowper became the first man to sail right through the passage from the Davis Strait to the Bering Strait and, as his crew, I became the first woman, which was fitting, since I was named after Jane Franklin. David doesn't seem to realise how to make capital when the opportunity presents itself, which is probably why he has not received the recognition he deserves.

ELEVEN

DUTCH HARBOUR IN THE ALEUTIAN ISLANDS

B Y FRIDAY, 14 SEPTEMBER, WE HAD ARRIVED at Dutch Harbour, an emerald-green island whose volcanic peaks were carpeted in a velvet wrap devoid of trees. After a world of snow and ice and constant fog, it was balm for the eyes. Two humpback whales were sporting about in the bay chasing krill as we entered the harbour at Unalaska Island, part of the Aleutian island chain. The harbour was full of large fishing boats offloading their catch of brown crab to the processing plants. The poor, spiny things of enormous size, weighing well over 2 kilos each, were held in vast, circular mesh bags and unloaded by crane into the sea secured by a tether until the processors were ready to handle them. The entire town revolved around the catching and processing of fish and crustaceans, although there was a threat of the oil industry taking over and usurping them to more remote areas. The staff were catered for in purpose-built service apartment blocks, complete with laundry, showers and a free canteen so they need only concentrate on the job in hand. The whole air was permeated by the revolting stench of boiling vats of crab.

David had been in here several times and knew exactly where he was going, so we proceeded through the harbour following the channel in a circuitous way, and round the final corner we came to a small private dock of uninviting great baulks of slimy, aged timber standing like sentinels. Here the *Lady Gudny* lay alongside – a large, smelly boat with a huge hold into which was discharged a soup of fish waste from the processors, pumped into her holding tanks night and day. As soon as the tanks were full, the Icelandic owner, Kristian Laxfoss, would take off three miles out to sea with his two crew to pump it out. This process, while the crab season is on, is continuous. Irrespective of the day or hour, the thud of boots on the coach-house roof would mean instant evacuation from a nice warm bed and sweet dreams, to a hurried call to don all clothes and heavy-weather outer clothing before venturing on deck into freezing-cold temperatures. Then we had to cast off our warps from the *Lady Gudny*, to whom we had secured ourselves, and chuff off into the bay to allow them to depart, then slide back into their place for the next three hours alongside the damp, smelly wooden piers. This required lassoing a rope, deftly catching the other end and bringing it back on board to secure us in position; this manoeuvre was usually done in dripping oilskins and freezing rain or sleet with frozen fingers.

It seemed that David had made friends with the manageress of the fish-processing laundry service. From the moment we were tied up, he started gathering up everything he could find to be washed and in due course it all came back to us in two huge polythene bags, marked 'Captain – *Polar Bound*'. What a godsend this was. There was also a shower facility in the office block; David knew his way about. He made a recce and when the coast was clear we dived in and had a lovely, splashy, hot time together – pure heaven. We sat for two weeks like this while gale succeeded gale, all the while entertained by a string of David's friends and acquaintances met on earlier trips. He had known Kristian and his Texan wife Teresa since 1989; Kristian was most kind to allow us to lie alongside his boat because not only did it save us the huge charges levied by the harbour authorities, it also meant that we did not have to lie off the 'spit', a good two miles out of town along a sharp stony road.

They were very generous and invited us out to a treat lunch at the local hotel, a self-service buffet laid on once a month for a given sum per person, and you could have all you wanted. The alcoholic drink was brought with the meal instead of being served first, and in place of whisky, it was Bourbon 'on the rocks'. It seems that Americans have always puzzled over why the English like their drinks at room temperature. David tucked into huge crab claws and I opted for scampi in breadcrumbs with various salads. There was roast beef, which I would have loved had it barely seen the inside of an oven. As for crab, I had had an allergic reaction to it when I was in my twenties and didn't want to risk that either.

Later Teresa gave us some warm hats and jumpers, and Kristian gave me a survival suit made of neoprene – this was to be donned before jumping into a liferaft to help ward off the cold. However, as the survival suit got stored in the forward hold and the liferaft is kept near the stern of the vessel, it is unlikely that they would be united in an emergency situation.

Kristian had two crew – one was an amusing young American called Michael, ex-Hell's Angels from San Francisco, and covered, everywhere on his body we were told, with tattoos, and the other a retired Vietnamese grandpa, a small, wiry man with quick movements and a shy manner. He was laughingly referred to by Michael as 'vermin' while wiggling his fingers in the air like a scuttling spider. The Vietnamese man was well able to stand up for himself, and in fact they got on very well. Michael is 'agin' virtually everything, but very funny with it. He thinks the world is run by Rothschild.

Both crew members were very helpful with our ropes every time we had to relocate ourselves against their huge steel hull, and retied the fenders as buffers again and again. It turned out that Michael was rather a wizard at chess and I was looking forward to a game. Eventually the opportunity arose and we sat down at the board. I started to concentrate, but all the while I was thinking of my move, I was aware of his eyes boring into me. I found this disconcerting. During the long pauses while he was waiting for my move, he had already decided his next, so there was no release from the stare. I was soon defeated. He then set to work on David, who seemed oblivious to his piercing stare, did his usual slow moves, and proved quite a match for Michael, though eventually he, too, succumbed.

We were introduced to Dutch Harbour's excellent library, which we went to many times to send emails. David was able to use Skype to make calls to various people. The library was a good mile's walk, and we ran the gauntlet of the numerous rain and hail squalls that arrived from nowhere. Halfway along the route were warning signs: 'Danger – beware of nesting eagles'. The warning was not to be taken lightly; they had indeed set upon someone passing nearby whom they viewed as a threat to their young. There is no knowing why they may take exception to you, but they can and do dive down and attack. This seemed unlikely in such cold weather, but these bald eagles – so-called because of the white patch on their head – were as prolific as wood pigeons and perched on every vantage point. Their beaks looked decidedly sharp and their long yellow talons could certainly do some damage.

Walking back in the biting, horizontal icy rain and wind on my own one day, and feeling quite miserable, I suddenly saw a figure in oilskins coming towards me. On close encounter it turned out to be David, who grabbed my arm and the bag I was carrying – never was I more glad to see his chirpy figure. We have a strange telepathy. Frequently, when back in England and thinking about him, the telephone will ring within the minute – sometimes to within five seconds – and there he will be on the line. Our walk took us past a stretch of rushing shallow river full of spawning black-crested salmon, known locally as 'humpies'. The female laid her eggs and the males vied to fertilise them, covering them over with shingle to prevent them receiving a rival. Death then came swiftly. As the days passed so the fish, floating on their sides, were attacked by myriad gulls and some eagles that stood ankle deep in the swirling water, carefully picking their way about to consume both the prized eggs and the dying fish.

One of David's friends was James Mason, aged sixty-four, a very kind, thoughtful and amusing reporter who, on first calling on us when we arrived, brought a large bag of lovely big oranges. We made pretty short work of eating them. James had met and interviewed David on several earlier trips and he put himself at our disposal as an unpaid chauffeur. He dropped by most days to see what we wanted to do, and ferried us about to the chart agents, the Alaska Ship Supply Stores (a huge local supermarket, run by the Inuit, as opposed to an even larger Safeway's down the road). He even took us down to the Spit, where we should have stayed had it not been for the kindness of Kristian allowing us to go alongside his *Lady Gudny*. This would have been about a 45-minute walk away, past a forlorn scrapyard of rusting cars, boats, bicycles and fridges, and alongside where a whole lot of factory boats were moored, processing their respective catches. A cab from there to town would have cost $50 for the round trip.

David and I both love looking at chandlery and we spent hours in the Alaska Stores combing the shelves – chandleries have the same fascination to me as hardware stores, where you find all kinds of things you didn't realise you needed. David once told me he had always coveted a stainless-steel lifting swivel shackle for the bower anchor, so I decided to buy him one when he wasn't looking. The lifting capability gives a better pull on the chain attached, and doesn't snatch at an angle, which can dislodge the holding. I felt it would be a great improvement. Parting with a great number of dollars, I bought the biggest one I saw, and he seemed very pleased when I gave it to him one evening. However, it didn't prove large enough, and in due course was stowed away in the hold after I suggested that we would see if we could change it for a bigger one on our return voyage the following year; this, of course, would set me back another couple of hundred dollars, as turned out to be the case.

The *Bertholf*, the United States Coastguard cutter that had intercepted us in the Beaufort Sea – the only vessel we ever saw other than a mysterious, unlit warship – had arrived the day before us. As they had invited us to visit them, while David and James sat in the 4X4, I rather brazenly walked across the berthing pontoon in pouring rain, dodging muddy puddles. In scarf and dark blue wool jacket, I was trying to look as if I was on business. I marched up their gangplanks, arriving on board followed hotfoot by a rather breathless man with a proprietorial air. As there was no one else on hand, I turned to him and said, 'Are you the captain?' to which he replied, 'I am.' Shaking hands at once, and delighted to have found my quarry so speedily among 150 men, I introduced myself, whereupon immediately David and I were given a warm invitation to be shown around.

I hurried back to the car to fetch David. When we returned to the cutter, the captain said he remembered the encounter with *Polar Bound* very well.

An hour later, following Captain Tom Crabb's conducted tour of the ship's three first Interceptors in the dry dock on the stern, the helicopter pad for two and the bridge with its dazzling array of navigation equipment and friendly staff who all shook hands, and with the ship's photographer taking a succession of pictures the while, we finally descended the bridge to the captain's cabin. Here a signed photograph of USCG cutter No. 750 the *Bertholf* was signed and presented to David – an excellent picture, showing her rakish lines and listing to port with streaming wake, passing under the Golden Gate Bridge in San Francisco. The captain's silver electric guitar lay on his sofa where it had been tossed and he was persuaded to give a short strum before we finally returned to the ever-patient James, who meantime had gone to sleep in his car.

Three days later, and this time dressed in mufti, the captain paid a return visit to *Polar Bound* and was shown over by David, who gave him a copy of his book, *Northwest Passage Solo*. That afternoon the *Bertholf*'s navigator also paid us a visit aboard *Polar Bound* with an up-to-the-minute weather chart, and a promise of more to come by email, to be forwarded to us by satellite via David's office.

One afternoon at long last, after a fortnight's delay, we finally left. We said lengthy goodbyes to Kristian and Teresa and their crew, with the ever thoughtful James photographing us from *Lady Gudny*'s bridge, having first given us a bag of paperbacks and two packets of crème caramel for me to make. As an afterthought, Kristian most generously presented David with a great white fender of gargantuan size, reminiscent of an enormous chorizo sausage. When you have a vessel with wide flared bows, high up from the water, a fender of such extraordinary dimensions can be invaluable. It was so large that David had to strap it up on top of the mounting for the gantry, under which he wedged it, above the wheelhouse, where it remained until *Polar Bound* returned to Scotland the following year.

We retraced our entry route down the harbour in the sunshine, once more encountering James standing forlornly in the distance, camera at the ready for that final shot, before we gathered momentum and started to pitch and roll once more as we re-entered the Bering Sea. After a couple of rather uncomfortable hours during which quite a bit of chewing gum was sought, we spotted a tug pulling not one but two container barges, one behind the other, loaded sky high and even with a car or two and a couple of fishing boats perched on the very top. The whole caravanserai was over a mile long. Meantime it was getting darker and murkier by the minute. You could have nothing but admiration for the skill of the tug master; it was clear he was heading for the Unimak Pass too, like us, no doubt to make deliveries to outlying settlements ahead. The Unimak Pass is relatively wide and allows passage through the chain of the Aleutian Islands, which stretch out in a great curving sweep – and were no doubt at one time joined together – from the Bering Sea to the Pacific Ocean.

We slowly overhauled them until we were ahead, but this clearly worried the tug master who, seeing the tide turn in his favour, flashed his searchlight at us. David made contact with him on VHF Channel 16 and volunteered to alter course by 20 degrees to let him pass on the inside. For the next eight hours or so the uncomfortable weather continued until finally we reached the Unimak Pass. After a further two hours we were through the notorious passage, respected for its fearsome current in certain conditions. We emerged out into the great depths of the Pacific Ocean and gained some lee from the Aleutian Islands chain.

Several hours later we arrived at a sheltered passage through the Shumagin Islands – a series of seemingly deserted volcanic remnants from prehistoric upheavals. We speculated as to what creatures might have found an existence there, and David, with his much-travelled eye in remote places, sighted three brown or black animals foraging on the foreshore. The soft grey shadows of the hills and the snow-capped peaks behind faded and a full moon emerged to bathe everything in its remote silvery beams. David, after standing a long trick at the wheel, finally turned the engine off and a wonderful silence took over. Only the gentle slurp of an almost motionless sea made itself audible and the boat rocked gently.

'I think we'll have a few hours' sleep now,' he said. It was heaven.

TWELVE

CROSSING THE GULF OF ALASKA

IT WAS NOW THE EQUINOX AND winter was just over the horizon. David had planned to leave the boat in Vancouver, from where we would fly back to England. He decided we would enter Alaska's Inside Passage at Icy Strait (Cross Sound); we had heard that this was very beautiful, and it would also be a more protected route. We appeared to be unique on this ocean. We did not see a single vessel, nor any whales; just a few birds on occasion spiralled around. The skies were dull and grey, and every now and again there was an ethereal swirl of cloud or mist which reduced the horizon from a quarter of a mile to 100 yards. At least it was a little warmer, the daytime temperature rising to about 10°C. However, the downside of this was that the big stove was only lit for cooking the supper, so there was no homely warmth during the day.

Polar Bound's rolling was remorseless, and with the seas coming beam on, she was possibly at her most wayward. This, coupled with the unpredictability of the vagaries of the seventh wave, made cooking and moving about generally a hazardous exercise. Every action had to be planned. For instance, a roll to starboard could facilitate pulling on your trousers, while on the return journey you might find yourself standing vertically gripping the central pole and making a quick reconnaissance in the galley cupboard for a wayward saucepan.

A few nights into the journey the swaying bag of wet rubbish hanging on a hook attached by shock cord to the side of the galley sink became unacceptably antisocial and David kindly moved it up to the heavy outer door, where he hitched it on to one of the securing 'dogs'. As the seas became bigger and the wind strength increased to force 8, the swaying bag liberated itself. Meanwhile an opened glass jar started a rival distraction in the lobby area. I climbed out of my bunk and found the jar firmly wedged behind the inner door, and the perforated rubber mat well endowed with a chicken carcass, porridge scrapings, tea bags and peelings. Donning the rubber gloves and approaching with caution, I scooped up as much of the contents as possible with one hand, my head between my knees, while firmly gripping the edge of the seat with the other. A searing pain shot into my hand as a shaft of chicken thighbone pierced the glove and went into my finger. All this activity brought on a need to visit the heads and, while swaying along, sometimes weightless, on the lavatory seat, I was able to retrieve my first-aid box from the cupboard under the basin and apply sticking plaster.

The next morning the lurches became paralytic and my bowl of porridge, unattended for two seconds, tossed out half its contents in a big dollop on to the seat between the two of us, and the other half somewhat maliciously down the leg of my corduroy trousers and on to the top of my shoe, where it worked its way under the tongue; troubles never come singly.

When the sea quietened somewhat, David and I donned our waterproofs and made our way along the deck. We climbed on to the coachroof where he unlocked the forward hatch and swung back the lid, while I climbed down to forage in the deep freeze. He stood guard above, opening the lid at intervals to see how I was getting on. Armed with supplies for the next couple of days and a replenishment of fresh fruit and veg from this cool, dark area, I re-emerged. It was useful storage down there. Potatoes, onions and carrots, if separated, could be kept for quite some time. Separators used by supermarkets to divide melons, avocados, etc, were very helpful in preserving vegetables stored below.

I cannot imagine what it must have been like for David on his 2011 voyage from the Falkland Islands to eastern Australia, well down in the Roaring Forties and at sea for a hundred days without stopping. He had to make all these forays unassisted; it must have been an intrepid undertaking. Apparently it can blow so hard that the ship is pressed over at quite an angle, but it doesn't roll so at least he can drink a cup of tea without any of it spilling over.

At last, during the first week of October, after a ten-day passage across the gulf, we reached Icy Point on the west coast of Alaska, arriving in darkness and thick fog, which had dogged us so much of the way. We cautiously approached Cross Sound, the northern gateway into the Inside Passage, with Vancouver lying 700 miles to the south. Here we encountered a contrary current and overfalls, where mirror-calm sea broke into short, steep waves and swirling eddies. The effect was that of sailing over a bed of rocks. However, their presence was clearly marked on the chart, and we had to trust our navigation. At spring tides, there can be a current of 8 to 10 knots, against which you would make little headway.

We came across a humpback whale, our first sighting of one during the journey across the gulf, which had apparently been somnolent until we disturbed it. Soon to follow was a small group of ducks flying low into a break in the cloud over the water. Deprived of wildlife for nearly ten days, it was quite reassuring to connect again with a tangible world. After lunch we were surrounded by about eight young humpback whales, revealing their presence by spouting vertical plumes of white spray like geysers; these jets gradually dissipated into vapour but at least they gave you a rough idea of where to point the camera next. Further afield across the sound, we could see the vapour from other pods of whales. David lent me his Lumix with a Leica lens, the first time I used a digital camera. Just as you focused on one area of water, so they would surface ahead or behind, or even the other side of the boat, all the while emitting grunts and sighs. Occasionally, as if communicating one to another, they would give an unearthly resonating trumpet, not unlike that of a charging elephant.

The sound was quite wide at this point, about 8 miles, and as the afternoon progressed, we drew near the shoreline and found an almost deserted, sheltered bay: Whitestone Harbour, with an otter playing in the seaweed by a rock outcrop. We decided to go in and anchor for the night. Far in a corner was a private fishing boat, also at anchor with a gantry out to each side. As darkness fell their riding light was switched on and we followed suit with ours. This was our first anchorage, and so the huge CQR, which had been chained to the side of the deck ever since we left Whitehaven in Cumbria, had to be prepared. First it had to be liberated from its restraints, then coupled on to the short length of cable which in turn had an eye spliced on to a huge rotating drum of rope in the forward hold, led up through the hawse pipe. When all was ready, the anchor was unceremoniously hoisted over the edge, and *Polar Bound* finally had her engine silenced. We settled down to a cosy evening for once. No fish came our way from the other boat, so we had some nut rissoles which I had made earlier with a tomato sauce.

The next morning at about 6.30 we were on our way again down Chatham Strait in lovely warm sunshine, having been shrouded in gloom and low cloud the previous day. The strait was very wide here and we were bowled along at about 5 to 6 knots. I was not too pleased at such an early start. I had been hoping to have a lie-in, and David did say, 'No need for you to get up,' but I felt I had to. This was a memorable morning as humpback whales arrived on both sides of us and gave us a stately and dignified display of spouting geysers and slow surfacing and rolling, their elegant scimitar tails slipping silently beneath the waves; strange shuffling sounds and great gusty sighs followed. Everywhere we looked there were these majestic creatures; David turned off the engine in order to watch them. We could have sat there all morning but we did not have the time and eventually had to get going again.

Later, we passed, far in the distance, a small cruise ship coming down the other way, and a busy little tug pulling what appeared at first to be a haystack, then a block of flats and, by the time it got level with us, which must have taken about an hour, turned out to be a giant barge covered in containers stacked six deep, together with heavy machinery interspersed.

We reached White Water Bay, with high forested hills around, described in an old marine atlas as 'a beautiful unvisited wilderness area, with a deserted Indian village and many brown bears'. The water was immensely deep, 80 to 100 feet. We navigated past a few rocks and outcrops, and sighted a small animal, maybe a type of deer or a wild cat, then eventually, where the hill dropped down to a grassy shore at the head of the bay, we found a gently shelving perch for the anchor. When all was secure, we finally sat on top of the folded dinghy in the sun eating ginger cake and drinking lapsang souchong tea.

That evening, our trust in the atlas, with its romantic description, was misguided. Sudden strong gusts of wind came sweeping down the hillsides, causing *Polar Bound* to rock wildly on her anchor, twisting and turning. She gave great shuddering tremors as her rope stretched and tensioned itself, groaning with the unexpected load. We might have to get out before the situation became worse, a difficult manoeuvre in the now pitch dark and with hidden rocks to negotiate. All became quiet by bedtime, thankfully, but the tranquillity was short-lived. At 3.30 in the morning, disturbed by the arrival of a bright moon shining over the bay, I felt the wind come back, and *Polar Bound* rocked and snatched and pulled on her anchor once again. I got up and stood in the wheelhouse, marvelling at the wild solitude and the starry panoply above, and wondering how it was that by some unforeseen force I had arrived where I was. Presently David came up too, and we stood on the bridge, leaning together in silence for a few minutes to assess the situation. David didn't think it was getting any worse.

We weighed anchor at first light and, chuffing down the bay, kept a good lookout for early morning brown bears grazing, but none seemed to have woken. However, there were numerous bald eagles sitting on the foreshore, which was littered with clam shells – evidence of their stronghold. Rounding the bottom of Chatham Strait, we turned into Frederick Sound and saw through binoculars a huge section of aeroplane wing raised up like a giant white motorboat, leaning against a backdrop of fir trees – presumably someone in authority knew of this incongruous sight. On the southern point of Admiralty Island, we saw a solitary wooden cross erected on rocks and speculated about it, later reading the marine atlas, which declared bleakly, 'Murder Cove'.

This confluence of Chatham and Frederick Sounds gave a great vista of open water with a rolling backdrop of forested hills and mountains and numerous islands dotted about, all wreathed and threaded with floating wisps of cloud. Most spectacular by far was a great range of snow-clad mountains reminiscent of the Rockies peaking in the distance – our first sight of British Columbia.

I was interested in the number of Norfolk names that have been given to various capes and bays in this area. Where Frederick Sound merges with Stephens Passage is a Holkham Bay, marked to the northeast, and, nearby, Coke Point (the family name of the earls of Leicester from Norfolk). The next inlet to the north is Point Snettisham, and to the south is Point Houghton, with Walpole Point nearby. Other Norfolk names include Labouchere Bay, Hamilton Island, Hancock Peak, Franklin Peaks, Windham Bay, Dawes Glacier, Point Anmer and so on. Captain Cook voyaged along this coastline in the *Endeavour* in the eighteenth century; his hydrographer, First Lieutenant Vancouver, was an Englishman born in King's Lynn, Norfolk, who, when creating the charts, seemingly appropriated any names that came readily to mind – including his own.

As we progressed along Frederick Sound – a long haul and in a glowing red sunset and gathering darkness – two huge whales, one perhaps 70 feet or more in length, rose from the depths in a slow but purposeful way, travelling close together in the same direction. This is a migratory route for whales at this time of year, and they were heading north. It got later and later, and we began to get anxious that we were not going to make it to the next anchorage, but the entrance was just still visible and so we entered Portage Bay in the gloaming and noted the welcoming twinkling warmth of the lights from three other boats already settled for the night. Anchoring in about 6 fathoms, we looked at our surroundings and felt a certain relief to be safe and snug. Next to the entrance was a little A-frame log cabin, half concealed by a peninsula of trees extending to one flank of the opening. It is possible, by arrangement with the Forestry Department, to rent one of these; they are dotted about all over these islands. The remainder of the circular bay was surrounded by a foreshore of stones and random dead pine trees with a backdrop of spruce trees. We felt secure, glad to have finally arrived after a long day. The bay gave us a friendly feeling, in contrast to the savage squalls of the night before. We were looking forward to a drink and supper and a good sleep.

THIRTEEN

LEAVING *POLAR BOUND* IN PETERSBURG, ALASKA

ONE OF THE BOATS HAD ALREADY GONE by the time we surfaced the following morning. After breakfast we too left, motoring on down to the bottom of Frederick Sound. David had mentioned a small fishing village on the chart called Petersburg, and on impulse thought we could call in there. We had read quite a good description of it in the guidebook we had been given by Kristian back in Dutch Harbour. As we turned off Frederick Sound into Wrangell Narrows, a very large buoy, leaning heavily to one side with the surge of the tide, marked the channel to take, and as we passed it we counted about fifteen enormous, whiskery sea lions, all piled up in a huge slithery heap on top. How they are able to heave themselves out of the water and climb up on to such a tipply platform is a mystery. We learned later that they are called Steller Sea Lions, and are known as the 'grizzly bears of the sea'.

We rounded up against the visitors' pontoon, and walked along the slippery surface and up a ramp to the Harbour Office. Here we found a charming woman called Glow, who turned out to be the harbour master. This was quite a job; she had to control a lot of very individual characters who had berths in three harbours, all adjacent. One of the harbours was for very small craft, another had quite sizeable vessels of long duration, but we were allocated a berth nearby in the principal harbour below her office window, with not too far to walk to the supermarket.

We learnt that the charges for leaving *Polar Bound* to overwinter here were about one-fifth of those we had heard were charged in Nanaimo, Vancouver. After a peaceful night we decided there was nothing wrong with where we were, and so David made arrangements and booked a berth for her, against a nearby pontoon; this was also going to save another 450 miles of motoring.

The three harbours were all interconnected by walkways and ramps, and one of the harbours had housing and an especially large pontoon for small float planes, which could be heard roaring up their engines intermittently throughout the day, and taking off like angry wasps up or down the inlet according to wind and tide. They gave sightseeing rides to tourists who might have arrived in town in a small cruise ship and who wished to go and see the famous Le Conte Glacier nearby; they were also used for business purposes, and surveying.

To access the float-plane pontoon, you had to run the gauntlet of a particularly notorious bull sea lion, which always seemed to be keeping guard. In semi-upright mode, with mean little head atop its huge bulk and a thick whiskery neck it could twist through 360 degrees, it was a hideous sight. Despite its massive size and ungainly flippers, it could hump along in quite an intimidating manner, making threatening grunts. Every now and again when you were minding your own business, on board your own boat, it would surface from the depths of the harbour and appear by your side, swim along quite silently and sink down again, reappearing the other side of the pontoon with a backward, baleful eye which seemed to say, 'I'll get you one day.' You had to be careful, too, having got into a dinghy, not to sit with your bottom over the side or you could have a large chunk taken out of it by this aggressive sea monster. It had done just exactly that to a poor young man the previous year, who ended up in hospital having a great many stitches.

The ramp leading from the floating pontoons up to the harbour office and the village could sometimes, depending on the phase of the moon, be extremely steep, and it was quite an effort to push gear up it that you wanted to get ashore. Helpful trollies were provided for the purpose, but they could prove remarkably wayward.

Petersburg was located on an island called Mitkof, and it proved to be a delightful, friendly place with a true village atmosphere – more provincial than Nome or Dutch Harbour, both of which had had a frontier-town feel, though nonetheless with a certain charm. The place was also known as Little Norway, and you could quite easily imagine you had been transported there. A number of its residents were descended from the original Norwegian settlers, and it had an intimate atmosphere, with small individual clapboard shopfronts, all selling a variety of different things. There were two supermarkets, a travel agent, a computer shop, an 'antiques' shop, and everything imaginable to do with boats and fishing gear, around which the small town has grown up, including electricians, marine welders and even a blacksmith. Seven churches of different denominations, a post office and some hairdressers' completed the scene, along with an excellent library, where we spent a good deal of time Skyping and sending emails.

After a day or two it began to dawn on us that we were surrounded by rainforest, and the preoccupation now, besides trying to keep warm, was to continually mop up the condensation that gathered below each window in the saloon where we lived. The drips splashed relentlessly from the hatch above on to the saloon table; it was evident we couldn't leave any electronic equipment in the boat over winter. The next task was to learn about the requirements necessary to protect the boat from a possible 26 feet of snow, which was what they had had the previous winter. Some people appointed a watchman to keep an eye on their boat and remove any excess snow, but there were several rogues around who would like to take dollars off you in exchange for little more than the occasional glance at your vessel. We also had to focus on eating up our frozen stores and any opened packets of groceries.

We noted that all the boats that had already been put to bed for the next few months had been covered with some kind of sheeting. It seemed a good idea to follow suit, and in the big, general purpose local store, Hammer & Wikan, we found what they call a 'tarp', which would cover about half the boat – at least the central part, which would make it awkward for any intruders, not that we particularly feared those. At least it was paying lip service to the possibility of heavy snow, which could compound and create massive ice build-up.

We had several days and nights of rain and low cloud, watching dripping figures passing to and fro on the pontoons made slippery with algae, smashed mussel shells and bird lime, before we decided to move off *Polar Bound* and find accommodation ashore to enable us to work more freely on our final chores. We followed up a recommendation from the friendly librarian and found ourselves with a delightful and comfortable self-catering unit right in the centre of town and only 10 minutes' walk from the boat. It was very quiet and peaceful, with the odd deer roaming down the road having a nibble at some of the residents' flowerbeds. We had plenty of hot water, a washing machine at our disposal and the luxury of a bath, which we revelled in. The owners of this establishment were away on holiday and their very great friends, Chuck and Mary Susan, were taking care of it on their behalf. We were most fortunate to find such kind people, and considered that we had fallen on our feet.

We managed to get all our personal laundry done, and I was able to iron it. We also washed our sleeping bags and tea and bath towels, and finally visited the travel agent to book our return flights to the UK for a fortnight ahead. It meant three connecting flights to get back, and the runway for the local airport was right next to the supermarket – you couldn't have anything more convenient than that. We also booked return tickets to come back in mid-May the following year, 2013, which would allow us the opportunity to make a mini cruise of our own and explore this beautiful region we had arrived at with its wonderfully friendly inhabitants.

David was something of a legend in this part of the world, and there had been considerable media interest in him. A personable young reporter from the local radio station had called on us while we were eating a late lunch and quizzed David about his sailing adventures. David rather baulks at these moments and is inclined to pass them over to me to deal with. However, in due course he was encouraged to contribute to the interview as well, and later this went on air in Petersburg and locality. The interview was played through four times during the day, with the result that several people stopped and congratulated us, and *Polar Bound* drew quite an admiring crowd down on the jetty. The ever-patient David was more than happy to show off his engine room and pretty little boat.

Our final morning came, and within ten minutes we were at the airport, driven by kindly Chuck, who was filled with advice about which queue we should stand in as we took our shoes and belts off and were processed through all the security checks and other formalities. Before long we were airborne for Sitka, where we had an interchange for our onward flight to Seattle, and then the long haul home.

FOURTEEN

THE NASA BEACON

D AVID IS A VERY UNUSUAL CHARACTER. He does not fit into any particular category. He is highly intelligent, sensitive to criticism, warm and affectionate, but never the less appears to be perfectly content to be completely alone for months at a time. He is self-reliant to a degree, and supremely confident in his own ability. Notwithstanding all this, he is humble and not in the least boastful about his achievements. Somehow his exposure to the loneliness of the oceans has imbued him with a remarkably intuitive perception of the moods of others. He is meticulous and conscientious in all he undertakes, and has the ability to think through everything he plans to do and anticipate all the difficulties that may come his way, making provision for most unforeseen eventualities. One of the more remarkable accounts he told me of was an experience he had in *Polar Bound* not too long ago, in which all these qualities came into play. It is not easy to get these stories out of him for he doesn't set much store by past events, but, if questioned, he might drop a few words about his experiences.

He was in Hawaii in 2011 on another circumnavigation, and called in at the Waikiki Yacht Club, where he was spending a few days. When it came near to departure time, he went across to the other side of the harbour to fill up with fuel, taking on about 1,800 gallons. The manageress of the fuel depot came across and handed David a slip of paper, which she said she had just received from the Hawaiian University. The university were putting out a request for any boats willing to go and try to find a beacon, which had cost the Americans two and a half million dollars, or thereabouts, and was in the sea approximately 900 miles due west of Hawaii. They could give the coordinates for the location a little later. As encouragement, a $20,000 reward was offered.

The beacon had been dropped off in the sea as part of a NASA programme to record depths and currents; it was brought up to the surface to send back its messages. However, it had a battery problem and the next time they remotely brought it up they would have only seventy-two hours to locate it. Local people wanted to charge $200,000 to attempt the rescue, arguing that they would need to hire special divers, RIBs and support entourage. The two scientists from the Hawaiian vessel came over to see David and declared full confidence in him and that he was the answer to their prayers, if indeed the beacon was findable and retrievable at all. That's the kind of man David is – inspirational. The other hopefuls tried to implement the Davy Act, which would exclude any non-American from making an attempt at the rescue. Needless to say, David was not deterred.

He anticipated that he would need an extra block and tackle, tyres and plywood to protect his hull and the beacon at the point of contact, and an extendable boathook. The grappling hook he already possessed would be sufficient to grasp the beacon once he had managed to hitch a strop over it.

It took him the best part of a week to arrive at the destination. He kept in touch by iridium telephone with the two scientists, who were able to monitor his position. Unfortunately, they made a couple of mistakes, including a mix-up over David's coordinates and the coordinates of the beacon, thus sending David 60 miles in the wrong direction, which amounted to twelve hours of steaming.

David calculated the position of latitude and longitude to within three decimal places. When he reached the position in which he thought he would find the beacon, the scientists brought it to the surface, leaving David seventy-two hours in which to locate it. The beacon was 8 feet 1 inch in height, 3 feet 3 inches in diameter and weighed 200 pounds. The only part visible above the waves would be an 18-inch black antenna, about the thickness of a little finger. The weather conditions were not ideal; about 15 knots of trade wind was blowing (roughly a force 5), so there was a bit of sea running.

David took up station at the external steering position and moved up and down the track for a short distance, then quite suddenly, at about 20 yards, he spotted it in a breaking wave. Without taking his eyes off it, he managed to steer the boat alongside, putting her in neutral, then went along the deck to the lowest point, midships at the waist, which he judged would be the best place from which to retrieve it since the decks forward and aft are considerably flared. Lying on his stomach, with the boat continually moving with the momentum, he managed to place a sling over the beacon and put a hook on it, through which he could pass a rope, then finally he could relax.

He swung the boat's gantry over and lifted the beacon out of the sea with the aid of a couple of handy bill-hooks, then got a third attached to tip it at an angle to clear the lift aboard, and on to the waiting tyres with a protective covering of foam rubber. There were six tubes on either side of the beacon, pressurised to 2,000psi, and David had to be extremely careful not to puncture them. Very soon after this he had a telephone call from the two scientists, who were overjoyed to receive the news.

After he had secured the beacon on the after deck, he wasted no time in getting under way to Midway Islands and then on to Dutch Harbour in the Aleutian Islands, over 2,000 miles away. The two delighted scientists had flown over to meet their precious beacon together with a custom-made crate for shipment back to Hawaii. Certainly it was a very sophisticated prototype, and the scientists were most anxious to get it back, and David was pleased to receive the reward they had agreed to.

His was a triumph of pin-point navigational accuracy, particularly bearing in mind that his charts for this area were only small scale. David is one of the best navigators to be found anywhere, and it is not for nothing that he was appointed an Honorary Life Member of the Royal Institute of Navigation.

Another experience came on his very first circumnavigation in the *Mabel E. Holland*, a 42-foot ex-RNLI lifeboat. He had recently left Cape Town and visited St Helena, where he met the owners of a sailing boat with whom he had become acquainted in Cape Town. The wife was probably in her early forties and her husband nearing sixty. They intended sailing over to Rio in Brazil, but before doing so they joined David in looking at some of the historical sights of St Helena – namely the houses where Napoleon had been held in captivity, one of them being Longwood. They also saw where

Napoleon had been buried; he was later exhumed and reburied in Paris in the catacombs.

Eventually the sailing-boat owners set off for Brazil. David was not quite ready to leave; he was awaiting a decision whether he would be required to carry Christmas mail to Ascension Island, 500 miles away, and to pick up mail there and bring it back to St Helena, as the islanders were keen to see their Christmas post. Had he done so, he would have received the status of a mail-carrying ship, which would have priority.

Polar Bound always had her radio switched on to Channel 16, the emergency channel, and during that night there was a distress call from the sailing boat. The husband had had a heart attack and his wife had turned the boat around and was heading back to St Helena; she was requesting medical assistance. David contacted the medical officer on the island, but was told that the officer could not leave the island at any time. David thought this was a bit pathetic, as he could have taken him out to liaise with the returning yacht. So David set off on his own to rendezvous with the yacht, and escorted them back to the mooring. On the way back, the wife attempted to massage her husband's heart, and kept him warm, but six hours elapsed. On arrival at St Helena, they wrapped the body in blankets and lowered him down into David's dinghy. David rowed him to the steps, but there was quite a swell running and it was difficult to land him. However, the doctor was waiting for them and, with correct wave timing, they were able to transfer the body to the shore, where he was put in a Landrover and taken to the small hospital. When they examined him, they pronounced him to be dead.

It was tragic for the wife. At that time there was no airport, and she could not take the boat back to Cape Town herself. New crew were brought out to St Helena and eventually they got back to Cape Town against the southeasterly trade winds.

The husband was buried on St Helena. A few years later David met up with the widow in Cape Town, who asked David, who was en route to the Northwest Passage via St Helena, to take photographs of her husband's grave. He did, and sent them to her. Sadly, shortly after, she herself died.

PART THREE

BRINGING *POLAR BOUND* HOME

FIFTEEN

RETURN TO
PETERSBURG

OUR JOURNEY HOME WITH *POLAR BOUND* IN 2013 was about much more than safely bringing the vessel back to her base in Scotland. David's ambition on the return voyage from Petersburg was to make the first ever transit of the Northwest Passage by a private vessel via the two-mile-wide Hecla and Fury Strait. This narrow channel, where the current flows fast, would allow – when not choked with ice – passage from the west through the Gulf of Boothia into the Foxe Basin, across the Arctic Circle through the Foxe Channel, thence into the Hudson Strait and finally the North Atlantic. This transit, coupled with the route we had traversed going the opposite way the previous year, would also make for the quickest route home.

We arrived back in Petersburg in early May and were welcomed to the same comfortable self-catering apartment we had rented before, only this time we had the added bonus of the presence of the owners Grant and Lila Trask, who could not have been kinder. After a few days under their wing we got *Polar Bound* aired and were able to return to life on board. Despite telling all enquirers that we would be off in a fortnight, no one seemed surprised that we continued to busy about getting back into the old harbour routine and taking advantage of the useful shops and varied artisans in this small town, and showing no hurry to leave.

We returned to the wonderful hardware shop that goes by the name of Hammer & Wikan. It is laid out in grid form with a central paint-mixing counter and row upon row of alleys selling everything the fisherman or hunter could possibly want, not to mention the local builders, welders, handymen and their wives and children. The staff speed about dressed in red cotton aprons and shirts with the name emblazoned on their pockets. You only had to ask at the till and they would call up their driver located a mile out of town at their sister company, an enormous supermarket, and within five minute the free cab service would swoop down to collect you and your dollars and whisk you up the hill to replenish your larder and drinks cupboard. No wonder the Americans find quaint little old England so lacking in commercial enterprise.

We had quite a social time despite the preoccupation of getting *Polar Bound* ready for sea. Everyone seemed intrigued by David's boat, and an endless stream of people were shown around and taken down into the forward hold and the engine room – the most rotund guests declined the latter as they might have become wedged in the hatchways and, like a cat with its whiskers extended, they knew their limitations. I did become quite annoyed sometimes at David's inability to recognise time-wasters. Once he got chatting, he could be out of orbit for well over an hour. He does really like talking. I put this down to the fact that he has spent so much time in a cocoon of his own, completely isolated from the world, and needs to make up for it.

We walked about the harbour at night, arm in comforting arm, up and down the pontoons, taking note of arrivals and departures. During our daytime perambulations we received invitations to go aboard various boats that we had paused to scrutinise. Very soon, David, who has a remarkable ability to remember people's names, was on first-name terms with a good many fishermen, and girls too, who also made fishing their livelihood and hauled all the gear about with just as much resolve, and somewhat more noisily. There was Dave and Paul and Rick and Chuck; then Dan and Don, Mike and Doug and Scott, not to mention Miranda, a lone fisher-girl who, together with her shaggy and eager large dog whose parentage had known a husky, frequently walked up and down the pontoon. One day she passed *Polar Bound* wearing a very scant pair of shredded blue shorts over her substantial thighs and beamed a huge, friendly smile at David. When next I saw her, she was sitting alone outside a café in the main street, adorned with silvery sparkle on her cheeks and incongruous high-heeled boots. Then there was Kate and her friend, a hard-working, noisy pair of hoydens who laughed and chatted as they baited the hooks with salmon heads and tossed them into a great vat.

Apart from this colourful assembly, there were 'gentlemen fishermen' from Kupreanof Island, who accessed their boats in Petersburg by fast little aluminium skiffs which, with throttle fully opened, reared up on their sterns and bounced over the waves. Among them was an amateur classical guitarist, Bob Dolan, who had dropped by our boat when we first sailed into Petersburg the year before, settling down in the corner of the saloon to play a succession of classical romantic pieces to me in the fast fading light as I cleaned the galley for the final time before our departure back to England. He needed no second invitation to bring aboard his very special guitar. Then there was Wayne, a figure reminiscent of Kirk Douglas the film star, with chiselled face and manly ways, whose boat was named *Hoyden*.

'Do you know what that means?' he called out to me.

'Yes,' I replied. 'An unruly woman.'

He was stunned for a moment, then said, 'I like your pearrrrls.'

We met, too, Ranger Doug Leen, philanthropist and retired dentist, who had had a practice in Barrow and had also worked in Antarctica, caring for the dental needs of the scientific community. His charming wife Martina was German, from Bavaria, and he was a self-described Ranger of the Lost Art, among whose many interests was saving for posterity, by reproduction, the few surviving posters from the Works Progress Administration Federal Arts Project, an organisation that between 1935 and 1943 printed two million copies in 35,000 designs to inform the populace about education, theatre, health, safety and travel – among other things. This most original pair live in a snug log house on a promontory of land backed by a small river and fronting Wrangell Narrows, with a spectacular view across the water of a range of snow-capped mountains, and only a fifteen-minute skiff ride away from Petersburg Harbour, where we were moored.

The large open-plan ground-floor room of their house had windows overlooking the foreshore, and housed a grand piano with music cabinet adjacent, filled with well-thumbed volumes of the classics. Doug seldom referred to these as he had quite a mastery of the keyboard and his hands and brain told him where to go next. He is in fact extremely musical, a thwarted prospective concert pianist with a remarkably retentive memory, which also embraces limericks and enabled him to break into a recitation of 'Albert and the Lion', all about a boy eaten by a lion when he went to Blackpool for the day. He would introduce this into the conversation at a moment's notice, and he had others he could regale you with too. Bob Dolan, who lived in a nearby house, was usually there too, and would sit in a corner of the sofa, one leg crossed over the other, a dreamy look in his eyes as he serenaded us. Evenings at Doug and Martina's were always very musical.

There was no ceremony about the washing-up after dinner. This was tackled with gusto by Doug, under running water at the kitchen sink, even as his guests were still scraping their plates for the last mouthful. That way, he could ferry them back across the narrows and then get off to bed. I hoped David had been watching this division of duties and display of capable manliness – Martina doing the cooking, Doug the washing-up. I'd come to the conclusion that David was not familiar with either end of a washing-up brush, despite plenty of encouragement; I think he views it as part of the kitchen décor, like a Japanese flower arrangement.

We were invited to supper on several occasions, which always necessitated Doug fetching us across the water in his skiff. We donned sea boots and waterproofs, and on one occasion were entrusted with one of his skiffs to make our own adventurous way back to the harbour through dark choppy water, twinkling lights, tide rips and mid-channel buoys. Quite hazardous really; I had to hope we weren't going to end up as supper for that evil sea lion, guardian of the harbour we were aiming for.

The first time we were invited to dinner, we wanted to take a nice bottle with us, so we went to the local drinks shop-cum-bar, where we researched Ranger Leen's favourite tipple. It was amazing how everyone knew everyone else's business. We baulked at the single malt and came away with something rather less expensive. Parting with a good many dollars, we clutched our bottle tactfully secreted in an unobtrusive brown paper bag and went back to the pontoon to await the arrival of our chauffeur. On reaching the homestead and scrambling up the slippery foreshore, we were immediately confronted by a small black baby bear, which took one look and then beat a hasty retreat, but it didn't stop me looking over my shoulder every five seconds – just in case. It turned out that Doug was actually a gin drinker, so I ended up drinking the scotch myself.

With black bears roaming around, Doug and Martina were on occasion imprisoned inside their cabin. This meant they were also unable to reach their visitors' hut, in which they house guests on the point, down through some huge mysterious fir trees, nor even their own vegetable plot. Their skiffs are secured to an outhaul offshore among the kelp, enabling them, at any stage of the tide, to access them by pulling the dripping wet line hand over hand. This is a sea-boots operation, and necessitates picking your way across cast-up clam shells of enormous size, slippery rocks and seaweed, among which some strange wriggling creature, which burrows into the mud, will rise up like a bursting bubble with a loud popping sound. Having negotiated all that, you then climbed into the boat over fuel cans and fishing impedimenta, surreptitiously wiping the seat clear of mud before finally sitting down, accompanied by wild rocking as the next passenger boarded.

One morning, Doug rang us to announce that the following day, Norwegian Day, he would be bringing along six traditional antique canoes, the design of which was based on a Viking ship with swept-up bow and stern, and extremely tipply. He challenged us to a race out into the Wrangell Narrows around a large green can buoy (pronounced 'booeey' in America), a quarter of a mile off and back again. In the event there were five contestants, and David's competitive instinct was aroused.

The next morning, in slight drizzle, we went to inspect these pretty little boats, which Doug had towed over from his boathouse. They were each slightly different, made of larch or pine; he had bought them all and had had them renovated. Clad in lifejacket and oilskins, I sat in one behind David's broad back, facing forwards so that I could guide the strokes to keep a direct course. I crouched low in the bows to reduce windage, and gripped the sides. David set off with such relentless energy that he might have been a Rowing Blue maintaining his reputation.

We rounded the buoy by a whisker and set off on the return, viewing the laggards way behind and way off course. As we neared the finish line, the three US coastguards who were positioned out in the middle of the channel stood up and clapped, as did a small group of onlookers standing, in the rain, on a pontoon nearby. David fell on his oars as all the best men do in the Boat Race. The coastguards were there for good reason: they were seen waving their arms frantically at a few speeding mariners who otherwise would have engulfed the canoes with their wash. There were many events going on all round the town that day, and it was very good-humoured as we paraded up and down the main street looking at all the stalls and bunting.

Doug had a great sense of occasion and was the ideal PR man for any event. Once a year he holds an Open Day aboard his enormous old tug *Katahdin*, dating from the 1920s, and about 90 feet overall. On the appointed day, we were invited to go and see over her, and this was to be followed by cocktails. We disappeared down the steel companionway into the bowels of the ship to walk all around the huge, throbbing monster, which Doug had started up specially for the occasion. We examined the dinosaur of an engine, which was juddering away with pistons pulsing up and down and oil squirting and oozing from everywhere. The tug had a bunk room and heads for the engineer, with old-fashioned wooden seated box closet, and massive bulkhead lights with bold brass switches. The remorseless thunder of the engine made it impossible to have any conversation as we toured around.

The tug was truly impressive. She had a smooth, wide, polished wooden handrail right around the circumference of the deck, and a charming self-contained cabin with its own private facilities, perched high up above, for the exclusive use of the captain. If you wanted to go into reverse, you had to stop the engine altogether to make the adjustment, then restart it; not a boat for close-quarter work. It seems, having brought her here from who-knows-where some years before, she had never been moved since. She would do well on the Thames in London as an exclusive floating restaurant, where you dine on the after deck and watch the world go by.

With *Polar Bound* nearly ready, we decided to go and look at the nearby Le Conte Glacier, several hours' motoring away. We invited our 'guardians', Grant and Lila, who had smoothed our path in Petersburg and been endlessly kind to us, to accompany us for a couple of nights. They had not been overnight in a boat since their fishing days, and eagerly anticipated the outing. It would be rather a squeeze as we were really a two-man boat, but there was a quarter berth up in the wheelhouse, and Grant insisted on taking the 'berth' on the cabin sole, where we put the saloon bunk cushions out for him. They were the perfect guests, arriving with minimal baggage, their own sleeping bags and cushions and, best of all, two large crab pots, a very large stainless-steel saucepan and the all-important irresistible bait.

It was a beautiful sunny day. The surrounding snow-covered mountains sparkled like jewels in the azure sky. Grant recommended a bay called Ideal Cove, and on arrival we put our anchor down, having first laid out the crab pots and buoyed them, then spent a peaceful evening keeping an inquisitive eye on the two other boats in the same anchorage, one of them a large red private motorboat. The following morning came the great excitement of the crab pots. Grant, who had been a fisherman in the area for some thirty years, took charge of this operation.

We grabbed the crab pots with the boathook and lifted them out. There were about five occupants in one and eight in the other, one of whom was making a valiant bid for freedom through the compulsory hole left for the purpose. Unhappily for it, the crab was too large, and failed. They were Dungeness crabs with very big claws and had to be handled with caution. First a plastic gauge was placed across the carapace. Anything under five and half inches in diameter had to be sent back immediately to the safety of the sea; all females, irrespective of size, were also returned for future breeding. The males have a long pointed section of shell on their undersides, whereas the females have a shorter wider arc – this connection is how they mate. The crabs were put in a couple of buckets, from which they kept trying to claw their way out, and in the end we had to place large, heavy-duty polythene bags over the top and weight them down.

The great stainless-steel cauldron, which seemed to take most of our water ration, was put on the Wallis paraffin stove. After quite a long time, and with some regret on my part, the water was boiling and Grant announced that he would administer a quick death. He advised me not to look. Of course I did, and was duly horrified to see him place his feet either side on to the crab's legs and, bending down, take hold of the back and with a quick wrench pull the whole shell entirely off. He assured me death was instantaneous. They then had to be cleaned out inside before being lowered into the pot. After 15 minutes' cooking, they were left to get cold. Meantime, I made some French mayonnaise to accompany them.

We all sat round the saloon table with the saucepan placed in the middle and everyone, bar myself, tucked in. I was amazed at the quantity David managed to eat and hoped very much that he wasn't damaging his cholesterol level. After about ten minutes I tried a tiny piece, but it was really an excuse to sample the mayonnaise. At any rate, despite my previous reaction a great many years ago, nothing untoward occurred. The feasting went on, with Grant and Lila proving equally enthusiastic. When all was finished the saucepanful of discarded shells was returned to the bottom of the sea where brothers and sisters, aunts and uncles were waiting to pick over the remnants.

Finally, we reset the pots, as we had the intention of returning to the anchorage that night, and got under way for Le Conte Glacier. The face of the glacier has retreated nine miles from the outfall into the sea, three miles of which has occurred in the last hundred years, and is now up a winding river full of chunks of drifting ice driven by the wind. It is a safe refuge for seals to give birth to their pups where orca whales are unable to reach them. We spotted one or two seals fairly far down the river, and in one spot we found a dead pup lying on the edge of an ice sheet with blood coming from its eye socket, its body bloated, and the piteous sight of the mother swimming desperately round and round rearing up to see why her pup didn't follow her into the water.

The premature sight of small lumps of bobbing ice floating on the surface of the inlet, led to thoughts of a gin and tonic with glacier ice and lime, as a treat, though not for the captain – he was made of sterner stuff. First we had to capture the ice, which was not as easy as it sounds when you are quite high up above the water. Everyone wanted to try their hand at throwing the heavy rubber bucket into the sea upside down. With a lanyard attached to the handle and a deft little jerk on the line, the object being aimed for will hopefully be captured, but most of the pieces of ice were too large. With some difficulty, we landed a suitably sized chunk. Pretty soon we were chinking our plastic glasses at each other.

Grant and Lila's evident pleasure at accompanying us was delightful. They had only been to the glacier twice before, and Grant had long since sold his immaculately kept varnished fishing boat, *Hazel B*, in which he and his wife had worked as a team for some thirty years, fishing for a living. They had contributed to an excellent short film about the life of the Petersburg fishermen, in which the pair of them featured quite a lot, Lila entering into the whole thing with enormous enthusiasm and energy. We wondered how many other women spent their working years united with their husband in such an arduous activity. We enjoyed their company immensely.

After several hours wending our way up river around several bends and through quite a lot of bergy bits, where *Polar Bound* came into her own, we reached the face of this formidable glacier. David took the boat to within a hundred yards of it. We were delighted at the amazing sight of this 'birthing ground' for baby seals: the whole area was covered in small islands of ice, and nearly every one had a seal with a newborn furry and whiskery little pup by its side. Some of the large shelves of ice housed three or four mothers with their young. The cliff face of the glacier was crisscrossed with crevasses, and was dirty and grey. It was imperceptibly flowing steadily down to the sea, although we did not witness it calving.

By now a chill wind was blowing and grey clouds had overtaken the sunshine. Rounding the first bend on our return we were dismayed to see the scattered floes all pushed up by the wind into what appeared an impenetrable impasse. David went outside up on to the higher external steering position, which gave him a better view, and with some crunching and grinding we made it back to Ideal Cove for the second night.

On lifting the pots the following morning we had another haul of crabs – many were returned as unsuitable, but the losers in this lottery were put into a bucket and had to await their end when Grant and Lila got back to base in Petersburg. I would never have made a fisherman. I felt so sorry for the crabs who kept trying to escape from their temporary prison, scrambling over each other's backs to claw their way out only to be pushed back down again.

Grant had been encouraging David to give a presentation to the local population by way of reciprocating some of the kindness and hospitality we had received; many of the fishermen were greatly interested in the boat that had carried David so many thousands of waterborne miles and marvelled at her construction, and at her Gardner engine, now quite a rarity since they have ceased production. After some persuasion, he agreed to do so. Grant made an arrangement with the Lutheran church, who had a spacious, comfortable, well-appointed hall, and an evening was set aside in early June.

Pretty soon the local radio station sent their reporter along to *Polar Bound*. We were finishing a late lunch when Joe Viechnicki from KFSK radio station came aboard and settled across the table from us, microphone at the ready, his handsome face beaming from one to the other of us. We both spoke, and answered his questions, then, leaving him to hurry back to the studio, we set off to the church hall for the first rehearsal. A huge window from floor to apex ceiling presented a problem as the large viewing screen did not cover it all and we were anxious about the effect of dazzling light from behind. We were assured that on the day the window would be blacked out. It was agreed that any donations would be given to the Petersburg Marine Mammal Centre at the Sea Grant University of Alaska.

We were lent a sophisticated projector and David's digital photographs were linked up to it. It was lucky he had brought them with him. He says these impromptu lectures can happen quite often, so he comes prepared. After a lot of playing around with the projector, and careful placement of a small screen at an angle near to the podium, on which he could see what was being projected from the ceiling on to the huge screen in front of the audience, he took up station, while I retreated to the back of the hall and found a comfortable seat to be his imaginary audience and see how he came over. He had obviously done this many times before, and was very calm and measured, knowing exactly what he wanted to say and using the photographs in sequence as an anchoring point. We had a couple more of these sessions, and one thing I learnt was just how much work goes into an informal, 'spontaneous' lecture given without payment of any kind – it is most time-consuming. He was not particularly looking forward to it, as he had no idea what kind of a reception he would get nor how many would attend – it might all go off like a damp squib. However, I kept on encouraging him and told him how well he came over.

In the afternoon, we went up to the hall for final adjustments and arrangement of the chairs, the latter being undertaken by at least three of us. Surreptitiously, when the other chair-placers had retreated, I had a rearrangement. With the best of intentions, the other two had aligned the chairs in equal rows. When one chair is placed directly behind another you do not get an optimum view – it is much better to stagger the rows so that each chair is placed in the centre of the two chairs in front; that way everyone has a chance of a good view, although the seats may not look so symmetrical.

Leaflets were distributed, one on each chair, giving a resumé of David's biography. The audience started drifting up well before the appointed time; the four great laminated posters we had prepared and posted up around the harbours on sandwich boards had evidently been noted. Normally, we were told, these kinds of lectures were attended by only around twenty people.

We timed our arrival just before the commencement to find more than a hundred people in the hall. David took up position near the podium, dressed immaculately in a suit (so the extensive wardrobe had finally come into its own!), and I took a seat in the second row from the front at one end. I felt immensely proud of his demeanour as he was officially presented to the gathered assembly by a representative of the Sea Grant University. I was invited up too and we stood together for the initial introduction, and there was quite a lot of joking and laughter about 'coals to Newcastle' as David was presented with a lump of local coal, and I was given a pretty, hand-decorated mug.

The first half of the lecture was devoted to the Arctic. After a brief interval, the second was focused on the Antarctic, supported by a great many excellent photographs of the wildlife in South Georgia, taken by David. He gave a professional and polished performance, despite the maddening irritation of a man, sitting directly in front of him on the front row, snapping his knees together all the time in a compulsive way. This continued throughout both halves, and caused one woman nearby to lean forward and glower at him periodically. David told me later that he was on the point of asking him to desist as it was most distracting, and it was getting on his nerves. The lecture was, by anyone's estimation, a great success. Both during the intermission – when wine and sandwiches were offered – and after the lecture, David was button-holed by one or two enthusiasts and couldn't escape. It is only fair that anyone who wants to talk to the lecturer should be allowed just a few moments of his time. At the end, when one man monopolised him for 15 minutes, I chose to intervene, as David seemed impervious to the line of people queuing to speak to him.

Much later when we were back in England we received a wonderful email from Grant Trask in Petersburg in which he said, among other things, 'David, I hope you recognise the value of your on-board public relations department/health and social services/logistics and planning/comfort, companionship, communications – all in a tall, elegant and beautiful bundle. And,' he continued, 'I hope and expect many more voyages made even more interesting and successful together, as a team.' I was so touched that someone had noticed what I was contributing to David's success. This spontaneous and generous compliment boosted my morale no end, as I did sometimes feel that David did not appreciate the things I did for him, but rather took them for granted.

SIXTEEN

TOUR OF ALASKA'S INSIDE PASSAGE

I T HAD ALWAYS BEEN OUR INTENTION TO go on a mini-cruise of our own to see something of the beautiful scenery of the inland waterway before setting off for the return voyage to the United Kingdom, and as we still had plenty of time in hand waiting for ice melt in the Arctic, we set ourselves a short itinerary based on study of the two most helpful volumes that David had been given by his Icelandic friend, Kristian; we also received quite a few recommendations from our friends and acquaintances in Petersburg.

The first day, we set off down the Wrangell Narrows. The current was in our favour so we zipped along, and as we neared the first corner a small skiff beetled across our nose trying to attract attention. It was Doug and Martina, our friends from South Kupreanof Island. We slowed the engine and were able to shout across to them that we would be back in a few days. There followed an exchange of photography before we resumed our course. Wrangell Narrows is a 22-mile-long winding channel with fast-flowing current which reverses direction halfway through, rather like the Solent does between England and the Isle of Wight. It is well buoyed, and at about 6.5 knots we were soon through and ejected into Sumner Strait. We motored across to

St John's Harbour, which had been recommended to us; it was a small bay on the north of Zarembo Island. Here we tucked in behind some islets. There were three or four other boats going to bed as we dropped our anchor in the fading light and rising mist. Irritating insects, the no-seeums, caused us to retreat inside rapidly.

After quite some time, David said, 'I'm sure the man in that boat over there is dead.'

'Why do you think that?' I replied.

'Because he's had his generator on for hours, and he's sitting slumped in a chair in the saloon – I can see him through the stern cabin door.'

'Don't be silly – I'm sure he's not dead,' I said, but I was left with a slightly chill feeling and the anchorage took on a more sinister atmosphere.

A short time later, he continued, 'I suppose we'll have to blow up the dinghy and go and take a look.'

'Why should *we* do it?' I said. 'There're several other people here with solid tenders – we could call them up on the VHF.'

The matter was left in the air for some time, and then David came back to the attack again. 'I'm sure he's dead.'

'Why *on earth* do you think that?'

'Because he's not moving at all, and he's been like that since we arrived.'

I continued to busy myself with supper preparations, then, 'Perhaps he's asleep,' I said hopefully, reaching for my binoculars and going out on to the bridge deck to have a better look. The generator was still throbbing away and its vacant sound seemed to confirm that somehow this lone traveller had arrived, anchored, sat down, 'slumped' and died.

'If he's still there in the morning,' David said firmly, 'we shall have to blow up the Tinker Traveller and go and make an investigation.'

'Why can't you call the coastguard if you're that worried?'

No answer forthcoming. We slammed the bridge deck door – one cannot close it gently as it forms an airlock with the massive outer door – and retired to bed to the now somewhat muffled pulse of the hapless man's generator, feeling rather uneasy.

The following morning, the motorboat had disappeared. The 'corpse' must have risen from slumber early and sailed away. Relieved of this onerous duty, we got under way for Point Baker on the north-west corner of Prince of Wales Island. En route we encountered our guitar-playing fisherman, Bob, who we knew was in the vicinity, in his distinctive salmon-fishing troller covered in pink and red buoys. We called him up on the VHF and then motored over towards him. We shouted a few exchanges across the water, and hoped to meet up later that evening, but he never appeared. He was evidently immersed in his fishing, which was his livelihood. We learned later that he caught 35,000 pounds of king salmon over the next few days.

At Point Baker, we snugged into a small cove that opened out on to a narrow channel with a couple of floating pontoons, to which were tied two or three scruffy boats. Accommodated on pilings attached to the pontoons were a few wooden huts and cabins. There was a nice empty space inviting us to sidle up to it, but a large sign announcing 'Float Planes Only' drove us on alongside what turned out to be the tiny post office. A wizened old man with a long, white, flowing beard to his waist and wispy hair appeared and said that we were fine where we were, so, having secured ourselves, we went on to the pontoon to explore. We were told that you couldn't get ashore and that you could 'help yourself to any book in the library' that was housed in one of the wooden cabins, and that there were 'only six residents in the area'.

Somewhat improbably, the library housed the muster station. At one end of the hall was an array of firemen's oilskins and heavy fire helmets, all hanging in a long row on old-fashioned hooks with a few faded sepia photographs of long-departed old worthies. There must have been at least a dozen outfits awaiting new owners since there were now so few remaining residents. Feeling a little like thieves, we helped ourselves to a rather interesting book about all the presidents of the United States of America who had occupied the White House, and replaced it with one or two surplus volumes from *Polar Bound*.

We found the old man again in a shed at the end where he was doing repairs to the fire engine. This was a barge with a large Yanmar diesel engine sitting in the middle, and a huge reel of canvas fire hose adjacent. It was amazing to me that these six residents should have such a facility in their midst. I asked him who the firemen were, and did they do fire practice, and he said they used to but now that there weren't many residents it was a case of, if the spirit moved you, you did it yourself. It all seemed improbable. He pointed out his 'old boat', which looked much newer than the 'new boat', and I admired the cranky stack pipe. 'I expect that keeps you warm,' I said, glancing at a huge heap of wood filling the saloon to the detriment of anyone wanting to shelter within it. 'Oh, I can carry a lot of wood,' he said, and continued, 'Aren't you those people who go up north? I've heard about you on the radio. They were saying something about a "talk".'

Later, while we were walking further along the boards to which one or two little fishing boats had tied up, a rough-looking fisherman stood up in his cockpit and accosted us.

'Wait a moment – I've got something.' He reached down into a cool box and came up with a beautiful, gleaming king salmon with baleful blue eyes, and thrust it gruffly into our hands.

We were quite overwhelmed. David chopped it up into lovely steaks on the jetty, and so supper was secure. I made some French egg mayonnaise, and the remaining steaks were individually wrapped and put into the freezer.

Much later that evening we walked back towards his boat, but he'd gone below to sleep, ready for an early start the following morning, no doubt. However, his Inuit crew took charge of David's reciprocated offering, which was a couple of boil-in-the-bag apple dumplings and custard, as issued to the British Army. It didn't seem much of an exchange, but then everyone gets tired of their own fare, and this was something quite different for him. We explained the intricacies of preparation to the Inuit and warned him to take care of his fingers as the foil edges were razor-sharp.

The next day, we set our course south down to Shakan Bay, Hamilton Island and on into the somewhat feared El Capitan Passage. This is about twenty-six miles long and we caught the current through it. Some sections were quite fast, and one area in particular pulled the boat this way and that as we encountered tumbling overfalls, swirling eddies and miniature whirlpools. You had to keep your nerve as you had the impression you were being swept along over huge, unseen rocks. At the entrance to El Capitan David had seen our first otter, and so at the other end of the narrows we decided to head for Sea Otter Sound. However, the bay on the north coast of Heceta Island proved a dull anchorage and the only wildlife was a distant whale and one otter, tantalisingly out of clear sight.

The day after, we crossed the southern end of Sumner Strait via Cape Decision and out into the open sea across to Cape Ommaney and Baranoff Island. Encountering blanket fog, we crawled up the coast past Puffin Bay to Redfish Bay and crept in using the newly downloaded charts on the computer, which have revolutionised coastal navigation, and found, as we closed the rocky entrance, the cloud thinning and a watery sun, which lifted our mood. Having anchored, we sat out on the afterdeck housing, leaning against the liferaft and deflated the Tinker Traveller dinghy, enjoying the warmth and blessed silence after the many miles of motoring we had done, and shared a beer. Glancing around at the steep mountainsides, completely covered by firs, we wondered at the trees' ability to take root on such hostile terrain and to achieve great heights of 150–200 feet. Quite a few dotted about had been assailed by termites, wind, drought or some other cause. Some seemed to have gathered by the foreshore, lying longitudinally as if man had had a hand in their placement.

The Forestry Service do quite a bit of their harvesting by helicopter, selecting a swathe of hillside from which to fell timber while still leaving a protective belt, so that the visual impact is not too startling. They collect the trees they have felled by grabbing them in a sling with the aid of a helicopter, then lifting them on to a nearby barge. These, having such shallow draught, can almost beach themselves. We timed a helicopter, and the round trip took the pilot just two minutes.

As we were sitting in sociable silence enjoying our surroundings, David announced, 'You know, you have absolutely no annoying habits.' He went on: 'It is quite unusual, as you find most people when you come to know them do do certain things which begin to grate.'

'Oh, I know exactly what you mean,' I replied. 'I remember a girl I used to share a room with when I first lived in London, and at bedtime we both read our books. All the time she was reading she would flick the top of the page she was on with her forefinger, and it really began to get irritating – so much so that I found I couldn't read myself. In the end I had to ask her to stop, and she readily admitted it, so it seems I wasn't the first to complain.' I continued: 'And then there are people who sniff all the time, or have a nervous cough, or play with the cutlery on the table or, worst of all, beat time to the music at a concert.'

We spent a whole day here and, although David hadn't said why, I knew it was because the next day was going to be quite arduous. He works all these things out but keeps them to himself. I suppose this is a habit from all the years of self-imposed solitude.

Sitka was our next destination; this was some 60–70 miles distant, but still on Baranoff Island. As we approached, we noticed a couple of small cruise ships who had been directed to anchor off. Those passengers who wished to go ashore were ferried over in a succession of small but rather smart lighters in their mother ship's livery. We went into a marina located on the edge of the channel. Having tied up alongside we went over to the office to be officially recognised and allocated a berth. This was conveniently located on a pontoon near the pedestrian entrance, so we had a succession of boat owners passing our beam and pausing to admire *Polar Bound* or chat to David, who was frequently on deck. There was also a supermarket nearby, an Aladdin's Cave which brought us back to earth with its bright lights, and variety of fresh fruit and vegetables after the wildness of the surroundings we had been passing through.

We stayed here for two or three nights, rather against David's inclination, who was viewing the disappearance of his dollars with some dismay, the rate of exchange being so poor. This was the former capital of Russian America and is now known principally for fishing and tourism, although it has also built up something of a reputation as a musical centre. We saw remains of Byzantine architecture in the old part, and since large cruise ships are not permitted, the more intimate character of the town is preserved.

The Sitka Music Festival, founded in 1972, attracts some fine classical musicians to the auditorium near the water's edge; the backdrop for any performance is a huge floor-to-ceiling window through which the audience can see any small cruise ships that may be in port. Perhaps this helps the musicians to give an exemplary performance, since the attention of the listeners is not focused on them exclusively. I noted that Piers Lane was the pianist one evening, whom I last heard in Norfolk giving a wonderful performance in the Marble Hall at Holkham. Unfortunately, we arrived too late for his concert. There had also recently been a Chopin recital by Natasha Parenski, which some sailing friends we met in Petersburg attended; they lived and worked in Sitka.

These friends, John Totten and his wife Kristy Kissinger-Totten, took us out in their 4X4 pick-up to the top of a nearby peak, stopping en route to visit a supermarket, which must have had one of the most spectacular views of any supermarket in the world, across the water of Sitka Sound. Here we armed ourselves with an instant picnic and drove to a nearby peak, around tortuous bends for several miles on a dirt track, gaining altitude all the time. We sat at a picnic table in brilliant sunshine, which proved almost too hot, and admired the view out across the water of the sound. There was total silence and no annoying insects to disturb us. John Totten, originally from Scotland, was a retired general surgeon from the hospital in Sitka, where he had practised for some thirty years, and Kristy had been a nurse. They also owned the local clinic, a large building in the centre of town on a dual carriageway, and which was for sale; their home was also about to go on the market as John had decided to return to his native Scotland, to Dumbarton on the west coast near Glasgow. John had earlier very kindly spent a considerable amount of time helping David to make some adjustments to his NOAA chart system on the computer.

Another interesting man we met as we explored some of the pontoons at a nearby harbour was Brent E. Turvey, Ph.D – a specialist forensic scientist and criminologist, who was throwing beer cans into a freezer box as we passed by his motorboat. It transpired that he is one of only five specialists in the world in his particular field; his expertise lies in looking more deeply into what would appear to be the obvious causes of death in a criminal case, and searching out the truth. He was evidently much in demand where the wrong conviction has been made in a murder trial, or an easy solution presented in what turned out to be a more complex case.

Another evening was spent with a retired surgeon and his son-in-law and son, who had been walking past *Polar Bound* the previous day and had stopped to admire her. Having then wandered on, they suddenly came back to ask us if we would like to join them the next day for dinner. The hospitality and friendliness of Americans is something quite special. The surgeon and his family rent a condominium in Sitka every year for one month so that they can have a month's fishing, and he keeps his motorboat alongside one of the pontoons in the marina. We had a wonderfully amusing evening in civilised surroundings and an excellent dinner of their freshly caught, barbecued salmon and crab with inviting fresh salads. Fresh food was not easy to keep in *Polar Bound*, so a salad was a very tempting thing. Like our dental friend, Doug Leen in Petersburg, this surgeon also washed all the plates under running water, and then to our amazement put them in the dishwasher – belt and braces! I would feel quite safe being operated on by him.

The Sitka Fur Company was an irresistible draw for me with its fox fur stoles, Inuit fur moccasins, hats, rugs and every other kind of enticement. There, we were met by a smooth-talking and charming man with swarthy skin that gave a clue to his local origins. David got into conversation while I drifted around the rails and tentatively tried on a cashmere cape trimmed with dark fox fur, with poppers on its folds to form sleeves. It simply fell into place, and swirled around me as I tested my mannequin's stance in front of a big mirror. Emboldened by this, and since the salesman made no move to try any sales pitch, I began to try on jackets and fitted waistcoats in Persian lamb's wool trimmed with sable. (The Persian lambs have tightly curled, short, furry pelts of natural brown shades.) I picked up a luxuriously soft rug with a rich sheen, at which point the salesman said, 'That is an otter-skin rug, or throw.' It was incredibly soft and warm, and apparently had over one million hairs per square inch; the otter has no blubber and has to eat its own weight daily in order to keep out the cold – this was priced at $17,000.

The shop had been empty up until now, when another woman came in with a small, multi-coloured bundle of fur and whiskers on a lead. Her golfing peak was pushed back on her forehead, and she had her sunglasses on. Small of stature, she drifted around the store with the little dog faithfully in her wake, trailing its lead along the floor. Like me, she fingered this and that until eventually we collided and I smiled at her and looked down at her dog, saying, 'You'd better watch that pooch of yours, or he'll end up at the taxidermist.'

She gave a laugh. 'Ah don't know why Ah come in here – Ah have so many furrrs, an' Ah neva wearr them.'

'Why is that?'

'Ah liive in south'n California.'

'Oh,' I said sympathetically. 'I can understand that then.'

The furrier salesman broke off his conversation with David to pay homage to this newcomer, with whom he was obviously well acquainted; I guessed she came from a cruise ship. She had a certain charisma, and I spotted a jacket that I thought would perfectly suit her artfully coloured hair.

'Do try this on,' I said, thrusting the coat into her arms. 'I think it would suit you.' She slipped it on, then wandered off to find something for me to try on. It was fun flaunting around the shop and not being bothered by any sales patter. He probably knew he didn't need to try.

Soon we discovered that she was indeed off a boat – her own.

'Have you got any crew?' asked David.

'Five,' she replied. 'A captain, a navigator, an engineer, a chef and a steward.'

We looked at each other, and asked where her boat was. Apparently it was near us in the marina, but so large it had to lie alongside on the outer edge. We learnt that her boat was called *Golden Boy*, and that she was Wendy.

Coming out of the shop empty-handed, we decided to search out her boat. It was second to the largest vessel in the marina, which was only fractionally bigger, called *Cocktails*. They were both accommodated on the outside pontoon. Wendy's boat had two huge white satellite globes among its array of antennae, and we decided she must come from Silicon Valley. We never saw her again, but we met the boat a couple of times with crew busying about hosing the decks and fussing over the fenders.

The following morning I weakened over the furs and telephoned the smooth salesman at the Sitka Fur Company. The owner of the store himself drove down to the boat bearing the cape and waistcoat in expensive dress bags and after some negotiation a deal was struck and the furs were transferred to David's tiny wardrobe, where they nestled comfortably up against his Browning 270. I hadn't given much consideration as to when I might wear them, but was sure that an occasion would present itself one day. The purchases lent a little glamour to my otherwise spartan existence and made me feel like a woman again.

Up early the next day in the anchorage – we had moved to save another expensive night of marina fees – and with the tide under us, we set off to the Olga and Neva Straits, narrow Passes with swiftly flowing water and navigation marks to guide us in the channel. We were closely followed by a fisherman who appeared intent on trying to ram us, crossing and re-crossing our wake, and who dogged *Polar Bound* until David got fed up with this seemingly drunken man's game and upped the revs until we had gained a healthy distance.

This was proving to be a bit of a whistle-stop tour, and we were certainly covering some ground. We spent that night at Schulze Cove in readiness for the long day to follow, and made a good start in the morning, finding that the alarmingly, and aptly, named Peril Strait was well marked with port and starboard hand buoys all the way along. We safely navigated our way around the narrow bends, meeting one or two strong pulls from the current, through which we had to hand-steer, at times reaching over 9 knots.

Coming out into a wider section where Peril Strait meets Hoonah Sound, we unexpectedly encountered first whales, then a group of five or six otters with little whiskery faces and beady eyes, playing in the fast-flowing water of a tide rip. They seem to like fairly boisterous conditions and would lie on their backs to observe us; they can swim strongly like this but as we closed the gap, they would sink below the water, only to reappear tantalisingly in another quarter to continue their inspection. We spent at least half an hour otter chasing so that David could photograph this elusive creature, but it is very difficult to spot them in the midst of small waves. At one time the otter was hunted almost to extinction as fishermen viewed them as a threat to their own livelihoods. Although they are supposedly protected now, we wondered if the hunting continues, as there seem to be remarkably few.

The next port of call was Cosmos Cove – a useful, safe anchorage with quite a number of fishing boats taking shelter and resting before their early dawn start. The following evening we arrived at Baranoff Hot Springs, eleven miles further south. This is a deep anchorage with high mountains all around, and you can normally tie up alongside a pontoon while you go ashore to sightsee and enjoy the springs.

However, the pontoon was crowded and there were numerous fishing boats present, so after admiring the waterfall thundering down the rocks we motored off to a cove nearby, which shallowed up at the end, and passed *Golden Boy* anchored nearby. David would not let me call Wendy on the VHF so I had to content myself with waving at the crew. The next day we ranged alongside as we were leaving to ask if Wendy was aboard, but she was either still in bed or had been whisked to the shore to take advantage of the hot springs issuing from fissures in the rock just above the falls.

This stretch of Baranoff Island coastline on Chatham Strait between Cosmos Cove and down to the junction with Frederick Sound is described in the marine atlas we used to navigate our way around as having grand scenery, 'with the steepest mountains and the most waterfalls tumbling their foaming white water into the sea'. Soon after leaving Baranoff we turned the corner from Chatham Strait into Frederick Sound. This junction is called Point Gardner, and Murder Cove lurks nearby – we never found out what had occurred there, but this was the same point we rounded on our arrival the previous year following our transit of the Northwest Passage via the McClure Strait.

We were beginning to head back to Petersburg now, and our next call was forty miles beyond, which brought us round to Cannery Cove in Pybus Bay on the southeast corner of Admiralty Island – a lovely, gentle, open bay with a shallow sweep of grassland at its head, several high mountains surrounding the sides clad in fir trees with a rocky foreshore, and the remains of a canning factory converted into some kind of lodge. Admiralty Island, whose Tlingit name is Kootznoowoo (which means 'Fortress of the Bears'), is reputed to have the largest concentration of brown bears in the world. It seemed to us that many of these islands were making the same claim, while we had yet to see a single brown bear.

We motored up to the head of the bay, which looked rather too shallow for comfort, I thought, and could have proved mosquito-y too. We passed a rather smug little Canadian sailing boat, the owner sprawled in a hammock on the after deck smoking a pipe, his wife sitting nearby, both wearing Tilley hats and appearing to be engrossed in their books. New arrivals at an anchorage are always a source of great interest to those who are already comfortably settled, having bagged their perch much earlier, their own anchoring dramas long forgotten.

We let the anchor down, then David decided it was too shallow, so up came the rope, which had to be coiled down on the foredeck. We started to motor a bit further out and passed the smug couple, who by now had lowered their books to observe our activities. At that moment a fisherman in a small motorboat came speeding up to us and told us that there was a brown bear eating grass on the foreshore. In some excitement we had another stab at anchoring.

'Here, do you think?' asked David, and then, answering himself, 'Yes – this looks a good spot.' I agreed, but by the time all was ready on the foredeck and the anchoring paraphernalia was in place, we had overshot, and now we were too close to another boat. Of course it was my fault. Up came the anchor again with a lot of muttering about the 'wrong advice', but on the third attempt we got it right, and the 'hammock' boat, rather disappointed, slowly lowered their eyes and reverted to reading their books.

This time we were close enough to the shoreline to make a prolonged study of the bear, which turned out to be a young one. We took endless photos of it munching the grass as it wandered myopically around, every now and again sitting down on its haunches to take stock. It seemed wholly unconcerned about noise nor about some kayakers who had paddled over to take a closer look.

We had been away from Petersburg for nearly two weeks on our sightseeing tour, and now we needed to return and prepare for our departure through the Northwest Passage. Taking advantage of the early morning current, we headed back some 54 miles to our berth at the north harbour in Petersburg.

SEVENTEEN

DEPARTURE FROM PETERSBURG

OUR DEPARTURE WAS TO BE TUESDAY, 9 July, and we had just over a week to get organised. At the eleventh hour the Jabsco pump on the heads seized up and David decided to take the outflow pipe off to investigate the cause. He said it would take him four hours, and that we'd have to leave the following day instead. Half the trim and fascia boards in the heads had to be dismantled to access the heavy corrugated plumbing pipe, which over the years had become silted up with scale from sea water. Once he had got it off, I draped it round my neck, and in pouring rain carried it up to the harbour master's office, where I was able to borrow a high-pressure hose. I spent a good twenty minutes squirting it through from both directions, with one end draped over the wooden walkway to the grid below. A lot of sediment was dislodged.

David appeared clad in oilskins and ordered me to take one end so that he could whack the pipe up and down, banging it on the concrete pavement by the road outside. The first whack nearly took my wrist off and so I had to go in search of a strong man to help David; mercifully, there was one just round the corner. (I always make my approach by asking, 'Are you a strong man?' Few can resist this.

163

However, one must size up one's specimen first.) We put the whole thing back together again, and put all the trim in place, but still the system was very stiff, so David then took the pump itself to pieces and put some special lubricant on the plunger. After that we had the clearest plumbing and the smoothest pump handle in Petersburg.

We had already been to the Hammer & Wikan supermarket out of town, next to the airport, and placed an advance order for a quantity of minced beef, steaks, chicken thighs and thin pork chops. All these had to be accommodated in the freezer, so we went armed with the measurements. The helpful and friendly butcher at the store had entered into the spirit of the thing and removed all the fancy packaging, on his own initiative, so that not a millimetre of space was wasted. He was very considerate. David had quite a following at the store, and some of the staff had heard our interview on the local radio. Everyone we met assumed we were husband and wife. The first time it happened, in some store or other, I was stunned for a moment, but tried not to react. Countering this misconception would only involve complicated explanations; however, we never referred to each other in this way. To other people, we referred to each other by our Christian names.

Apart from the last-minute stores to stow away, there was also wonderful freshly frozen halibut, which I bought, and super prawns, full of flavour, which as David had to watch his diet where they were concerned I packed in small bags, six or eight together, so there would be no cheating. As I was doing this, he came over and tried to get a larger number into each ration. I had to be firm.

We finally left at 3pm on 9 July in light drizzle, seen off by a small deputation who helped us untie the warps. Our wonderful hosts Grant and Lila Trask arrived to say goodbye, and also the kindly fisherman off a nearby trawler, who gave us a special jar of his own salmon. Joe Viechnicki, the local radio reporter, turned up with his microphone, and Doug and Martina Leen, who had come over by skiff specially from South Kupreanof Island, were bearing two burgees, which they wanted flown from *Polar Bound*'s rigging – one was the flag of the Ross Island Yacht Club of Antarctica from the three years Doug spent as a dentist in Antarctica and represented a group of of men hauling a sledge across ice, and the other was the flag of the South Kupreanof Yacht Club, whose seven members were the only island residents. Grant and Lila came aboard to have a huddle with us in the wheelhouse, our arms around each other's shoulders, all of us facing inwards. Grant offered up a short prayer for our safe-keeping and thrust a small wooden cross into our hands, which David placed in the paws of a brown teddy bear mascot that was wedged next to Reeds Almanac above the chart table. We were quite touched and emotional, and felt truly sorry to say farewell to this kindest and most Christian of couples. Doug Leen pressed a small coin he had found in the road into my hand as a keepsake for my security. Cameras were brought out on both sides, and eventually we got away, eight weeks to the day since our arrival back from England. We were quite overwhelmed, and busied ourselves coiling up warps and putting away fenders as we passed the huge can buoy heaving with sea lions.

With the tide under us again, we were soon up to Portage Bay for our first night, and away early the next morning – this time going north through Stephens Passage to visit a few new places along Alaska's Inside Passage on the way to Icy Strait and our 1,200-mile crossing of the Gulf of Alaska. Our first call was at Taku Harbour, where we had hoped to meet up with guitar-playing Bob. We went alongside a well-constructed and maintained wooden jetty in the peaceful bay near a log cabin owned by the Forestry Service. These types of cabin can be occupied by anyone. There is a fixed sleeping shelf, on which you can lie in rows (take your own bags), a stove, an outside privy and, along a short winding track in a carpeted forest clearing, a great swing suspended on two very long ropes from a pair of extremely tall fir trees. The silence after the constant engine noise of *Polar Bound* was eerie and all-embracing, just the pine needles crunching under David's shoes as he pushed me higher and higher. A pair of bald eagles guarded their nest nearby. I read a comment from an earlier visitor to the hut who said she was 'spooked' by the bears. Although we saw none, there were references to sightings right by the hut from other contributors.

In a new anchorage the next day, in Auke Bay near Juneau, the capital of Alaska, we tried to go alongside the pontoons, but when David called the harbour master on the VHF, he said they were full up and it was on a first-come first-served basis. I had never seen so many fishing boats before. There was a constant procession of fishermen returning to base, nose to tail, as the Fisheries Protection had decreed that the season would have to close early because of a shortage of fish; the remaining fish in the waterway were to be given a chance to escape. I respected their vigilance on this matter. The fishing boats were rafting up six and even eight abreast and there was certainly no room for us. David stood off, with *Polar Bound*'s engine just turning over, and at that moment we spotted the shiny topsides of the immaculately gleaming, enormous private yacht *Cocktails*, last seen in Sitka; our friendly smiles were met by a blank stare from a member of the crew, who took up a rather negative stance on the after deck, which discouraged us. Instead, we made our way over to Indian Cove across the bay, and once the rocking wash from the endless procession of returning commercial fishing boats had finally died down at dusk, we spent a peaceful night. The following morning we finally managed to secure a berth alongside one of the outside pontoons in the main harbour.

We decided to take the bus into Juneau to see the bright lights after our period of reclusiveness; this took about an hour as it was some 40 miles away and necessitated a change of bus. We got off at a downtown stop and by then had managed to make contact with our gentleman fisherman friend, Bob of guitar-playing fame, who met up with us later that evening and gave us supper at a bistro called El Sombrero. Bob had a good rapport with the charming and chic Mexican owner, and quite a number of beers were consumed before the end of the evening. Bob was in relaxed mood, having just caught 35,000 pounds of salmon (and sold them too), and he became more and more gregarious and flirtatious as the evening wore on. It was good to meet up with him again. We would have been sorry to leave the Inside Passage without saying farewell.

The next day we reached Hoonah in Icy Strait, after a long stretch of spectacular scenery and beautiful sunshine, seeing several whales on the way. Hoonah is a native village supported by fishing and has its own cannery. It was a calm, still evening and we tied up to a pontoon ahead of a vast great tug. We were impressed by the quantity of rubber buffers and overlying platelets around its bow and stern – it was a very purposeful vessel. After supper that evening, we walked ashore in the darkness and saw some of the local population crouched in doorways slightly the worse for wear. We found a large silent marina, almost devoid of life, despite being crammed with private boats; few owners seemed to be aboard. There were just one or two twinkling lights giving a sign of life. It showed the government were doing their best; it must have been a very expensive operation, requiring millions to be poured into the infrastructure to preserve traditional ways and to support the native Indians.

While we were at breakfast the following morning, a diligent young man arrived to collect our harbour dues. After he'd gone we decided to go ashore again to revisit the marina. Here we met up with the great red private motorboat last seen on our visit to the Le Conte Glacier, when we were anchored in Ideal Cove on our short sight-seeing trip. The *Engelbank* remembered us and invited us aboard. We were filled with amazement at the luxurious interior complete with spiral staircase, huge galley and bar, and a grand sitting room, whose sole occupant was a fluffy cat with squashed oriental face and paws folded under, adorning the back of a sofa. We marvelled at the state bedrooms with island-sited double beds, en-suite bath and shower rooms, a grand bridge deck with seating for eight or ten, and their paper charts rolled up in static circular slots above the console, which had a bewildering array of switches, buttons and instrumentation. Two floors below was a vast engine room with machinery, pipes, electrical cables, stabilisers and workshop, all with watertight bulkheads.

While we were admiring all this, and David was privately speculating how she would stand up to a seaway with all her top hamper combined with a huge after deck, another couple joined us who had a slot on the pontoon just behind the *Engelbank*. We had last met them in the main street of Petersburg, and I remembered them well as when we introduced ourselves, standing on the street corner, they appeared to have heard of David. She had said in an excited way, 'Oh – you're royalty!' She was young with a gamine hairdo, and he was a handsome, lean, grey-haired man, considerably older. They had trailed their little, so-called 'tugboat', barely 30 foot, from Florida, launching her up at the northern end of the Inside Passage, leaving their 4X4 on the dock and setting off to explore the area.

They admitted that they needed to be very tidy and had very few clothes aboard, cooked on a single-burner Wallis paraffin stove (such as we had ourselves), slept in two single bunks and employed a 'bucket and chuck it' system – and were having a wonderful time. She was a pharmacist, and he probably retired – Casey and Mary Casebeer.

I must say we thought that was real enterprise, trailing their boat all the way from Florida. We had to admire their initiative; it brought home how little one needs to have just as much fun. By comparison, the shiny red *Engelbank* with so much luxury and complicated electronics and machinery, seemed a big maintenance responsibility.

After our tour around the *Engelbank*, we set off for our final port of call, Elfin Cove on the northwest corner of Chichagof Island, before leaving for the 1,200-miles crossing of the Gulf of Alaska. A lot of people had recommended this place. As we approached through the narrows of the South Inian Pass, we encountered an enormous school of humpback whales – everywhere we looked there was a whale, but there was also a lot of wind and the sea was choppy, which made it hard to capture them on film. They seemed preoccupied with one thing, and that was to stock up on king salmon, which were entering the Inside Passage from the open sea to return to their birthplace to spawn, then die. The unfortunate salmon are at the head of the food chain, with whales, bears, seals, otters, eagles and mankind all intent on capturing them.

We rounded the corner towards Elfin Cove and found the entrance so narrow that we could barely believe it was an entrance. It had rocks on both sides, and not too much depth by the look of it. Initially there seemed nowhere to tie up, so we went alongside a rickety pontoon that was the fuel and water dock. These moments are always somewhat fraught as nine times out of ten we are unsure which side to place the warps for throwing ashore, and similarly which side to tie the huge fenders. The long lines on the fenders, which are needed for security, take far longer to tie on than a handy short one would, and to make matters harder, they cannot be tied to the stanchions, but have to be passed through metal freeing slots in the capping rail – this entails standing on your head and trying to do everything at once. This isn't the end of it, either; you then have to execute a long jump on to, quite probably, a slippery pontoon, having first untied the steel core 'gate'. This involves facing inwards and balancing along the outside of *Polar Bound*, like a tightrope walker, carefully placing your feet on the capping rail and carrying the fag end of the warp with the loop in your hand, waiting for the moment at which you judge you can step boldly backwards out into space from the mother ship, to rush to some securing point, quite likely only to receive orders – 'NO! Not that one – further aft – quickly!'

Quite often there are minor repercussions and explanations afterwards when order is restored. This is all quite normal, and a captain at these times is always delighted to have someone to blame if things don't work out quite as expected.

EIGHTEEN

ELFIN COVE, AND ACROSS THE GULF OF ALASKA

ELFIN COVE HAS OVER A MILE OF WOODEN WALKWAYS
serving visitors and a tiny indigenous population, which
number approximately twenty-five year-round. The walkway
had been constructed round the forested shoreline and is the only
means of getting about, so locals have to use trolleys to transport their
belongings, and children play on their bikes and trikes. We walked
ashore after we had made fast to see if we could find a better perch
for the night and passed a group of three hippyish men and a woman,
all with roll-ups hanging from their lips. We enquired from them
where we might go, and the woman said, 'You can go anywhere you
can find a spot.'

She continued, 'There's no harbour master, and don't listen to any
of those people who tell you you can't tie up there – take no shit from
anyone.'

Feeling somewhat comforted by this sound advice, we saw a spot
on a pontoon around the back of the promontory and, after we'd moved
Polar Bound around, two rather rough, gnarled-looking fishermen

171

came along to take our warps. After tying us up, they eyed the boat for a bit in silent contemplation, conferring between themselves, then one came back. 'Where yew folks from? Are you the people who go up north to the Arctic? Fuckin' Jesus.' He continued, with an embarrassed, self-deprecatory laugh, 'I'm just a backwoodsman – that's all Aah do. Just a back woodsman.' It was muttered in a self-comforting, confirmatory sort of way, and he went shambling away to tell the others, who were all working on their respective boats but had stopped to have a tea break and size up the new arrivals.

We had occupied the single remaining spot. To go ashore, we had to negotiate the fishermen's outstretched legs, among other obstacles along the walkway. It was a hive of organised chaos, little regard being paid to the notice posted at one end telling the berth holders to keep their property within the confines of their respective boats. Electrical leads trailed along the route, along with discarded tools. One boat had a floating workshop attached, with an itinerant cabinet maker complete with bandsaw and jigs, who was clearly being employed to fit out the interior of the vessel to which his workshop now clung. A very, very large dog named Nelson, with a huge, seemingly endless chain, stood guard overall. We wondered how people could afford to feed such a vast animal. We weren't sure whether it was a St Bernard crossed with a husky, or an Alsatian – at any rate, he appeared to have eaten, and gave a perfunctory sniff at David's proffered hand as we squeezed past.

We walked to the small store and bought an expensive orange, and then were almost swept off our feet by a child on a trike clattering along the boards. We walked right around the bay and photographed some of the little wooden houses and cabins – each so individual. One house was decorated entirely with the beautifully architectural horns of small deer and roebucks, another with gaudy ceramic shoes and clogs filled with plants. We saw a calabrese plant, elevated from culinary use to ornamental purpose, sitting grandly in a large terracotta pot, its knobbly buds awaiting their flowering time; it was surprisingly effective.

The wooden walkway gave out here and there and was replaced with a needle-coated earth path that traversed massive roots from sawn trees, which still lay where they had been felled to make room for the track. The track itself came to an abrupt end up a slope with barking dogs in attendance. On our return we met a very nice man and his wife who had built quite a set-up for themselves over the last thirty years. Her love of horticulture was in evidence everywhere you looked, each nook and cranny taken advantage of with ferns and plants, some wild, all very colourful and attractive. Her husband operated the pilot boat, for which he had built his own pontoon and a terrace above, with more flowerpots sprouting wherever the opportunity presented itself.

We mentioned a company, much in evidence, who had evidently acquired a good deal of the local property and who were exploiting the unique setting of the cove. We learned that there was much resentment from the year-round population, who received no benefit from the summer invasion this company attracted, and were not employed by the company, who imported staff to run their business, which amounted to a grand, comfortable fishing-lodge with their own skiffs, laundry service for guests and young staff to clean, process and package the guests' daily catch ready for them to fly back in the company's own light aircraft to the point of entry.

Later, back on our boat, a large motorboat came in with a party of Americans on board, about eighteen of them, all with cameras slung around their necks, who were apparently expected for dinner at the company's lodge. We waved to them as we helped the crew to take their lines, and they started snapping their cameras at *Polar Bound*, desperate not to leave anything out of their holiday experience.

'Where've you come from?' I shouted out.

They looked at each other and shifted uncomfortably while they tried to remember; they weren't too sure, and one man started arguing with his wife as to where it had been.

We got ready to leave on the evening tide, but not before motoring right up to the head of the bay and circling round in the golden sunshine and lengthening shadows to wave goodbye to our new-found friends, the pilot and his thoughtful wife, who had given us a bag of freshly picked lettuce and herbs from her greenhouse, knowing how they would be appreciated.

Chichagof Island is yet another to make the claim that it has one of the largest populations of brown bear in north America, and you are advised if you go hiking in the forest to take bear protection, travel loudly and dress appropriately. I wondered what sort of sartorial elegance is acceptable to a bear.

We slipped out of Elfin Cove on the ebb tide, and saw the whales again, although they were less in evidence. A photographer had positioned himself on an inaccessible crag to get our picture, and I pointed him out to David, who was concentrating on avoiding a huge raft of kelp in the rather tricky, narrow entrance. Once clear of this, he turned *Polar Bound* around, and with much waving and smiling we made a pass right across in front of the photographer's perch, which he must have taken some trouble to reach, and hoped that he captured the image he wanted. Picking our way through more rafts of giant seaweed, which had long, thick stalks that could easily entwine themselves around our propeller, we were pushed and spun around in circles by the swirling eddies and overfalls in the narrows as we passed clear of the Inside Passage. We felt rather lonely and isolated as we motored out by Cape Spencer into the vast arena of the Gulf of Alaska, with 1,200 miles to go to our next port of call, Dutch Harbour via the Unimak Pass in the Aleutian chain.

It was a beautiful golden evening, and as we reached further and further out into the ocean, we passed several fishing trawlers hurrying home with their catch. A thin wispy haze formed over the water, and coming up to the bridge during supper to check on rogue vessels, I spotted a long log floating almost in our path, and in the wreathing mist realised that it had two big seabirds roosting with their heads under their wings, standing on one leg at each end, with the log submerged between them; a delightful sight and so unexpected. They were as surprised as we were and took off in alarm from their slumbers. I did manage to get a picture, but we were almost upon them before they took flight into the swirling bank of rising sea fog.

The next eight days were spent in heaving seas as we punched directly into strong northwesterly winds. With a 10-foot swell, our speed fell from an average 6.5 knots down to just 4. We gradually acquired our sea legs, but little was eaten for the first forty-eight hours, and the only way we could get some sleep was to pack ourselves into my bunk in the saloon, jammed up against the table flap to stop being thrown around. That way, nested together, we could relax from constantly bracing against the roll. Moving about in the cabin was an adventure in itself and required agility; standing at the sink or stove one had to adopt the pose of a young giraffe with legs splayed, and hip wedged. The saucepan and spice cupboards were another challenge and had to be opened with great caution to prevent a cascade of lids, herbs, plastic pots, butter dish and a hail of other items from within. Everything was a huge physical effort. Similarly, a visit to the essential offices was an undertaking; even to open the door and get around it was a struggle. Then came the lowering of trousers and knickers, one hand grappling the belt, then lowering yourself gently on to the seat, which got colder and colder the further north we went.

To minimise the discomfort David decided to head up a bit, to close the land south of Kodiak Island, which would give us a bit of lee. We entered the Unga Strait on arrival and found relatively tranquil water. We passed one or two settlements and wound our way through a series of islands. Near Popof Island we encountered a mass of seabirds in a feeding frenzy, having located some krill. Wave upon wave of birds rose up as we passed among them – they were for the main part the little puffin with its colourful, fat bill. During that night, lying awake in my bunk, the faithful Gardner engine's *chonk, chonk, chonk* turned to a splutter. I called David urgently, and he dashed up the companionway to the bridge deck to shut down the system and prevent an airlock. We then had to go up forward in the dark night and a heaving sea in our thermals to open up the forward hold and turn on some levers to access fuel from a different holding tank. I merely held the torch to highlight the area, while David contorted himself among the pipes and wrestled with the valves.

We entered another sheltered area of water within the Iliasik Islands, and David wanted to transfer some fuel from the jerry cans on the after deck into the ship's holding tanks. We got out of the strong wind and flow of current, which had been sweeping us along under the lee of a high peak, and turned off the engine. Such a contrast – here the sea was mirror calm and the silence was magical. In the distance, slowly approaching us, was a gigantic delivery barge pulled by a gallant little tug, one third of a mile ahead with a long steel hawser attached to a towing harness. This took about twenty-five minutes to reach us – an unstoppable load. It was necessary, when encountering one of these mobile monoliths, to call up the tug master on the VHF to enquire which side of your own vessel he would like to pass. The vast, unhurried procession sailed by with load upon load of containers piled high, and bulldozers, cars, diggers and skiffs atop and between the containers. There is evidently great skill in loading these colossal equipages, leaving gaps between categories so that individual sections can be accessed without disturbing the whole edifice, and also to allow a space through which the wind can pass. A tug master in charge of one of these deliveries has to be one of a rare breed. The job requires great judgement and skill, and no doubt commands a commensurate salary.

Not long after this we had a wonderful visit from the deep. A vast humpback whale announced its presence with a huge sigh, and circled the boat, coming up for air then gently submerging again, investigating *Polar Bound*'s underwater surface in the greatest detail. There commenced a slow ballet of stately majesty with turns, arabesques and great elegance; in an unhurried and dignified way this vast mammal, quite as long as *Polar Bound*, made a careful and courtly inspection of every orifice and external fitting, submerging again and again, never once touching us, and with a final gentle slide of the vast tail fin sinking below the boat and up the other side. The crustaceans and molluscs served to show the stature and age of this leviathan of the deep. On each surfacing, the eye was focused on absorbing the whole structure of the vessel, and the gills exhaled a great gusty sigh audible below the water, notably fetid, and with the appearance on the surface of a great yawn.

This silent scrutiny continued for well over half an hour, as David and I ran from end to end of the ship to capture the magnificent spectacle. We were hugely privileged, and any thought of topping up the fuel tanks was abandoned in our anxiety to photograph this presence from another world. Perhaps the whale thought it had found a mate. We shall never know, but eventually the twists and turns came to an abrupt halt, and as silent as the arrival, so the departure, and we were left to continue with our back-breaking work of carrying the five-gallon jerry cans forward from the stern and carefully tipping the contents into the filler hole using a simple but effective siphon and, finally, a gigantic funnel for the dregs.

We had almost completed our long haul through the Pacific across the Gulf of Alaska up to the Unimak Pass, the three- to four-mile-wide opening in the chain of the Aleutian Islands that allows you passage from the great Aleutian Bank in the Pacific Ocean with depths of over 3,500 fathoms (21,000 feet) to exit into the Bering Sea, with depths of only 10–15 fathoms. What an extraordinary sight it would be if the seas ran dry. It would leave an immensely high cliff face and then, way below, a vast expanse like the Rift Valley in Africa, and all in the space of about four miles. Small wonder, then, that the Unimak Pass is to be respected on account of the immensely strong currents that swirl through it.

A day or so after our encounter with the whale we arrived at Castle Point at the eastern entrance to the Unimak Pass, and here we awaited the turn of the tide to catch the current through into Bristol Bay, a vast, shallow area of water constituting part of the Bering Sea. The sun shone and once again the engine was turned off as we drifted on the counter current very close to the shore near the entrance of the pass. We bobbed gently on the wavelets and sat sharing a beer on the after-cabin coach roof, while I took the opportunity to cut David's hair, amid a great deal of advice as to how to taper it, and how he didn't want 'to end up looking like a monk'.

The steep hillside opposite still bore the scars of the Second World War, with gun emplacements, bunkers and heaps of rusting machinery – a somewhat incongruous sight nearly seventy years after the ending of hostilities. Why doesn't mankind clean up after itself? Several waterfalls cascaded down the slopes, as they had done for aeons, sparkling and jumping in the sunlight, unmindful of the desecration amid their beauty. It seems the Japanese, once the Americans had entered the war, were determined to obtain a foothold in the Aleutian chain, hoping to gain territory and to deflect American troops from other key points. They established themselves on one or two of the islands, including Attu to the west of the Unimak Pass, and the Americans launched a counter-offensive. However, poor intelligence meant that the Americans stormed the island only to find the Japanese had left the day before. Over four hundred American troops were lost as they tried to land: drowned in the strong tidal currents, killed by aerial attacks or dying in planes that got lost in the deadly wreathing clouds and mist that lay within the folds of the mountains, radar still being in its infancy.

During our enforced period of peaceful contemplation, David told me the story of an experience he had had in Durban, South Africa in 1984, when he called there for a week's break or so on his circumnavigation of the world in the old lifeboat, *Mabel E. Holland*. He had been out sightseeing and then to supper with his cousin and, tired at the end of the day, had retired to his cabin in *Mabel*, which was tied up alongside the pontoon. There was no electricity supply to the boat from the shore.

He was soon in a deep sleep, and some time later he had a vivid dream in which he could hear a tinkling waterfall. After about sixty seconds he came to his senses and realised that it was not a dream at all. A big black man, clad in dark clothing, was crouched by his bunk in the tiny cramped cabin of *Mabel*, within a foot of his head. David started up in surprise and asked him what he was doing. The man said he was hungry. David, very calmly, said, 'Come with me and I'll give you some food.' Without stopping to put his trousers on, David proceeded out of the cabin through the heavy, watertight door, which had been left ajar on the warm night, followed by the man, who was aged around twenty to thirty.

They made their way to the forward hold, where standing height was only four feet six. This was entered through a small hatch and down four steps to land on top of a fuel tank, from where there was a high step down to the tiny cramped space below the hold, which served also as David's galley. The man followed him down and David put on the lights and gathered up some food in carrier bags. The man stood silently by watching for about ten minutes. When David had got it all together, he said, 'I'll pass it up to you, if you go up first.' David followed him out and lowered the food to him over the side when the man had stepped on to the pontoon. 'Thanks, man,' the fellow said and disappeared into the night.

David told me that he had never had any rapid heartbeat, despite the experience. He said, 'I was quite young then and probably a bit naïve.' Apparently when he got up and put his trousers on in the morning, he realised that all his loose change had disappeared, which no doubt accounted for the sound of tinkling that had woken him in the first place. He was very fortunate indeed that nothing worse befell him as there were many stories of knifings.

When the current turned, we proceeded through the Unimak Pass on a diagonal course from the southeast to the northwest corner and the exit into Bristol Bay, with the current sweeping us along at over 9 knots, and kept going for the next two hours or so through the sea fog that arrived once more to blot out our landfall. David's diligent navigation was spot on yet again and amid a mass of homecoming fishing boats and a confusion of navigation and shore lights, we entered Dutch Harbour in the small hours of the morning, picking our way through the red and green buoys that marked the channel and kept us off rocky promontories and isolated shoals.

If David had not, by chance, on first entering Dutch Harbour so many years ago, discovered the kindness of Kristian and the ample sides of his fishing trawler, *Lady Gudny*, against which to tie up, we would have been banished to the impersonal and distant location of the Spit. Now, just as in the previous September, we were delighted to see the vessel and happy to lie up abreast. Currently no one was aboard and she was all newly painted. We secured ourselves with fore and aft lines and placed our vast fishing buoy fenders over the sides to act as buffers between us. It was 3.30am, and we had finally arrived at Unimak Island, connected to Unalaska Island by bridge.

NINETEEN

DUTCH HARBOUR

T HAT MORNING, SOME HOURS LATER, we were awoken by an insistent singsong. 'HEL–LO–HO! Anyone there?' I climbed out, throwing a towel around myself and went up to the bridge deck. There was the welcoming, beaming smile of James Mason, resident (on the island) journalist, standing expectantly, just as before, with canvas bag and all his camera impedimenta slung around him, part and parcel of him, without which he could go nowhere. The appearance of this somewhat scantily clad and dishevelled woman did not disconcert him, and he said he would be back about 1pm. James was an ex-war correspondent and had been out in Bosnia, where he had seen some horrific things; he was now renting an apartment overlooking the harbour on one side and the airport runway on the other, giving him instant visual access to all comers, and had started his own online newspaper called *The Dutch Harbour Telegraph*, of which he was the editor and sole journalist.

James once again became our daily companion-cum-chauffeur, meeting us every morning on the boat at 10am, normally while we were still at breakfast, and waiting patiently while we cleared up and made a plan for the day. His attempt to mimic our English pronunciation with a crystal-cut accent, and his light-hearted observations of the human race and its frailties, kept us vastly entertained. On occasions we were so absorbed by his stories that we forgot what we should be doing. He once told us he had flown into London and stayed in a hotel on the Embankment. Suffering jet lag, he had gone for an early morning walk along the Thames. He sat down on a bench, and along came a man with a little dog. He recognised the man as James Mason, the actor. They got into conversation and our James said, 'My name is James Mason too,' at which the actor seemed quite surprised. He tethered the dog and sat down, and they talked for about fifteen minutes.

There is no proper provision on Unalaska Island for yachts in transit, as the island does not need, or appear to want, visitors. The economy is sustained by the fishing industry, and there are several Unisea fish-processing plants with workers hurrying about in white overalls, their hair in white nets, the men with white caps. Unalaska is a place where work goes on round the clock. The workers are housed in purpose-built blocks, and all their needs for food, laundry, showers etc. are provided by canteens and a laundry service. Some of the long-term resident managers have their own house, but all are wooden shacks and there is no feeling of permanence.

The men have come to do a job, and for the main part they arrive on the island, work hard, earn good money and, after a prolonged stint, return to their homes and families elsewhere. Linking all the areas are hard stony roads, dusty and muddy and painful to the feet – there are few paved roads. Great billowing clouds of white steam gush out of vents overlooking the road. A stench of processed crab lies over everything – a nauseating smell that would deter the keenest crab eater, though it did not seem to put off small birds that darted in and out through the louvres, either nesting in the confines of the building or picking up what they could find to eat.

The docksides by the processing plants were lined with large ocean-going fishing boats, each shinier and bigger than the one before, and all costing millions of dollars. The decks were packed with cranes, derricks, fish pots and cages, and the docksides were busy with electric carts and forklifts trundling to and fro. Overhead, the huge bald eagles I remembered from our earlier visit floated majestically, scouring all this human activity for their opportunity to swoop down and scavenge for food.

A new mooring facility has recently been constructed at considerable cost with state-of-the art floating pontoons, built to a very high specification, but this is not for transient yachts, only for the big fishing ships. We noted only six or seven taking advantage of this new facility, although we were told it was occasionally at full capacity. At least David had managed to obtain tickets for us to use their excellent, spacious showers with endless hot water that were, above all, spotlessly clean.

The dominant feature of the factory town is a nineteenth-century Russian Orthodox church, with a fine wooden, blue-painted, late-Regency house adjacent for the resident priest, when there is one. The house, which appeared to be empty, is much in need of attention, and is the principal focal point on entering the harbour. Inside the church an American woman was lecturing a rather untidy group of tourists. We wandered into what might be termed the lady chapel, but were peremptorily instructed by the guide, no doubt suspicious that we might be going to make off with the sacramental silver, to go over and join her group. So we retreated and walked along the grey sand beach below, with lapping wavelets and cast-up timber and shells.

The two large and expensive supermarkets, the Alaska Stores and Safeway's, are placed at some distance either side of the Grand Aleutian Hotel, which would be better named 'the Grand Illusion'.

The prices are sky-high, like everything on this island. Upon enquiring about availability, we were told they had a waiting list of eighteen. Nearby, on an isolated site, is a small shop run and leased by Veeda, an Englishwoman from Essex, though you wouldn't know it. Now naturalised, having married an American, she reigns supreme over all the necessities and accoutrements of the world of information technology, plus stationery supplies, cards, writing equipment and all manner of such things, and is also the local grapevine, with whom James checks in on a twice-daily basis. She knows every boat that is in harbour, which ones are expected in, which have departed, where they're going, whether there's been a punch-up in a local bar, and she told sixty-five-year-old James that it was time he found himself a good woman to care for him. While David and I wandered about window shopping, they discussed the finer points of an attractive-looking lady doctor recently appointed to the community.

It was from Veeda that David bought a new visitors' book for the Hudson's Bay Company hut at Fort Ross, a place at which we would be calling on our way back; this was at the instigation of Douglas Pohl, whom we had never met, but who has great admiration for David's achievements. Doug, together with Peter Semitouk, had given us much helpful advice about ice conditions. He was insistent that the old visitors' book, a school exercise book, was full up with signatures and needed replacing. So after a careful selection of what was available in Veeda's shop, we chose one with a firm hardboard cover and put it in a clear, plastic sleeve.

James was very helpful in making us a couple of labels to stick on the cover and inside, and after much discussion and some healthy argument about the wording, it was finally achieved, although James got fed up with my Virgo attention to detail and abandoned us to cope as best we could, which left us both feeling somewhat uncomfortable. However, the air was soon cleared and we rather thought that we had been taxing James too hard over the last few days, as he had been most attentive to all our needs, and extremely thoughtful.

When Safeway's was in the course of construction, the workforce uprooted five sinister wartime bunkers, or pillboxes, from the site area, which ended up in a hastily dumped line at the back of the stores, where they remain, tilted at curious angles like some modern architectural sculpture, adorned by Michaelmas daisies sprouting from the slit windows and bastions; a botanical redoubt. Beyond these is a line of light industrial buildings, each providing a vital back-up service for the fishing industry. We went into a few of them – LFS the Chandlers, Lunde North who specialise in navigational electronics, and Tim who does hydraulics.

Then there was Seamus Melly from Ireland whose main business, Swan Net, was in Seattle, but he also had a branch in Dutch Harbour, where he had discovered a niche market employing the indigenous Aleuts; they were to be seen in all weathers laying out and repairing vast fishing nets on the waste ground between the Grand Aleutian Hotel and the foreshore. First they had to stretch out a tangled web of damaged net, over 1,000 feet in length, some of it wound on huge drums at one end, and with a wide trace attached at the other. They would haul it along the rough ground with one of their trucks – it was far too heavy for even a team of men to haul by hand. It was painstaking, back-breaking and complicated work. The Aleuts were bent over double in cruel weather, wielding their large wooden needles, working from late dawn long into the evening, supervised by the ever-patient and skilful Seamus, who was pretty hardy himself. When a fisherman has caught his net on the rocks or snarled it up in some obstacle, it has to be repaired immediately, as the fishing must go on and they cannot put out to sea without it. Bald eagles are ever present at this operation, and unwittingly cooperative too, spotting as the net is laid out that it is full of rotting fish carcasses that they can alight upon and pick over, quite unafraid of the men absorbed in their work.

Seamus was another admirer of David's, and when he was shown the very large substitute stainless steel lifting, swivel shackle that I had been fortunate enough to swop for the smaller one I bought for David at the Alaskan Stores the previous year on our outward voyage, Seamus very kindly volunteered to splice the end of *Polar Bound's* anchor warp on to it, a very hard and difficult job as the rope was so thick. He arrived later that afternoon and he and David disappeared down into the forward hold, where I later found them, David seated on the drum of coiled-up anchor rope and Seamus perched on a fishing buoy wielding a huge steel fid. With this he parted the fixed coils of warp to form a hole through which he could force the loose, unwrithen strand of rope – this tough splice was being put at the neck of the loop thimble through which the swivel shackle passed, linking the short section of anchor cable to the rope.

Later on when I was left alone on the boat, I went to inspect the substantial neat splice, and seeing its huge size began to have doubts, but in case I was wrong fetched the plastic tape measure from my bag and went aloft to look at the fairlead. No way was that thimble going to pass through the cheeks of the fairlead and, with heavy heart, as David was so pleased with this new improved shackle, I had to break the news to him on his return. The shoulders of the thimble at the widest point were 5/8 inch too thick to pass through the fairlead. David disappeared aloft immediately to check and came to the same conclusion, so the following morning I had to deliver the bad news to Seamus, feeling somewhat foolish. He very kindly said that he would come back in the next day or two to redo it, and in the meantime we went to visit Tim of the Hydraulics, bearing the now naked-looking splice, as David had removed Seamus's first one, still made up around the thimble, but severed from the cable on the drum.

David felt that the jaws (shoulders) of the shackle, now less slippery with the rope wrapped around, could be put into a vice and pulled up, thus reducing the girth, so we went along to Tim's workshop. It was a dark, cavernous place for 'real men', with all kinds of fittings strung from the rafters, and pieces of unrecognisable machinery of gargantuan proportion. Rows of vast spanners clung to the walls on hooks. We stepped over pieces of work in various stages of completion until we found Tim, a giant of a man with a grey beard, who thought the steel would stand being compressed, and also suggested an additional small linking weld across the neck to prevent the shackle from springing open again. He took the fitting and approached a vice of a size I had never seen before. Placing the halter-shaped thimble between its jaws, he applied his massive strength with one or two turns of the screw while we stood well back, then the machinery for the steel weld was heated, and protective helmet and shield donned. We were told to walk way, turn our backs and shut our eyes. A few minutes later the job was done and we emerged out of the gloom into the sunshine with the readjusted shackle now ready to receive its new splice, and this time were confident of success.

In due course, kind Seamus returned to *Polar Bound* and applied a new splice – this time it slid between the jaws of the fairlead, and all was well. Seamus had a warehouse a short distance away where he stored vast reels and bags of rope of all sizes, and most generously gave David a huge length of rope (about 160 feet) as a contribution to the cause; this was dragged out along the entire length of the building up to a painted line on the concrete floor. We came away with this vast coil over David's shoulder, two warm, bonny bob caps and three little serrated kitchen knives for the galley, which have since proved incredibly useful – indeed, one has found its way into my kitchen drawer at home.

James Mason's apartment became our home-from-home. Through his internet access we could make contact with the outside world. We had to pick our way gingerly through his flat as there were books, papers, trailing wires and camera equipment everywhere; also eight bicycles – three in the hall, one in the kitchen, one in the bathroom, one in his bedroom and two in his computer room. (A legacy no doubt from the days when he owned a bicycle shop.) There was also a huge new mattress leaning against the wall, which had to be negotiated as you entered, but it had never advanced beyond this position, the frame still in its packing. Finally, after some cajoling, we were allowed to carry it upstairs for him, and a day or two later the old single mattress on the floor where he slept was exchanged – he did admit how much more comfortable the new one was.

He made us endless cups of tea and coffee and, while we dealt with correspondence and phone calls via Skype, he would take to his mattress on the floor with orders to wake him when we needed his chauffeuring hat on again. He ran us down to the quayside to see the *Healey* taking on fuel. The USA's largest icebreaker, she was topping up her tanks with 250,000 gallons of diesel to go up to the Arctic for seven months – she has the capacity to take on 1.2 million gallons, and a complement of three hundred crew. She can go through 6 feet of ice, though this is nothing compared to the Russian nuclear-powered icebreaker, which can cut through at least 6 feet of ice at 18 knots.

One Sunday, James took us to see an eagles' eyrie, where the parent birds had one fledgling – its sibling had been pushed out of the nest and probably fallen to its death. We drove for twenty minutes along the cruel stony road to the loneliest spot overlooking the bay through which we had entered Dutch Harbour, and were then guided through the mountain scrub with a wonderful, colourful variety of wild flowers and ferns, to the grassy cliff edge where we all three, with cameras ready, had an excellent vantage point. We looked down on the craggy pinnacle below with its precipitous drop of many hundreds of feet to the sea, where this young fledgling had emerged into the world. Only one parent was in attendance, and seemed unconcerned at the chick's lumbering insistence on hopping clumsily to the very edge of the eyrie, where it flopped down and went to sleep. The parent flew off finally and although we waited a good hour it did not return. It was a beautiful and remote location, and we thought James had been most observant to have spotted it. He said he had paid spasmodic visits to study their development and they had become acclimatised to him.

As the days passed, David became increasingly restless, frustrated by reports of a very late season in the Arctic, with nine-tenths ice thickness – *Polar Bound* struggles in anything over four-tenths; she can manage five-tenths but only for a short stretch – and two choke points that would prevent us from getting right through the Northwest Passage, but a date was finally set for departure: 9 August, four days away.

We went to the fuelling dock, by appointment, to top up with diesel and water, the total final complement being 10 tons of diesel and 65 gallons of water. This quantity of fuel gives *Polar Bound* a comfortable range of 5,000 miles, and can be stretched to 6,000 miles depending on circumstances. With the fuelling complete, the attendant simply disappeared, leaving us tied up to the dock fore and aft. The dock was far too high to climb up on to, and there was a strong onshore wind. Most annoyed, we called them up on the VHF but there was no response. My father's old naval whistle came into its own at last as a small truck pulled up. Seizing the opportunity, David blew several shrill blasts on the Acme Thunderer, and the surly man came grudgingly over to untie us.

The following day we invited our Icelandic host, Kristian, and his Texan wife to supper. I remembered that the previous autumn they had eaten like birds, so I decided to give them stuffed peppers and rice, with fruit salad to follow. We warned them in advance that we had no vodka aboard. On arrival Kristian gave me a magnificent bottle of Veuve Clicquot, chilled and ready to go, but they refused to let me open it. They had also brought a bottle of vodka, upon which Kristian immediately embarked. David and I stuck to our respective whisky and glass of wine.

The evening progressed happily. Kristian had returned the day before from a month in Iceland and looked well and bronzed. He had been doing the rounds of his friends and relatives, having not been back for ten years. He was the epitome of what one imagines an Icelandic captain to be: filled with bonhomie, generous to a fault, broad, expansive and genial with a delightful twinkle in the eye; frequent replenishments to his glass added to the jollity. Teresa had had recent medical treatment and had to be more restrained.

They both picked at their food, as expected, despite my giving them small portions and making it as attractive as possible.

'I remember you gave us a stuffed pepper last time – very good,' said Teresa, pushing it round her plate.

I felt mortified. We were now on to a bottle of wine and Kristian's glass continued to rise to his lips. When that was finished we moved on to a cubibox of vin ordinaire. Then came the fruit salad, and the conversation continued to flow - mostly Kristian reminiscing rather fondly about his travels and talking about the work he had had done on his boat, *Lady Gudny*, and how he had had to sack the man from

Seattle who had come to do the joinery as his charges were exorbitant and out of all proportion to the daily output.

By now, tiring of the wine, the vodka came out again for a nightcap or two, and the level was getting dangerously low. Teresa's restraining hand came out.

'No, Kristian,' she said, 'you've had enough.'

In full spate, Kristian paid no regard to the words of warning. Finally Teresa said, 'I'm going – I'm sorry, folks, but Kristian doesn't know what's good for him.' She stood up, reaching for her jacket. 'I've got my own car here,' she said, then added, 'I'll send a taxi for you, Kristian.'

He appeared not to hear. I followed her outside on to the deck, into the squally rain and blackness of the night, and led the way round through *Polar Bound*'s exit gate, on to the huge steel after deck of *Lady Gudny*, then up the vertical iron ladder on to her higher bridge-deck level and over to the railings on the port side.

The wind was blowing quite hard and the ship's stern had swung out away from the wooden baulks topped with huge lorry tyres, which we had to negotiate every time we went ashore. There was a long drop down against the steel sides of *Lady Gudny* into ice-cold water. I scrambled across in front of Teresa, who was looking somewhat apprehensive, and took firm hold of her arm as she ventured across the yawning gap.

'I'm sorry to wreck your party, but I know what he's like – he'll have to get himself home. I've got his keys,' she added, jerking her head at his pick-up truck and patting her pocket.

'Does he often get like this'? I asked as she tried to light a cigarette and I cupped my hands round the flickering flame for her.

'Oh – quite a number of times,' she replied, drawing on her cigarette. She pulled out her mobile and dialled for a cab. Thankfully, the phone was answered and arrangements were made for him to be collected. 'He won't be long coming.'

'I'm a bit worried as to how we're going to get him ashore.'

'Oh, the cab driver knows him well – he'll manage,' Teresa replied, and with a peck and an apology, she was gone.

Returning to the saloon, David, ever the English gentleman, was endeavouring to carry on as normal and pretending not to notice that Kristian was *hors de combat*. I noticed that Kristian still had some vodka in his glass. I whisked the bottle, which by now had only one inch remaining, off the table and sat down next to him, patting his hand and hoping I was exuding confidence in his sobriety and good-will. He spotted the removal and said, 'I think there's a bit more in that bottle,' his inquisitive eyes following my arm into the galley, then rumbled on with his reminiscences.

We went on cajoling him until there was a thump on deck announcing the arrival of the cab driver; we searched around for Kristian's coat and hat and struggled to put them on his huge frame – it was like dressing a child, all arms and protruding fingers. He cast his eyes around for the bottle.

'No, Kristian, come along; you can have that next time you come, and here's your friend to drive you home – you can collect your car in the morning,' I said in an authoritative sort of way, filled with apprehension. How we managed to get him up the iron ladder of *Lady Gudny* I shall never know – he had tremendous girth and took some considerable manoeuvring. He would have crushed David, who was pushing him up from behind, like a fly; and if he had done so, he would have taken me with him as I had a firm hold of his clothing.

The next hurdles were the iron railings and the gap between the ship and the vertical baulk on to which he had to step. Suddenly, like an elephant on must, he gathered himself and was up on to the railings, all restraint cast to the winds. He struggled round to face the other way (as you do when climbing over railings). With one foot on the outside lower rung, he slung his other leg over the upper rail and flailed in space, unable to find a landfall. We all gave warning shouts. 'No! Kristian – no! You won't make it. Come back!'

The cab driver, anxious to get out of the rain and get home, was making encouraging noises from the safety of the concrete pier but could not help.

I said wildly to David, 'We ought to get a harness on him or it's going to end in tragedy.'

'I'll go and get a sling.'

I turned back to Kristian, who was still holding on to the railings. 'You don't want to end up in the water down there,' I said, pulling him out of the rain and away from the railings, back into the lee, while we waited for David to return. 'I'm so happy,' he went on, muttering to himself as he remembered his holiday.

Then he said quite suddenly, 'Give us a kiss.'

Just at that moment David came back bearing the sling, which we struggled to put under Kristian's armpits. It was like wrestling with a great bear. We finally got him on to the railings and managed to get the first leg over, but the other waved wildly in space, whereupon David hauled on the sling, which fell down around Kristian's knees, effectively hobbling him. I reached down to pull it up, and the next minute, miraculously, we had him landed, home and dry, like a huge carp, and finally got him into the cab.

We retreated rather shakily to *Polar Bound*, somewhat stunned at the turn of events. David was distressed to see his old friend in his cups, and we went below to do the washing up, hiding the dregs of the culprit bottle of vodka in the middle of the saloon table locker.

Two days later, we made ready to leave. Both Kristian and James Mason came to say goodbye and helped to untie our warps. Hooking up the steel safety line across the access gate and coiling the warps to store in the stern locker, I then went round untying the fishing buoys, which make excellent fenders but are huge and heavy, and so cumbersome to lower down into the forward hold where they have to be secured.

We were off by 8am, heading for Nome, just before the Bering Strait; the start of the Northwest Passage transit route on the Arctic Circle. James and Kristian, both looking a bit wan, went their separate ways to take the final photographs of *Polar Bound*'s departure. I think they felt a bit lost that we were leaving. But it was mutual, and we, too, would miss James's jokes and comforting presence, and Kristian's warmth and larger-than-life personality. We waved goodbye repeatedly, as the pick-up was to be seen at each headland, following our course back out through the entrance.

As Dutch Harbour slipped behind into the murky fog and we got further and further out into the Bering Sea with a strong head wind, we were startled by the sight of a big fishing boat close to our starboard side, which came pounding by at speed out of the murk, belching thick black smoke from her stern. She appeared to be on fire, certainly a roaring fire was clearly visible in the boiler room. We had visions of picking up her crew in their liferaft, and called them urgently on Channel 16 several times, but there was no response.

That first night back at sea, we maintained two-hour watches, and with the aid of an alarm clock could snatch a bit of sleep in between. I went up on the bridge deck in the early hours of the morning, at half light, and saw another large fishing vessel a short distance due west of us, this one approaching on what appeared to be a collision course. Glued to the windscreen with binoculars at hand, I monitored it carefully and judged that the angle was widening as we converged, so no alteration of course was needed – they passed to port of us by about 200 yards. Then, out of the corner of my eye, I was startled to catch a glimpse of yet another vessel, larger and of somewhat sinister appearance, approaching obliquely from the starboard quarter at about 12 knots, apparently with no one on the bridge. The rule of the road is that the overtaking vessel keeps clear, but this was not the time to argue over niceties. Alarmed, I seized the wheel, cancelled the autopilot and went hard to starboard. It was a close call; its oblique angle of approach was so unexpected. It brought home to me how important it is to look behind you as well as ahead. David said later it was probably a vessel that had just come through the Unimak Pass and might have been heading for Japan.

Apart from these and a few other fishing boats that may have been returning from the Pribilof Islands, or the Saint Paul fishing grounds to the southwest, we had an uneventful passage to Nome, except that, once again, we had strong head winds blowing down from the north and rough seas. When the wind eased off a bit on the fifth day, although still from a northerly direction, we started hobby-horsing – a most uncomfortable motion, and one that can catch you off guard as there can be a sudden slamming jolt from a rogue wave. You know then that the plates you left balanced for a split second are going to slide on to the cabin sole, and that you yourself will be caught off balance and lunge into something, gaining yet another bruise.

TWENTY

NOME TO THE AMUNDSEN GULF

IVE DAYS OUT FROM DUTCH HARBOUR, we arrived in Nome. We telephoned the harbour master on the VHF to ask him where we should berth, and a new recruit to the harbour office arrived to take our lines. A fisherman off an exploration vessel adjacent to us came to help too, and wanted to know all about *Polar Bound*. David was awaiting some packages care of the harbour master, and among them we were surprised and delighted to find a large envelope containing four packets of different Yorkshire teas, which had been sent to us by Seamus Melly and his wife, Josephine. I must have said I hoped we wouldn't run out of tea, and he had remembered and despite all his work commitments had taken the trouble to send us some – we were very touched at such thoughtfulness. It always seems to me that the busiest people make time to go the extra mile.

It was fun to be back in this frontier town atmosphere, but we concentrated on doing our final shop ready for departure the following evening. We went to a café called Airport Pizza where we could use their wi-fi, and where David bought me some lunch – a delicious bowl of home-made chicken broth, and an oversized, greasy bacon and cheese sandwich with crusty toasted white bread. The place was packed. Our visit coincided with a huge party of Rotarians who had taken over most of the dining room with only a thin screen between us and them. They were welcoming four new women teachers. After the introductions, and with the aid of a microphone, the four new recruits each made a speech, one or two rather nervously, their voices at maximum volume and laughing inordinately at their own jokes in case anyone else failed to get them. We had to shout to each other above the din, and were also endeavouring to make telephone calls back to England, via Skype.

Later, we called at the visitor centre, where we could get no connection for wi-fi; a rather ineffectual young man, supposedly in charge, could do nothing about it, and the only other person was a tall, spindly man who was busy ironing lace tablecloths on an ironing board placed right in the middle of the floor. Finally, we went to the supermarket found the prices unbelievable – something like $10 for a pound of potatoes, while a small loaf of wholemeal bread was $6.50. We wondered how the local population could afford to shop there. I was thankful we had bought all our essential meat and fish stores for the freezer in Petersburg, which had seemed expensive enough. David topped up with fuel once more from a bowser that came down to the stony jetty; the diesel cost nearly three times what he had paid in Petersburg. The facilities for visitors were non-existent. Nome struck us as even more run down and expensive than it had before.

Just as we were hurrying back to the boat ready for departure, a pick-up truck pulled up next to us, and there was Rolland Trowbridge leaning out of the window with a big smile and an invitation from his wife Debbie to go to dinner. David wanted to get under way before dark so we had to decline, sadly, as we had greatly enjoyed the time we spent with them last September. However, we invited Rolland aboard for a cup of tea while David fired up the engine and I put away the stores.

Then we were away. Time was pressing on, with autumn not far over the horizon. For the most part these few days proved uneventful other than that we had strong winds – force 6, 7 and 8, which were to last almost the entire way to Point Barrow. We passed Cape Prince of Wales on the Seward Peninsula, and it was amazing to think that only 60 miles to the west of us, at this narrowest point, lay the eastern tip of Siberia. We advanced north another 30 miles and crossed the Arctic Circle in the Bering Strait. There is a firm boundary line on the chart here marked 'United States–Russian Convention 1867'. This was the year when Russia, almost bankrupt, sold the whole of Alaska to the Americans for $7 million.

The next landmark of any significance was Point Hope, where the Bering Sea becomes the Chukchi Sea. In the depths of the big winter freeze, it is possible to sledge from Siberia to Alaska across this 'ice bridge'; this was presumably how the Russians, and Laplanders before them, originally came to be in Alaska, claiming the territory as theirs.

Taking advantage of a lull in the near gale-force winds we had been enduring, we transferred some fuel from a number of the jerry cans strapped on deck into the main holding tanks. We have a neat little pump siphon for doing this. Poke the flexible pipe down into the tank and the other, rigid end down into the can, a couple of squeezes on the bulb, and the flow starts – there is no way of hurrying it, so you just had to adopt a comfortable pose and wrap up well. When the can is almost empty and the flow becomes a mass of bubbles, resort to a funnel for the dregs. A few of the cans had to be hauled up the twelve rungs of the ladder in the forward hold – this is back-breaking work. I wasn't sure whether I preferred to be at the bottom giving a shunt to the perilous load, having made fast a speedy bowline through the plastic handle with David hauling from above, his great long legs straddling the hatchway, or whether it was better to be above doing the hauling. When he was below, the advantage was that he could push the cans higher up the ladder, so there was not so far to haul them. Once you got a swing on, it was less of a strain; it certainly kept your muscles firm.

A few days on we were abeam of Icy Cape and saw a tug heading southwards towing a great barge, and two further tugs off Point Barrow – a desolate place stretching along the horizon, giving a strange mirage effect as the land is so low-lying. From a distance it appeared as if the shoreline was dotted with shimmering palm trees, but as we got closer the palms were superseded by large warehouses, oil tanks and other industrial impedimenta. It was a vast Indian settlement, supported by the American government. The sea was also incredibly shallow just there. David pointed out a marked line in the water where there is a sudden step in the ocean bed, the inky black of the deeper water giving way to translucence where you could see the bottom.

We were beginning to have misgivings about retracing our steps of the year before up the west coast of Banks Island and round the top through the McClure Strait. There was plenty of ice around already, which David thought unusual so early in the year. The ice reports we were receiving both from Peter Semitouk and Doug Pohl stated that there was nine-tenths ice to the west of Banks Island and it was still solid to the north. It rather looked as if that angle of the voyage would have to be bypassed. We could take the conventional southerly route, but at that moment there were still choke points in the Franklin Strait and Bellot Strait, and the whole of Melville Sound was blocked. Ice is so unpredictable. David said we could have sat around for two weeks hoping for McClure to clear, but his experience was that this was unlikely, and, if it did, by the time we had passed through it to the north of Banks Island and eventually reached the Hecla and Fury Strait, that would also be blocked as it would be getting too late in the season. At this point, we were running along the north coast of Alaska from Point Barrow and had passed Cape Helkett and the Franklin Mountains, named after one of Sir John's early sledging expeditions.

We continued on a course towards Herschel Island, where we hoped to meet up with the Reverend Bob Shepton and his crew of four. Bob Shepton is a mountaineer who lives in northwest Scotland and, in his 36-foot sloop, *Dodo's Delight*, takes parties of young mountaineers to climb the peaks in Greenland. Bob had made the westward journey from a starting point off the west coast of Greenland the year before and overwintered the boat at Nome. Now, with a more mature party aboard than the usual young mountaineers, they wanted to transit the Northwest Passage. David and Bob had known each other for ten years and had had much contact by letter and phone but had never actually managed to meet face to face. A much-hoped-for meeting was anticipated in Nome, but *Dodo's Delight* had left just before we arrived. Now Herschel Island was set to be the meeting place.

At this stage the ice density was about a tenth: more or less open water. The ice was loose and fluffy-looking – a stark brilliant white of floating meringues bobbing in a grey sea. We had no problem wending our way between them. Every now and then a smaller 'bergy' bit of glinting silver grey would come into our path. They are not so easy to spot, and are dangerous if they get into the propeller, where they can sheer a blade right off. We went through several rafts like this, but then came out into a great expanse of open water with not a trace of ice as far as the eye could see.

It was after we left Point Barrow and were beginning to take a slightly more northeasterly slant well to the north of the Mackenzie

River delta that we encountered a formidable barrier of ice right to the horizon, brought down on the relentless north winds which had been blowing for days without let-up. We had already entered the periphery through several leads and were hoping to skirt around it. I had never seen such density before. Some of it appeared to be multi-year ice, with pieces from earlier years on top of new ice, all forced down by the northerly winds into this monstrous and grotesque pile-up. Great lumps projected skywards at oblique angles like Exocet missile launchers; other slabs were akin to the flight deck of an aircraft carrier. It was an ice god's playground of discarded, glittering toys.

David had no option but to make a dramatic course alteration, from a northerly direction, on to a south easterly heading towards the Mackenzie River delta to the east of Herschel Island and keeping inshore to avoid ice concentration. The Mackenzie River is long and narrow, fed by the Great Bear Lake and the Great Slave Lake, and quite possibly exceeds a thousand miles in length, with a few Indian settlements along the way, Tuktoyotuk being one of them. On an earlier transit, in his old lifeboat the *Mabel E. Holland*, when conditions were against him, David had been forced to overwinter at Inuvik, about a hundred miles up this river, where he had her hauled out for the winter. The river is very shallow and he touched the bottom on several occasions.

The decision to alter course was made after consulting Peter Semi-touk on the satellite telephone. Peter tells you the facts, rather than gives advice. It is up to David to make the appropriate decision on the spot; the responsibility lies with him alone. We had to hand-steer to work our way free of the impasse. It is alarming to meet a barrier like this. Once you have entered it, following one lead through to another, you find yourself encouraged to venture on along the primrose path until suddenly confronted with, not open water, but a blockage. Meanwhile the wind blowing strongly will have closed up some of the gaps through which you came, making it difficult to retrace your steps. So it was with enormous relief that we finally skirted clear into more or less open water.

The external temperature had begun to fall markedly and was now down to 2 degrees centigrade. The following day we did a lot of steering through rafts of pack ice, which David thought at this time of year would almost certainly join forces with the large mass we had encountered to the north, and would quite likely block the exit from the passage to a few adventurous mariners who were even now heading west from Greenland. (This did indeed prove to be the case.) The outlook appeared set for an early winter, although miracles could still happen if there was to be a tremendous gale from the southeast.

August 24 arrived and I realised with some dismay that it was my seventieth birthday, which I had more or less forgotten – another decade was no cause for celebration, and I cannot understand why so many people like to throw a huge party when they reach these milestones. You don't feel any older than the day before, but at the same time the realisation that the years are passing, and the psychological impact this has, is demoralising to your determination to remain ever youthful and supple. David wasn't going to let the occasion pass without some acknowledgement; perhaps he was secretly pleased that I had finally caught up on his decade. Within five minutes after midnight, congratulations had been given, and at breakfast time out came a birthday card. I would actually have rather appreciated some champagne. We still had the bottle given to us by Kristian. It was down in the ice-cold lockers below one of the saloon berths. Finding it would be one thing, and drinking it another, as I would be the only participant. David doesn't even like it. I put it out of my mind.

We reached Cape Bathurst and passed though Snow Goose Passage between the Cape and Baillie Island. It was very sheltered behind Baillie Island, and also extremely shallow, with only about 4 feet 6 inches below the keel. I wasn't allowed to speak to David as he was concentrating so much. Looking through binoculars at some birds flying over, it seemed they might well be the snow geese with their long streamlined shape, elongated necks and trailing legs; perhaps they too knew that winter was coming early and were heading for warmer climes. Even in such a remote and bleak landscape of bare black rock and a windswept sand-coloured spit, there were some low-roofed domed shacks which appeared to have clods of earth over the tops. These were probably for the itinerant Inuit who use this island as a hunting base.

The menacing dark sky ahead met a distant horizon of pack ice, which appeared to block our path once again, but we came through and out the other side and started to head across the vast Franklin Bay, where we were confronted by even more ice to the north. It looked forbidding, with the sea breaking on the bar at the exit of Snow Goose Passage. However, the ice was still some distance off out to sea, and once we were clear of the passage we set our course for Cape Parry, the next landmark to the east. We had by now firmly decided on the southerly route through the Amundsen Gulf and beyond. As we crossed the head of Franklin Bay, David pointed out an extraordinary phenomenon: what appeared to be a semi-circle of smoking mountains in the distance. These are indeed marked on the chart as the Smoking Hills. They exude sulphur fumes through the substrata, which rise way up into the atmosphere in a continuous pall of black cloud.

At 11pm on the night of my birthday, and on the fringe of another vast area of five-tenths ice, David finally turned the engine off. We were both tired from the strain of dealing with such an unexpected quantity of ice, and we could not continue in the dark confronted with what we now saw. We decided to lie a'hull until the dawn – we were a good mile off the ice mass and there was no wind, so we would just drift. The silence came like balm, and darkness overwhelmed us like a giant blanket, giving no clue as to the potential of the vast forces of nature lying dormant just a couple of miles distant.

I was so pleased to get into my bunk that night, but I woke again at 3.30 and went up to the bridge deck in the faint light of pre-dawn to see what was happening. The ice was now within 200 yards, and it was obvious we would very soon have to be on the move again. I went down and called David. He went up to look and, after a long moment or two of silent scrutiny, he came down and said, 'Want to bet me your house or your car that we have been joined by another boat? But it's not Bob Shepton because it's a ketch, and *Dodo's Delight* is a sloop.' I dashed up in great excitement; it was almost impossible to believe that here, actually, was another boat – one of the adventurers attempting the Northwest Passage east to west. The boat, still hard to distinguish, came on towards us, swaying to and fro as it picked its way through the ice leads, under engine, and equally delighted that by pure chance, in these thousands of square miles of wilderness, such an encounter could happen.

There appeared to be three men on deck, clad in oilskins and looking ready for anything. Dressed only in my husband's old thermal underwear and bedroom slippers, I hurried out on deck to take some photographs of this apparition from outer space that had mystically arrived into our world of wilderness and desolation. I wanted to capture the apparition before it disappeared and we were left wondering if it had all been a dream. When they came abeam, I shouted out, rather idiotically, 'Livingstone, I presume.' The poor attempt at humour was lost as my fatigued voice came out only as a pathetic croak.

They were equally intrigued to see us, but we could make little progress with our shouted dialogue; they made a couple of passes alongside us, and we exchanged a bit of news about ice conditions, and said we hoped they would still manage to get through going west-wards what we had recently transited heading east. They said they had come from Resolute; we had heard that route was completely blocked but they must have had a window of clearance. At any rate they were very determined and business-like, and, as we did, they had a line of jerry cans with spare fuel lashed on deck. They must have been the first boat through this season, but they could have over-wintered at Cambridge Bay, to where we were now heading. There was a lot of waving of 'goodbyes' and '*Bon chance*' (for it seemed they were French speakers), and both parties were anxious to get on their respective ways, heading in opposite directions.

We subsequently learnt that they were Belgian. Their boat, whose name we couldn't make out in the dim light, was the *Pas Perdu le Nord*, and they later came to grief on Point Barrow, where they foun-dered, dragged on their anchors. Two of the crew were airlifted off, and the captain remained with the vessel, with the surviving bower anchor still just holding against the surge of the waves, until finally a day or two later a tug came and hauled her off. They were lucky to escape with their lives.

TWENTY ONE

THE SOUTHERN ROUTE

S TILL FEELING SOMEWHAT AMAZED BY our chance
encounter in this vast emptiness, we pressed on for Summer
Harbour at Cape Parry, where we were hoping for the planned
encounter with the elusive Reverend Bob Shepton, the previous one
having proved unsuccessful. He had telephoned very briefly, via
satellite, to say he was running low on both fuel and gas, and with
five people on board he was afraid they were going to be eating cold
bully beef. He asked David if he had any spare gas, and David had
suggested we meet in Summer Harbour so he could loan him a bottle
and ring.

There was much anticipation as we rounded every headland, only
to find yet another one, and another, and never any sign of a mast
showing above the topography. As we hove into sight, he must have
been rounding the next point. Summer Harbour is very hidden, and
you must continue almost in a circle past a succession of headlands
to access it. It seems Bob had arrived ahead of us and wanted to take
advantage of the weather before a forecast easterly blow of 25 knots
arrived. It was most frustrating to miss *Dodo's Delight* by such a short
head. We learned later we had missed him by only half an hour.

We spent an hour and a half in Summer Harbour. The wind was very fresh and *Polar Bound* tugged on her mooring line, which we had secured around a huge, old, rusty can buoy in the middle of the bay.

'Can you jump on to that?' David had asked.

I had stared in horror at it. 'No, I certainly can't, it might tip over.'

'No, it won't do that.'

Without further preamble he made a close pass at the buoy. I made a lunge with the boathook to grab it, but the wind was too strong. The quivering boathook was about to take off like an arrow, and I had to snatch it free before it catapulted into the water. I decided that leaping on to this tilting, slippery buoy in a biting cold wind, carrying a line to pass through a huge iron ring on top, did not appeal. On the second circuit, however, we had better luck and were able to manage by leaning over together to pass our warp through the ring.

We carried out a few useful boat tasks while secure and in calm waters, in the course of which David said in a conversational way, 'I spent seventeen days here in 2011 on my way back from Australia, via Cape Town, Antarctica, South Georgia, the Falklands, Valdivia, Chile, San Francisco, Dutch Harbour and finally Point Barrow.'

After that incredible itinerary, I was speechless for a moment or two. 'Why were you here for so long?' I asked, looking around wonderingly at the low-lying sandy escarpment, and musing over the fact that there was not a living thing, neither plant nor beast, to be seen.

'I was waiting for the ice to melt in the McClure Sound so that I could make the return transit via that route, and then I would have done all six routes.'

'What did you do all that time?'

'When I wasn't doing jobs on the boat I sat here in the sunshine in my shirtsleeves.'

'And were you the only one here?'

'Yes – there was no one else here.'

'Did you go ashore?'

'No, I didn't like to leave the boat – there were quite strong winds.'

It seems that Peter Semitouk had encouraged him to stay in the hope that the weather would come right and he would be able to fulfil his ambition, but it was not to be.

'I got fed up with waiting and decided to leave,' he continued.

There is no doubt that David is a very unusual person, with great inner strength and courage, incredible patience and self-reliance. I could not imagine how anyone could have been content to remain looking at that barren landscape for so long.

There is no doubt, too, that I had fallen in love with him. It was sobering to think that he had been circumnavigating the world in both sailing and motorboats, entirely alone, with all the difficulties of making landfalls without any assistance – which is where the real problems lie in any boating venture – and all the while I had just been carrying on my antique dealing business. I looked at him hard, wondering whether he was mad, and decided he wasn't, realising that I was looking at one of England's true eccentric adventurers of the old school. His tall, slender build and refined manners might cause some to doubt his achievements, but they should not be misled. His self-effacing manner belies his capabilities. He has none of the rodomontade of many who seek publicity and have gained their country's recognition through considerably less. David is self-funding and his financial acumen has enabled him to undertake these voyages without sponsorship, though there are several companies who, filled with admiration for his achievements, have offered refurbishment of some part of his vessel or other at nominal cost, and suppliers who have volunteered their equipment for the advertising kudos of claiming David as a customer who relies on their product.

There was no point in remaining any longer at Summer Harbour as it seemed that our quarry had given us the slip once more; The Rev. must have been motoring hard – we tried to make contact with him on the VHF and on the satellite telephone, but the VHF did not respond and Bob's telephone was in answer mode. We did, however, get an email from Bob via David's office, suggesting we meet up in Bernard Harbour on the north coast of Alaska, near Cape Krusenstern in the Dolphin and Union Strait. So we continued on track for this destination. That evening we decided, once again, to lie a'hull with the anchor light on and get some sleep as there was no wind and we would only drift about two and a half miles. Just as we were turning in, a huge tug appeared on the horizon with its tell-tale four large lights on, and the master called David on the VHF to ask if we were in position (in other words, parked), so that he knew how to manoeuvre the 1,000-yard barge he was towing. David said he would move, but the tug master said there was no need, and passed well off to our starboard side – once again, we were filled with admiration at the competence and skill shown by these lone individuals.

At 4.30am we were up and hurrying for our new rendezvous with the Reverend. The landscape was low-lying and, with a strong freshening breeze scurrying along behind us, we were chased into the open harbour. A low, protective stony groyne lay across most of the entrance and glistened menacingly in the bright early morning sun. A pair of large red and white transit buoys showed how careful you

▲ Enjoying the scenery at Petersburg, Alaska.

▼ A precarious barge haulage in Force 6 winds off Dutch Harbour as the tow heads for outlying settlements.

▲ *Polar Bound* at anchor, Fort Ross, after the first autumnal snowfall of 2013.

▼ *Polar Bound* lying off Fort Ross. In the foreground is the Tinker Traveller inflatable that has accompanied David on four circumnavigations of the world and all six expeditions to the Arctic.

▲ David testing the gun in Prins Christian Sund.

▲ Looking down at Port Kennedy where Captain McClintock overwintered with the *Foxe*, on the other side of the hill from Fort Ross.

▼ The two lonely cabins used by Hudson Bay Company at Fort Ross, abandoned in 1939 as ice conditions proved too difficult to enter the bay and relieve the occupants.

▲ The path between the two huts at Fort Ross, which have survived nearly 80 years. One of the huts would originally have been used as a depot by the Hudson Bay Company for storing animal pelts.

▲ One of the two Hudson Bay Company huts, with nice architectural features, but now vandalised by visiting polar bears.

▼ Me at the McClintock memorial, with *Polar Bound* at anchor in the distance.

THIS CAIRN HAS BEEN PROVIDED BY MEMBERS
OF THE McCLINTOCK FAMILY IN PROUD MEMORY
OF ADMIRAL SIR FRANCIS LEOPOLD McCLINTOCK-
THE DISCOVERER OF THE FATE OF FRANKLIN-1859:

JOHN O'NEIL McCLINTOCK	CAPTAIN HUBERT McCLINTOCK AND FAMILY
ANNETTE, MRS. FIRTH	ALAN McCLINTOCK
NICHOLAS, C. McCLINTOCK	DAVID C. McCLINTOCK
ARABELLA, MRS. CARTER	KATHLEEN, MRS. KINAHAN
PATRICIA, MRS. CYRIAX	PATRICK McCLINTOCK
SIR PETER GREENWELL, BART.	SURGEON REAR ADMIRAL CYRIL L. T. McCLINTOCK CB, OBE
JOYCE, MRS. MILES	CANON JON McCLINTOCK
BARBARA, LADY WILLIAM POWLETT AND FAMILY	SHEILA, MRS. STEWARD
BETTY, MRS. CASEMENT AND FAMILY	ANDREW McCLINTOCK
DIANA, MRS. R. S. McCLINTOCK	HUGH McCLINTOCK

BELLOT STRAIT
1979

▲ The plaque erected at Fort Ross by members of the McClintock family in recognition of their ancestors' search for the Franklin Expedition.

▲ The only way to bury people in the permafrost was to place stones over their coffins to protect them from marauding polar bears. A startling sight to come across in such a remote setting.

▼ David made this grizzly find on Herschel Island, an old whaling outpost. The skull probably dates back to the late 19th century.

▲ Ice build-up on deck caused by spray as *Polar Bound* makes her way up Prince Regent Inlet.

▼ Tassellated fringe of ice on the handrail before we made our escape, just in the nick of time, from Prince Regent Inlet in 2013.

▲ Pack ice in Prince Regent Inlet, where we saw the imprints of a polar bear on a raft of fresh snow.

▼ Spotting an icebreaker in the Northwest Passage is always a comforting sight.

▲ The backdrop close to Pond Inlet, Bylot Island, with *Polar Bound* at anchor.

▼ One of the mammoth icebergs found in the Vaigat.

▲ Ice and snow on the superstructure of *Polar Bound* whilst at anchor at Fort Ross.

▼ Picturesque scenery down Navy Board Inlet as *Polar Bound* takes her departure from Pond Inlet with Mount Herodier to the left.

▲ David checking the anchor before returning to the wheelhouse in Navy Board Inlet.

▼ A spectacular glacier in Navy Board Inlet.

▲ *Polar Bound* moored alongside in Julianehåb for refuelling.

▼ Colourful wooden houses on the slope above the harbour, Julianehåb, where we took on fuel for the final leg of the journey back to the UK.

▲ Stern view of *Polar Bound* as she heads out into the Bering Sea.

▼ Stormy clouds over Lancaster Sound.

▲ Running before following seas in the North Atlantic.

▼ Posing for the camera in Dutch Harbour.

had to be as a lot of the anchorage was very shallow. Up until this moment David had had his main bower anchor catted, but in readiness for the passage he had prepared it for lowering over the side. This was the first time the new lifting shackle was put to use. We took careful note of our position against fixed objects on the shore because the tide was coming in, and anchored.

Of course, there was no Bob Shepton. We had put ourselves out to enter this rather perilous anchorage to give succour, motivated by visions of his crew all munching cold bully-beef, and once again he had eluded us. I'd earlier invited them all to supper, but my readiness to offer hot sustenance to an invasion of five was beginning to pall. We were getting distinctly annoyed.

We stayed for an hour and had breakfast, and meanwhile downloaded an email from Bob. It said, 'Sorry, David – didn't stop. Making all haste with fair wind to Cambridge Bay.'

Privately, I was of the opinion that they got cold feet at the sight of this exposed harbour, into which neither David, nor Bob, had entered previously. *Dodo's Delight* had probably thought better of running into a shallow, temporary refuge with covering groynes on a rising tide and with a freshening chill wind up their backsides. We did not have the luxury of such choice, as we had agreed to meet Bob there.

Bernard Harbour is a line site for Canada's Distant Early Warning system, and a bleaker, more desolate place would be hard to find. Yet more of the limestone-coloured soil and shale, and not a living thing – just a stack of container tanks lashed together against the wind. The anchor came up quite readily, and the new shackle passed through the fairlead without any hitch. We took the greatest care on leaving this treacherous anchorage with, by now, semi-submerged rocks across most of the entrance. Soon after leaving the exposed harbour, we rounded Lady Franklin Point, marked by a huge hangar which no doubt housed helicopters for the DEW line station.

I had nurtured a tomato plant all the way from Petersburg. It was secured with four plastic suckers to a perch above the companionway where it got all the rising heat from the saloon plus intermittent sunshine and light through the stern window next to it. *Polar Bound*'s hobby-horsing had been its undoing. It had been pitch-poled three times from its perch, generally flying straight down into the cabin during the night, scattering earth all over the carpet on the cabin sole. It had been repeatedly repotted, fed, watered, trimmed, put out in direct sun when conditions permitted and generally cossetted. Now, however, its three remaining tomatoes still resolutely green, the inevitable brown fronds had started to appear and my hopes for it had faded.

Both sides of the Northwest Passage southern route so far had been the same: all along the Amundsen Gulf, Dolphin and Union Strait, and Coronation Gulf, which also has a mass of small islands dotted about, with the Northwest Territories to our south and Victoria Island to the north, the topography is of low, smooth, sandy-coloured mounds and hillocks, one running into another, with here and there a low wooden hut, apparently placed at random by the Inuit, and lined inside with caribou skins for protection from wind and weather.

There had been no trace of ice, only a few small patches of blown snow tucked up on the shoreline here and there. The beauty of this area, if any, is in the vastness of the heavens: the constantly changing mood of the sky and the march of the clouds – sometimes a procession of small fluffy sheep, sometimes great tumbling banks of cumulus. Seen from a distance, with the sun now well below the horizon, they seemed filled with menace as they intensified and turned deep purple, accentuated by the contrasting streak of pale orange from below. As dusk fell and the new moon appeared, the banks of cloud started to build up, one upon the other in various hues of greys and blues. We kept going all night on two-hour watches, aided by the alarm clock, and made good time through a flat, calm sea. The following morning in the light of dawn, clouds appeared to billow from the depths of the sea.

As we neared Cambridge Bay in the golden evening sunshine the following day, a small Hanseatic cruise ship emerged from the bay, heading in the direction from which we had come. It was hard to imagine what entertainment the ship's company could have provided for these passengers who had paid huge dollars to embark, and whose only view was to be mile upon mile of small, low-lying isolated islands and a long, flat, limestone shoreline. They were taken ashore to have a look around from time to time, but as there was not much to see when you arrived except small wooden shacks, oil drums and general untidiness, it is hard to know what they got out of it all.

We arrived about 11.30pm, in pitch darkness, having spent the previous two hours navigating the long approach channel and steering on three or four sets of leading lights. This requires a lot of concentration. You have to keep each pair exactly in line with one another, and after quite a distance – perhaps a couple of miles, which at 6 knots would take twenty minutes or so – and just as you were thinking you must surely collide with the marks, you picked up the next two, quite possibly at right angles to the way you had been proceeding, and you were then obliged to alter course dramatically to follow the new direction, staring forward to see if the two yellow lights in the distance were aligned, one on the other. As we closed the shore, our observation was tested to the limit as street lights began to compete and night vision was eroded.

It was bitterly cold and dark. We thought we could see five sailing boats of varying sizes, but it was difficult to be sure. The main thing was to find a perch to tie up to. There were no quay-side lights here and, at first glance, no room for us either, everyone else having long ago turned in for the night. It was too deep to anchor. We got out a very large and extremely heavy torch – it has two million candle power, or so David claimed – and shone its light across the water. Then we slowly crept in on the engine, the wind blowing all the while and the bridge door slamming to and fro disconcertingly as I dashed in and out passing on information to David. Finally, when all seemed rather desperate, he came out of the wheelhouse and we discussed which vessel we would raft up to. We selected a steel sloop, *La Belle Epoque*, put ropes ready fore and aft, opened the safety gate and positioned three of the huge fishing-buoy fenders along the starboard side to act as buffers. I really hated tying these on as they were so cumbersome and heavy with long lines to make clove hitches through the cold metal freeing ports in the capping rail, and the darkness didn't help.

It is quite tricky, even in daylight, to manoeuvre a boat alongside in a confined space, especially when rafting up, and when there is a projecting vessel already rafted up to the one you are aiming for, but David managed to put me right up to it – after the boathook came into play and we grabbed their steel cap rail – I climbed over the guard rail, dodging all the paraphernalia on deck, including a haunch of caribou swinging from the boom, and secured *Polar Bound*'s bow line to our new neighbour's forward cleat. David, meantime, with *Polar Bound* idling in neutral, took the stern line and secured us in similar fashion at the other end of the boat. Just as we had finished, I glanced up from making some final adjustment midships and there, appearing silently, stood an apparition in white thermal pyjamas and a pointed white pixie hat with dangling wool ties hanging down each side.

'Can you manage?' asked the genial gnome sleepily.

'I'm most awfully sorry we've disturbed you,' I said and added, 'What time will you be leaving in the morning?'

'About ten,' came the answer.

I was greatly relieved that there would be no dawn start to wake us up, and with that exchange we retired to our quarters. We relit the cosy Dickinson stove and put some red mulled wine on to heat – very comforting when you are cold and tired – and sat in gratified silence, absorbing the stove's glow.

The following morning David was up just after six, and when I complained, all I got was, 'We're on Canadian time here; it's 8am, and everyone's up and busying about.'

David had absolutely no regard for sleeping hours. If he was awake, it was time to get up, no matter that we had jumped two hours to accommodate *Polar Bound*'s advance eastwards. Maybe everybody else was indeed up, but they had probably been sitting here for several days awaiting better weather, while we had arrived in the dead of night after having been on short sleep rations for some time.

He disappeared excitedly up the companionway and out on to the deck into what appeared to be the dawn. Emerging on deck myself a while later, I met up with the night-time gnome, who turned out to be a most charming and gallant man. He took my hand and said, 'You are a beautiful woman,' and added, as he allowed his hand to brush over my hair, 'and you are wearing these lovely earrings.' Feeling grubby and unkempt, I was of course delighted by these words, true or not, and replied, 'You must be a Frenchman!'

With so few words, he had transformed my feeling of being drab into a recognition of being chic and personable. In this stark environment, the quayside littered with gasometers and oil tanks on an industrial scale, it was very pleasing to be appreciated.

All through both our voyages I made an effort to put on my 'face' every day. I could see no reason to abandon feminine vanity just because I was in a boat, and I had no intention of becoming a hearty, unkempt sailor. So generally after breakfast, but sometimes before, if David was still somnolent in his bunk, I would sit at the saloon table and tip out the contents of my make-up bag. There followed about twenty minutes of careful application of face cream, a touch of foundation, eyeshadow, mascara and eyebrow pencil, and occasionally, if the boat wasn't bucking around too much, eyeliner. And, if it had been a sleepless night, a dab of rouge. Then, all that was needed was a careful selection of earrings and probably a pearl necklace. It certainly made me feel more of a woman and gave a touch of normality to our ocean voyaging. There wasn't much I could do about my hair. Although I had brought some dry shampoo, it made my head feel as if I had covered it in ash, which perhaps is the principal ingredient, so I didn't use too much of it. Luckily for me, in Dutch Harbour was a very good Inuit hairdresser, called Rosalind. She had a tiny establishment just opposite a fish processing plant, with one dryer. She was of the old-fashioned kind who knew about rollers and allowed the client to participate in the hairdo by handing up the desired roller at the required moment. Rosalind was excellent at cutting my hair, too. I visited her on both occasions we were at Dutch Harbour, and I always came out feeling good and confident.

TWENTY TWO

CAMBRIDGE BAY TO FORT ROSS

I T SOON BECAME OBVIOUS WHY DAVID had sprung out so early – he wanted to reconnoitre the quayside and see who was there. Most of all, he wanted to establish whether *Dodo's Delight* was among the gathering. After my encounter with the Frenchman, I peered out towards the knuckle of the quayside and I could just see glimpses of David's head bobbing about. He was locked in conversation with the very man we had sought, the elusive Bob Shepton, whom he was meeting for the first time after ten years of letter and email correspondence. I got on with breakfast preparations, and when David came back again, he announced that one of Bob's crew, Richard Nicolson, was coming over to see us. He turned up just as we had finished breakfast, and we learned that he had been the co-owner of *Belzebub II*, the Swedish sailing boat that had been about sixteen hours behind us through the McClure Strait the previous August.

Richard gave me some meat that was surplus to their own requirements. He said it was musk ox, and to watch out as there might be some grass on it as it had travelled a long way by sledge and in the back of a pick-up truck. I ferreted about in the hold for something to give them in return and found four tins of haggis (which I thought

Bob might like as he lives in Scotland); it certainly did not appeal to me. I also gave him some of the army rations of apple dumplings and custard in sealed bags, plus some soup.

Quite a lot of *Polar Bound*'s stores have made at least two circum-navigations of the world, but so far only one rusty tin of raspberries had had to be discarded. It gave a 'fssshing' sound when opened which was most unappealing. We discovered a packet of cheese biscuits with a Best Before date of November 2005, aptly named 'Dare' wholegrain crackers. We took on the challenge, opened the sealed pack inside and found them to be delicious; as crisp and crunchy as the day they were made. Some of the stores go back to 2002, and on this return trip I determined to make inroads into them, but I have to admit that the appeal of a newly purchased packet or tin dented my resolve.

The next twelve hours were spent in feverish activity. After Richard, we had a visit from Brent Boddy, a tremendously energetic man who had an 18-foot sailing boat on a mooring in an inner lagoon, and who also loved kite-skiing and bicycling. David had known him from a couple of previous visits; he lived locally and was extremely helpful by driving us to fetch fresh water from a nearby creek. They both stood rather perilously on stones while the sparkling water jumped all around them and soon filled the three containers we had brought to top up the main tank. So much nicer than the chlorinated, desalinated water available on the shore, which was also expensive. Brent then ran us over to the general stores where we were able to stock up on fresh produce. The further north you go, the higher the scale of charges in the stores. I spent $130 on groceries, but only got about half what I had purchased back in Nome for about $140.

Five boats that had recently come in were all making the Northwest Passage, and one of these was *Dodo's Delight*. That afternoon four of the boats left in a group together heading westwards, the direction from which we had come. We hoped they would be successful in getting through the Amundsen Gulf and around Cape Bathurst where we had encountered so much ice. (We heard subsequently that they did all manage to get through, with difficulty.) *Dodo's Delight* set off in the opposite direction, eastwards, about four hours ahead of us. Instead of laying up in Cambridge Bay as planned, Bob had changed his mind when he heard that David was planning to continue, despite inward worries about the choke points.

Eventually, after topping up with fuel from a bowser, we too departed in the low evening sun, and once again pursued the tortuous channel and waypoint transits – not easy with a glaring light in your eyes. We also had to look over our shoulder all the time to keep the transits in line. There was some confusion at one moment and we had to slow right down by one of the buoys to take stock. The mirage effect at the horizon in calm weather made it difficult to distinguish between land and sky.

We motored all night with no sign of *Dodo's Delight*, but the next morning we spotted their white mainsail through the binoculars; they held their distance steadily and it was obvious that they were motor-sailing. All day they kept ahead of us, first on one tack, then on the other, bearing away into the distance about five miles off. Late in the afternoon, and hour by hour, they came slowly across our bows about two miles off and went steadily forging along on our starboard bow. This was one of those occasions, and there were not many of them, when, with a clear wide-open stretch of water free of ice, it was possible to sail, aided and abetted by the engine if against a strong head wind.

Just as this happened, we spotted a large red Canadian coastguard ship, the *Sir Wilfred Laurier*, who called us up on VHF Channel 16;

we switched to Channel 6 (leaving Channel 16 free for emergencies) and they asked David about his boat, whether she was a class design, to which David replied that she had been custom built. We requested an ice report, which they kindly called us back with, and which sounded slightly hopeful. As David signed off, he asked them if they were aware of another vessel ahead of us, and there was a moment's silence while they confabulated; they obviously were not. Then *Dodo*, who had been listening to our exchange, called them up themselves, and in the course of their conversation Bob Shepton enquired if the search operation for Franklin's two ships, the *Erebus* and the *Terror*, was still going on. The coastguard confirmed it was. We would very soon be approaching Cape Felix on the north coast of the Royal Geographical Island in Victoria Strait – this was the area where it is believed the ships were lost, but up to this point soundings had still revealed nothing. I was, of course, particularly interested in this section. The fact that Sir John Franklin was my four-greats uncle was one of the reasons David had invited me to accompany him, so that I might see where my distant and famous relation had perished.

Finally, some time later, *Dodo's Delight* called us – now we switched to Channel 12 and Bob and David had quite a chat. Just as they were concluding their call, I made frantic signals about the meat, and David remembered to thank them for the musk ox. Bob said that they had had some for supper but that it was very tough. I suspected it might be and had put some aside in a marinade of Dijon mustard, honey, olive oil, pepper, cumin, rosemary and loads of garlic. The duty chef then wanted to know what my recipe was and David put me on the airwaves. After we had exchanged the niceties of preparing musk ox, we wished each other a good night, and I got on with the supper.

It was nearly midnight and we had been keeping an eye on some ice that had appeared from nowhere – very dangerous, damaging stuff. Suddenly there was an enormous *bang*, and a ghastly crunching noise under the boat from the propeller. I nearly lost my footing in the saloon, and everything got a great jolt. Thank goodness it was David on ice watch on the bridge deck. He threw the engine into neutral immediately and then tentatively gave a few gentle revs – more crunchings and grindings, but after a little gentle coaxing the cavity in which the huge propeller sat seemed to clear itself. I went outside to look and saw some small shards of ice bobbing away in our wake. After this sobering experience, David decided to slow down from his normal cruising speed of 800–850rpm, giving an average speed of 6 knots depending on sea conditions, to about 500rpm. Miraculously, with the same suddenness with which the ice had appeared, so it disappeared, and we supposed it must have been wind-blown ice trapped in the contours of the islands.

At first light on 31 August we were steaming up the Victoria Strait inside the Boothia Peninsula. There was no ice on awakening, and we had good visibility. I lit the Dickinson stove as it was very cold, logged our position, then felt guilty at waking David. However, I needn't have worried – a sleepy voice said, 'Have you increased the revs?'

I hadn't, but, given such a duty, I advanced on the throttle and watched the rev counter as I slowly pushed the lever forward, secretly pleased that David was entrusting me with the controls. We tended to reduce revs at night on the premise that if you are going to have a collision, it is better to have a slow one. There was no sign of *Dodo*, but as we had reduced speed, so had they kept the pressure on – with five of them to share the watches and the boat being a sailing boat, and lower in the water, it might have enabled the crew to spot any 'bergy' bits in the brief, pitch-dark night.

The visibility being excellent, we advanced all day, the wind freshening as we did so, up the Victoria Strait and beyond Cape Felix to the Tasmanian Islands. At Franklin Strait, which runs north between Boothia Island and Prince of Wales Island, the visibility began to close in on us. Sea fog had enveloped the islands in a shroud and David stood for the whole of this section glued to the windows on the bridge deck, keeping an eye on everything. Little surveying has been done in these waters and only the centres of the channels have been charted for such shipping as there is, the most important being the icebreakers who serve the small settlements. Peering into the ghostly shroud, one moment you could see nothing, and the next the curtain fell back and you could once again gauge distance. We were approaching the Bellot Strait and there were a few Arctic terns swooping about, with their sparkling white plumage and soft grey feathers on their wing tips.

You can only wonder at the courage of the early Arctic explorers who ventured into these hostile parts with no modern aids, with poor clothing, food and other equipment, in cumbersome, slow vessels whose only heating was coal-fired hot water circulating through piping around the ship. Certainly this was the case with both of Sir John Franklin's ships, the *Erebus* and the *Terror*. Their hulls were reinforced to 12 feet thick in the bows, built of English oak. Engulfed in ice, as they must have become, I puzzled that not even soundings had revealed anything of their whereabouts. The *Erebus* would be found within the year, and cause great excitement, but at this stage I was not to know of it.

We lay off the entrance to the Bellot Strait, which is the first bit of topographical interest for hundreds of miles, and more or less remained motionless until first light. This strait separates the Boothia Peninsula from Somerset Island, and is a narrow channel with fast-flowing current. The sea appeared to be bordered by dark brown-black igneous rock, and the low rolling shapes of the rounded hills were covered in a substantial dusting of snow lying wherever it could find shelter from the wind – the territory of polar bears and musk ox;

narwhal and saxifrage. Some of the gentler folds in the hills appeared to have a browny-green veil of vegetation, relieving the stark rock surfaces of this remote landscape. But no musk ox were to be seen, nor any school of narwhal. The sea in this channel and indeed in all the channels would shortly be frozen – normally this occurs from mid-October right through to May, but winter appeared to be coming early this year.

In the very centre of the channel, with creaming overfalls at the eastern end, lay Magpie Rock, a menacing trap which has ensnared the unwary and is very hard to spot. Although the location is given on the charts, more or less, it nevertheless requires great eyeball concentration, and David's concern was apparent. Just nearby was Fox Island, and the Port Kennedy inlet where Captain McClintock overwintered in the middle of the nineteenth century in the *Fox*, a sailing ship bought by Lady Franklin in order to search for her missing husband. McClintock made several lengthy sledging expeditions to search for Franklin from here, and it was during one of these that he and a member of his crew, Hodgson, found the cairn left by Franklin's men on the tip of Cape Felix. Beneath that lay a note revealing their fate.

Negotiating Magpie Rock, we passed Fox Island and the Port Kennedy Inlet, and rounded the point into Depot Bay. Here at Depot Bay was Fort Ross, with its two abandoned Hudson's Bay Company huts, in one of which David once spent a night before preferring to move into a tent while he worked on recaulking *Mabel*, many years earlier. This hut was where he took a photograph that was to become famous: of a polar bear looking through the window at him, reared up on its hind legs with its front paws pressed against the glass like two huge dinner plates.

Looking through binoculars at a pile of rocks, I saw a little white animal jump out and start to leap around in what seemed a playful manner. I said to David in an incredulous way, 'Oh! How absolutely adorable; there's a dear little baby polar bear playing about. Oh, do look, it's absolutely sweet – it's a baby bear.'

'What you are looking at,' said David, like a rather stern uncle with a frivolous child, 'is an Arctic fox.' It was almost entirely white, with flowing tail; just one remaining brown patch before its winter coat took over completely. Feeling rather foolish, I watched the fox trotting away, having failed to capture a small mammal sheltering in the rocks.

To our surprise, in this very lonely place we saw a pretty little fibreglass ketch, *Anna Vaareg*, which turned out to be owned by a Swedish man who had gone ashore to fetch water from a dew pond. After we anchored, he rowed over to see us and offered up a lovely silvery Arctic char he had just netted near the shore. The Arctic char is very similar to a salmon, but perhaps a little more delicate in flavour. It was very cold, and that day no snow covering had as yet fallen, but the temperature was such that we had a natural refrigerator and were able to leave the char lying on deck outside until needed.

We were both tired from the night before followed by a dawn start, so we had a hot toddy, then a good sleep, followed by onion soup, which was fast becoming a firm favourite. Then we set to work to unpack the Tinker Traveller rubber dinghy that David had had for over thirty years so we could row ashore to Fort Ross. We blew it up lying athwartships on the stern of *Polar Bound*. This is awkward and quite hard work. With the boom hoist, we lowered it into the water, then clad ourselves in layers of clothing – thermal polar wear, water-proof trousers, and my new and most comfortable Petersburg brown fisherman's boots, which are insulated and very substantial. These are de rigueur Petersburg kit, as worn by the whole town, and until you have bought yourself a pair you are noticeable as a visitor.

All the while I was feeling very uneasy about the impending visit to the shore and the thought that a large white furry face with twitching whiskers was about to come over the hill. We took the important new visitors' book, purchased in Nome, in its waterproof cover, together with camera gear, two plastic cans for water to refill from the dew pond, and the heavy walnut Browning 270 rifle in its canvas sleeve. David slipped four or five bullets into his pocket.

We rowed ashore. Feeling decidedly wobbly with poor land legs, I scrambled out into the shallow water with rolling stones beneath, and stepped up the foreshore, taking the painter with me so I could hold on to the boat and pull it nearer while David got out with all the equipment. Together we hauled and carried the dinghy up the stony beach below the McClintock Memorial flagpole with plaque beneath; we had arrived at Fort Ross, all two huts of it. One is an abandoned ruin, its dilapidated state much to be regretted. The other, quite well preserved, serves as a visitors' hut, a place of refuge for expeditions and parties of naturalists and sailing people. A narrow brick-lined path leads from one to the other.

A few old oil cans lay about, and a hand-riveted metal water butt with a small plaque and indecipherable impressed mark. David said there had been gardens neatly laid out when he first came here thirty years earlier: what a strange sensation that must have been, walking about in such desolate surroundings and wondering how long these two abandoned huts had remained like that before depredations by bears.

We went into the totally abandoned hut first, through a stiff and creaking door that was slightly ajar. There were wall divisions inside and two or three rooms, the main one with quite an elegant archway through to another section, and a ruined and rusted cast-iron range with stovepipe poking up, one or two pieces of broken furniture, upholstered chairs with their innards lying around, and a brass bedstead. Someone should be doing something to preserve this most interesting historical reminder of the early days of the Hudson's Bay Company up in these parts. (When I subsequently made enquiries, I was told that it was not the responsibility of the Historic Buildings department, but the Parks Department, and as usual no one wants to spend the money. This is a great pity as the hut is part of the history of the Arctic and left like it is, I suppose it will eventually disintegrate.)

When I saw what the bears had done to the contents of the hut, tearing the sofas asunder, dragging furniture around, the claw marks down the walls, I hurried after David, who had gone on ahead, and quietly pulled the door to on this somewhat intrusive visit into what had been another person's existence. Finding no bears, we approached the other hut, still used and of 'bear-photograph fame', and, climbing on to the water butt, David passed down to me, one by one, the wide lengths of hardwood boards slotted into sections of angle iron down each side of the door frame. These covered the full height of the door and were there to prevent bears from breaking it down. There were quite a number of boards and they were deeply lacerated with the claw marks of bears who had attempted to break in, or possibly who just enjoyed the sensation of sharpening their claws, as there was nowhere else for them to do so. It was alarming to see how high they could reach. Once inside, we peered around and David recollected the wooden bunk upon which he had placed his sleeping bag all those years ago – it had since been replaced with a much newer and smarter one. The wall above was covered with the scrawl of signatures of numerous visitors over the years – nothing, it seems, is sacrosanct from graffiti. There was a stove, and on a shelf along one side were numerous tins of food left by kind and thoughtful people, donating something for fellow travellers who might be hard-pressed.

This was the hut that David sheltered in when he made his first attempt to transit the Northwest Passage in 1986. He became iced in and then had two years, off and on, of struggle to extricate his old lifeboat, *Mabel E. Holland,* a 42-foot Watson, from the icy grip at Depot Bay. On waking up after his first night he had heard noises of oil barrels outside being blundered into, and the next minute a large bear face and huge paws appeared, pressed against the window panes. With great presence of mind, though frozen with fear, he had slowly reached out for his camera and, with the sole exposure remaining on film, took a photograph of it blinking through the window. It shambled away and knocked over some oil drums before returning to the hut for another look, and in the meantime David scrambled up into the loft area above. The bear could very easily have knocked the shabby old hut asunder in those days, and David had no rifle with him.

We took a number of photographs, then David, sitting on a simple wooden bench in front of a rough table littered with the detritus of various former visitors, brought out the replacement visitors' book. We each formally signed the new book, David first, appropriately as the donor; I followed. We photographed each other, and felt slightly self-conscious as if we were putting our signatures to the Magna Carta. We entered the date: 1 September 2013.

The old visitors' book (a school exercise book) had been instituted in 1985 by a cruise ship, the *World Discoverer,* who would bring clients ashore with a guide, while a marksman kept a lookout in case of unwanted ursine attention. A quick glance through it showed that several of the signatories had had encounters with bears; indeed, one party went into the ruined hut and found a polar bear in residence there. Only a handful of those who had signed were independent mariners. For the most part they appeared to have been exploration parties interested in marine biology, polar bear studies or botany. David's name was one of the earliest to appear; his first signature was on the second page, but altogether his name appeared six times on successive visits. Almost the last to sign was Peter Ashcroft, who took up half the last page to declare himself as 'Lord Ashcroft, House of Lords'. After much discussion, we decided to take the old visitors' book back with us and post it to Douglas Pohl. (He copied it, then returned it to us for onward transmission to the Scott Polar Research Institute, where it now resides.)

Lost in thoughts and memories, we were therefore somewhat startled when the doorway was darkened by the arrival of two men: it was the Swedish crew from the *Anna Vaareg*: Peter, who had presented us with the Arctic char, and his friend Pelly. They carefully leant their cocked gun outside against the door jamb; they were also armed with sharp knives in holsters around their middles. They were an interesting pair. We learned that Peter ran a garden centre supplying plants and gardening equipment to the residents of Gothenburg, and Pelly was a bricklayer and carpenter. They were most friendly and came and helped us to fill the water cans from a nearby marshy dew pond, standing wobbling on a stone – it was very shallow and you had to be careful not to stir up the moss at the bottom. The gun went everywhere with them, and I felt both relaxed and relieved that it was ready to fire, if needed. David's, meantime, was still in its canvas sling. It had a slug in it, but was not cocked. Apparently if I had tried to fire it, it quite likely would have broken my shoulder. We walked back over the stony terrain carrying our water supplies and chatting to the two men the while before rowing back to our respective boats.

Fort Ross, despite its stark beauty, has an air of melancholy. There is a strangely haunted feeling about it, a ghostly emptiness. You felt as if your presence was somehow violating the place, that you were an intruder. Periodically, I heard a noise like that of a boat's engine passing nearby, or it could also have been described as the sound of a light aircraft circling around to land. It was a disturbing 'thrumming' noise, which was unaccountable as there was nothing to see. It was only audible inside *Polar Bound*, and on each occasion I would rush up on deck to look, but the sea and sky were empty. Was it atmospherics, or what? I had encountered it nowhere else before, and it generally lasted about twenty seconds or so before fading away. Eventually I asked David if he had heard it too. He said he had, and that he had often heard it back in 1986, too, and had felt inexplicably uneasy. Certainly if I was totally alone in this wilderness, I would have felt distinctly so.

TWENTY THREE

PASSING TIME AT FORT ROSS

D AVID WAS STILL HOPING THAT THE Hecla and Fury Strait, way to the south of us, would clear of pack ice so that he could achieve yet another record by transiting it, then travelling on through the Foxe Basin and the Hudson Strait, and finally out into the Labrador Sea and the North Atlantic. As the time passed, it became less and less likely. Meanwhile ice was building up in the Prince Regent Inlet, through which we would have to pass to escape into Lancaster Sound, Baffin Bay and the Davis Strait, and home via Greenland and the North Atlantic. We spent altogether ten days in Fort Ross waiting for the weather to change and the wind to go around 180 degrees.

One grey morning we went along the beach for a walk and David showed me the site where in 1986, when making his first transit of the Northwest Passage from east to west in *Mabel E. Holland*, she had become ice-locked. He tied her up with about eight lines to survive the winter alone. In spring he flew out to monitor her state, travelling on a Skidoo across 500 miles of frozen sea, and found her in good shape, but when the thaw began, he was notified by a reconnaissance aircraft that she had all but sunk. David flew out and with the aid of a chartered Twin Otter managed to get dropped nearby together with a quantity of 4- by 6-inch baulks of timber on which to haul her out, and all the other materials, winches etc., that would be needed to effect repairs. He had to carry all the baulks, one by one, a quarter of a mile around the head of the bay to *Mabel*'s location. Everything had to be offloaded and moved within twenty-four hours as the pilot was anxious to be on his way for his next assignment.

After the roar of the departing Twin Otter's engines died away, David was engulfed in the vast silence of emptiness. He got to work, first setting up a small bivouac tent in which he preferred to sleep, encircling it with empty oil drums, rigged up so that any polar bear would knock into them if it came shambling around and alert David. On one occasion, lying underneath *Mabel* clad in a mosquito suit, he felt something that made him turn to look, and there was a bear, silently surveying him from 4 metres. He said he never moved so fast in his life as he leaped up into the safety of *Mabel*. He spent many months salvaging and repairing her, where most people would have abandoned her and declared her a write-off.

Now, twenty-seven years later, the timber baulks were still there, looking at us reproachfully. They had suffered no deterioration in this cold climate. Some way above, on a small hillock, David had built a cairn, and it was almost an obligation to carry up another stone or two and place them on the top. With this successfully accomplished, if not very willingly by me (I was beginning to flag), David wanted me to take a photograph of him on the summit with *Polar Bound* at anchor below, using his sophisticated Canon with its multi-lenses. I simply could not press the button – either my fingers were too cold, or the instructions were not explicit enough. Anyway, we both got cross before the job was finally accomplished.

Not content with that, he then wanted me to accompany him along the rocks to a considerably higher location, some distance away, to look over into the Port Kennedy inlet where McClintock had overwintered a century and a half earlier. Meantime, the gun was lying in its brown canvas bag some way below near the timber. After about five minutes of picking my way laboriously over stony obstacles, feeling most ill-at-ease and anxious, I finally exploded with indignation and said angrily to him, 'Look – what is the point of carrying this gun around in a canvas bag, not loaded, and now, not even *with* you?'

I pointed to the baulks of timber below, just out of sight, where the gun lay next to them.

'It's no good calling out to Brumas as he catches you unawares coming round the corner of some boulders. "I say, old chap, would you mind hanging on a moment, I'm not quite ready for you." Then struggling with freezing fingers on the zip, which might quite possibly jam, and fumbling in your pocket for the bullets, cocking the gun etc. – or whatever you do,' I added lamely.

Polar bears are highly intelligent, unpredictable and cunning, and should not be underrated; they can smell you from five miles' distance, and if there is snow, and they are on a higher ridge, they can curl into a ball and roll down the slope and be on top of you within moments. One swipe of their huge paws and they could easily decapitate a man. The reason why David was carrying a gun was purely in self-defence. If a bear approached him, his first reaction would be to fire the gun above its head to frighten it, but if the bear is hungry, or has cubs to feed, it may still come on. David's gun was particularly heavy and cumbersome, beautiful to look at but not very practical. I had noticed that Peter and Pelly's was much smaller and handier.

David, ignoring my outburst, said I should go back to the dinghy and wait for him there. I thought he was acting out of character, and was annoyed by his cavalier attitude, just to walk off into the blue with a vague wave of his arm, over a lot of stony, ankle-twisting terrain, leaving me to go down the hill again alone, recover his rifle – or not, as he hadn't even said what he wanted me to do with it – and walk all the way back along the shelving stony beach, covered at the fringe by mini-bergs. I thought it very irresponsible. Not only was he unarmed and going to be out of sight, but he was abandoning me. Although I would have the gun, I hadn't the least idea how to fire it – and now I come to think about it, he had the bullets in his pocket anyway.

Feeling very upset, I scrambled down the rocky slope to the baulks of timber below, picked up the Browning, slung the strap over my shoulder and walked back along the foreshore, picking my way. I was rather dismayed to come upon a long, rectangular heap of rocks and stones piled up above the shoreline, with the vertical half of a wooden cross pushed between them, crudely inscribed and indecipherable. The grave was on the surface, and peering through the stones you could plainly see the wooden box inside, left to the permafrost, the stones being protection against molestation from the bear. David told me later that it had been there just the same, twenty-seven years ago. At any rate, I found this sad little scene desolate in the extreme, and it only served to remind me how vulnerable we were in such a bleak wilderness.

I kept swapping the heavy rifle from shoulder to shoulder, and intermittently looking round to see if I was being followed. It wasn't many months earlier that a boy from Eton, on a school holiday to Spitzbergen, had been pulled from his tent and killed by a polar bear.

On finally reaching the dinghy on the foreshore, I placed the gun inside it, then went over to inspect and photograph the McClintock memorial plaque by the flagpole, and also took pictures of some of the beautiful lichens growing at its base. The plaque recalls the names of various members of the family, who had the pole erected there to commemorate McClintock's expedition in the *Fox* and his subsequent sledging forays, during one of which he made the discovery of the cairn left by the Franklin team. A large round white stone on the mound below stood out clearly against the startling red of the ancient lichen clinging to the surrounding ones. It was quite heavy, but such a lovely shape that I carried it down to the dinghy with me. I wearily sat down on the side, picking up two small stones in readiness, as David had told me that bears are nervous creatures and don't like the sound of two stones being clicked together. I presumed this was what he was doing himself, as he was otherwise quite defenceless. However, their favourite food is seal, and they are therefore most likely to be encountered along the shoreline – in fact, just where I was sitting.

Just as this realisation struck me, I was greatly comforted by hearing voices behind me, and turning I saw the crew approaching from *Dodo's Delight*, who had been to inspect the huts. I stood up in surprise and joy, and we all introduced ourselves. This was my first encounter with the Reverend Bob Shepton, as I hadn't had the chance to meet him when both our boats were moored at Cambridge Bay. We had not seen them arrive, although we knew they probably would call in here. I noted they were carrying a gun and, with gathering confidence and relief, I started letting my hair down about David's independence. At that moment his tall figure was seen striding along the beach towards us. I was so relieved to see him that I couldn't be cross any longer. However, the next time we were to go ashore, I was pleased that he took the gun out of its brown cover, and furthermore loaded it with a couple of heavy slugs, and that he stayed with me while we were on land.

We had to reposition ourselves twice in the anchorage. The first time we had gone close to the huts to save rowing; this was fine in calm weather, but when it started to blow, we pitched up and down on the steep, white-crested wavelets. David thought this might cause the anchor to trip and then we would have dragged, so we anchored further out in the middle of the bay. After that the wind really got up and the motion was quite violent, so we moved in closer to obtain some lee from the shore while remaining in quite deep water. The proximity of the shoreline and hills behind gave some shelter and reduced the fetch. Then, on a couple of evenings we had to let out more rope as it came on to blow with 35 knots of wind (force 8) – a full gale and great fierce black waves with angry white crests throwing our bow around, and all this despite being closer to the shore. We took careful note of our position so we could monitor whether we were dragging.

For ground tackle we had a 100-pound Delta anchor, and about 20 feet of heavy 19mm chain coupled to a swivel-lifting shackle attached to 500 feet of very thick rope cable (4.2cm in diameter). The reason for rope in lieu of chain is that if you became overwhelmed by pack ice, it would be possible to cut through the rope, whereas with chain your bows would be pulled down beneath; David thinks of everything. The wind came in great gusts, and blew hard in the chimney stack of the Dickinson while I was preparing supper. It was noticeably colder inside in these conditions, and food preparation took that much longer because the stove couldn't compete with the outside temperature. In the mornings we awoke to a mantle of snow covering everything in sight, and our surroundings took on a really bleak, wintery aspect.

One evening we invited the skipper and crew of *Dodo's Delight* to supper. They arrived at 6pm sharp and we gave them mulled wine, which seemed appropriate in view of the snowy transformation of our surroundings. This was followed by chicken soup, Arctic char risotto, then fresh fruit salad – they very kindly contributed a bottle of white wine. Besides Bob Shepton and Richard Nicolson, there was one other man and two women. Apart from one of his crew, none of us that evening was in our first flush, but I did envy Bob having four people aboard to share the chores and, most of all, the watches. We found that being only two aboard, we were always short of sleep. They also shared cooking and washing-up duties, of which I was also envious. David still has an outdated attitude that a woman's role is in the kitchen, though he seems pleased enough to have my help heaving oversized fenders out of the forward hold and staggering around with five-gallon diesel cans. He once informed me that I was a 'passenger'.

The next day *Dodo's Delight*, anchored nearby, was dragging noticeably, and they were getting rather too close for comfort. One by one, in the dusk, as the realisation dawned on them, Bob and the four members of his crew appeared in their heavy-weather gear and one of them went up on the foredeck endeavouring to bring up the chubbed anchor. It was freezing, and with newly fallen powder snow smoking along the foreshore in a blinding, stinging sheet, the wind was a real killer. A chubbed anchor is when you let a weight halfway down the cable, before the water level, so as to keep the line more horizontal, which gives better purchase for the anchor deep down on the sea bed. However, this obviously isn't effective if you have anchored to start with in too shallow water, coupled with not letting out enough chain.

Our most surprising visitor was a superyacht, the *Michaela Rose*, with the illustrious Crow family and guests on board. We were filled with amazement at the luxury of the vessel and at their appearance in this lonely spot. They went ashore in two fast Zodiacs, together with the obligatory marksman in case of predatory bears, to have a look at the huts. Nothing daunted, Bob Shepton called them up on the VHF to ask if they could let him see an ice report so he had some idea of what was going on with all these gales. The captain said, in a low drawl, that if they 'cared to swing by' he would be pleased to. David and I were eavesdropping on their conversation on our VHF, and grinned at each other at the dégagé manner of this invitation; we could only imagine the expressions on the faces of *Dodo*'s crew as they looked at the stiff breeze on the choppy water without. These luxury boat owners and their captains live in another world to the rest of us. They obviously had no idea what it would be like to chug in a small jelly baby right down the bay – a good quarter of a mile or more – and back again, with an unpredictable outboard engine and under the vagaries of an ever-freshening wind. However, Bob rose to the challenge and said he would 'swing by'.

Presently we saw him setting off with two of his crew aboard – so he wasn't going to risk all of them – for the long trek down the bay, bounding over the wavelets. We watched with binoculars as they arrived at the side of the *Michaela Rose* and disembarked, making fast their dinghy to the steps. The ship's crew then raised the steps with electrifying efficiency, which tipped Bob's outboard smartly backwards under the water. After a couple of hours aboard, during which they were shown on to the bridge, the owner, Mr Crow, said, 'Well – I'm off to the saloon. If anyone cares to join me, please do so,' and the three of them traipsed after him to meet the guests in the saloon. Most hospitably, they were given drinks, and also one or two bottles to take back home to the boat. When it came time to leave, the *Michaela Rose* had to ferry the crew back in their Zodiac, towing *Dodo*'s rubber dinghy ignominiously, with slightly less bounce than before and with a bedraggled outboard perched on the stern. *Dodo*'s crew spent the whole of the following day repairing the outboard. The *Michaela Rose* left Fort Ross soon after this and, despite claiming they could navigate through nine-tenths ice, they came unstuck in the Prince Regent Inlet and had to start zigzagging and backtracking, and eventually had to call on the services of a Canadian icebreaker, the CCGS *Amundsen*, to extricate them so they could continue to Resolute.

On waking early on the eighth morning, we saw a much larger ship out in the bay, the *Hanse Explorer*, who we learnt spent their winters in the Antarctic and their summers in the Arctic. They had a most efficient Norwegian crew aboard, who came over to visit *Polar Bound* in their Zodiac, bringing about twelve of their guests and, most obligingly, an up-to-date ice chart. No doubt this visit was by way of diversion for their paying guests, who needed variety and entertainment to break the monotony of the icy wilderness. We were still in bed and had to scramble up in a hurry. They had a nice young competent captain, with a firm handshake and excellent English. David took him down into the engine room to see the Gardner, and meantime I showed some of the guests round the small confines of our cabin; they had to come down the companionway in relays. Quite how entertaining they found us, I cannot say. At least our simple galley layout would have been a novelty after their sophisticated shipboard life.

We had been in Fort Ross for more than a week. When we arrived, the shore and surrounding hills were completely clear of ice and snow, except for some small lumps of grounded iceberg along the perimeter of the bay. Two days later the whole scene had changed. We woke up to find 4 inches of snow all over the ship and it became bitterly cold. It was not inviting to go out on deck to clear it, although it would have been wise to do so, as to leave it was merely building trouble for later on when the snow became frozen hard as we found to our cost.

We were at the point of no return, still hoping against hope that the weather would undergo a major change of wind direction and temperature and allow us to attempt the challenge of the Hecla and Fury Strait, 450 miles southeast. But as time went on and winter came closer, it looked less and less likely we would be able to head that way. David did not give up. He refused to accept he might not be able to undertake the final conquest on this voyage.

TWENTY FOUR

ON OUR WAY AGAIN

W
E WERE KEPT ABREAST OF ICE CONDITIONS via
Douglas Pohl, who was sitting on his boat in Panama
in the warmth (sensible man), and Peter Semitouk in
Winnipeg. David talked to both on the VHF radio, and received ice
charts by email, forwarded via his office. Nine-tenths ice was still
blocking the exit of the Prince Regent Inlet and also the eastern end
of the Hecla and Fury narrows. Northwesterly and northerly winds
remained predominant but the situation could easily change. Patience
was essential.

David was contemplating alternative options, such as leaving the
boat at Fort Ross, by putting out lines and anchors all around her
like a giant cat's cradle, then chartering a Twin Otter to fly us to Resolute at a cost of $10,000. As far as I was concerned, this was not an
option. In fact, I was quite startled when he broached the subject at
breakfast one morning. He put it in such a matter-of-fact way, almost
as if he was asking me if I had sixpence for my fare. There had been no
mention at the outset that if all else failed I would have to fork out for
an aeroplane. I told him firmly I would happily ride in the aeroplane
with him, but he would have to pay for the charter. I was crew and

expected to be looked after. The alternative, I said, would be for me to ride out the winter in *Polar Bound*. The subject was not raised again.

On 8 September we were not surprised to be awoken at 8.45am by a call from *Dodo's Delight* to say they had decided to leave and head up the Prince Regent Inlet on the east side. They had been quite fidgety for two or three days, and Bob Shepton had been in consultation with David about the possible outcome of the weather pattern we were having. They had already lifted their anchor and disappeared from view by the time we got their call, and their sudden departure left quite an empty feeling. We busied ourselves with chores in the boat and sent emails via David's office to our ice masters, Doug and Peter, and also later to Bob Shepton, to see how they were getting on. It was understandable that they had left; if you have several people aboard, all with their own agendas, it is always a compromise to accommodate everyone, and people have obligations and responsibilities they must try to comply with. We had the feeling that Bob would be pleased to get clear of the ice threat and get back to his more familiar Greenland. David, on the other hand, was ambitious to conquer the only route he had not yet claimed. Around the time *Dodo* left, another sailing boat, *Gitana*, a 43-foot schooner, entered the bay having arrived from Resolute. They were heading for Cambridge Bay with three men on board. We spoke to them on the VHF at about 11am and they said they were going ashore, but we saw no sign of them doing so.

Somehow the departure of *Dodo's Delight* heightened the threat of advancing winter, which was three or four weeks early. David anxiously made contact with Peter Semitouk again, both by email and also on the high-frequency radio; this communication was filled with crackles and noise like a machine gun, which David told me was a carrier signal. There was also an endless repetition of statements and a lot of *Affirmative, affirmatives*, and even a *Negative*. David was beginning to cough, which showed that he was under stress as to what decision to make – Hecla and Fury Strait, or the Prince Regent Inlet. I must say that the former did not sound like a very sensible option, even supposing there was a sudden change of wind direction and that a passage did open up in the narrows; there were still several hundred miles to travel southeast before we would even have a chance to make the attempt, and little is known of the waters beyond the main channel through the Foxe Basin. Other than a central channel for icebreakers, the remainder has not yet been charted.

On Monday 9 September we went ashore to close up the hut. David stood on the old hand-riveted barrel and I handed him the boards to slot back into the angle irons. I was reminded by the rasping claw marks on the boards that we had seen no polar bears while there, nor musk ox or caribou; only the Arctic fox we saw on arrival, along with some type of gull, and a tiny finch-like bird which was in the process of camouflaging itself and changing its feathers from brown to white – nature is very clever.

During the afternoon, while we were packing away the Tinker Traveller dinghy on the stern of *Polar Bound* – a cumbersome job, with David doing the major part – a black and white helicopter came whirring overhead. Not coastguard, said David, as they were always red. A bit later on, while I was preparing supper, David announced that a large blue boat, the *Octopus*, was in sight at the southern end of Depot Bay, where we were lying. This was beginning to become like Piccadilly Circus. I asked if I could call them up on the VHF. Privately I felt that they would have up-to-the-minute first-hand information that might help David reach a decision. After my third request, David grudgingly agreed, so I got on to Channel 16 and spoke to their ice master to ask about ice concentrations around the Hecla and Fury Strait, and in particular the east end. I also asked about ice density in the Prince Regent Inlet.

Reception was excellent; he was an Englishman, and concise and to the point. He thought Hecla and Fury had several problems and was quite a dangerous undertaking; he recommended the east side of the Prince Regent Inlet heading up to the Lancaster Sound while the going was still good, before the sea froze over. Nevertheless, even with this route there were going to be one or two areas where we would meet difficulties, and the ice was seven-tenths so we would have to skirt around these to find continuing leads. I felt quite professional talking to *Octopus* – apparently she was a private yacht, unless her 3,000 tons or so classified her as a ship. We thought she was probably owned by a Russian oligarch, but subsequently learnt that she was owned by Bill Gates's second-in-command at Microsoft. The boat had its own helicopter, which turned out to be the one that had flown over us earlier; this was, of course, a wonderful way of identifying ice concentrations – not many private yachts can boast one of these. Normally you had to rely on downloading ice charts from the American or, in this case, Canadian Ice Chart Service, but we did not even have this facility. We had to rely on what David agreed was an antiquated method involving his office forwarding the necessary information from a third party.

We finally made a plan to leave the next day, 10 September, and go north through Prince Regent Inlet (if we could!). Following a beef curry supper, and feeling more content after all the endless discussions and talking round and round the alternatives, we watched the second half of *The Horse Whisperer* on my computer. By bedtime, however, David, obviously feeling frustrated, started to resume thoughts of the Hecla and Fury. From the darkness of his bunk, a small voice asked me whether I thought we should consult a man to whom he had been given an introduction at the Canadian Ice Service in Ottawa, who might have better knowledge. I tried to knock this one on the head but was not sure I succeeded.

The following morning, departure day, which I was looking forward to after such a long period of inactivity, even before breakfast we had to send off an email via David's secretary to the Canadian Ice Service, seeking their apparently more informed prognosis of our chances if we were to proceed southeast towards the Hecla and Fury. Back came a very firm negative: any passage through the Hecla/Fury was totally out of the question – not just hazardous, but impossible. David is nothing if not determined, which I suppose is how he has achieved all the incredible solo circumnavigations he has made, and overcome seemingly insuperable setbacks. All along I had been very careful not to suggest what he should or should not do, as I had no experience whatsoever on which to base any judgement other than plain common sense. The decision had to be his; but it was exhausting!

David also managed to speak to Peter Semitouk, who told us the distressing news that a helicopter from the coastguard cutter *Amundsen* had crashed off the northern end of Banks Island that morning, killing the three occupants. This was the area at the western end of the passage before entering the Beaufort Sea, which we had successfully transited the previous year, the first private boat to do so. It was also just off Point Barrow where we heard that the Belgian boat, *Pas Perdu le Nord*, had foundered on the shoal. The strong northerly winds we had been encountering must have driven ice down close to the shore and they were evidently trying to escape this as they attempted to round the point – the shoal is quite clearly marked on the chart.

I don't know why it is but once a man has decided upon his course of action, it must be accomplished without further delay, and general agitation sets in. The galley secured and washing-up done, engine started, a final visit to the heads, a quick shave and teeth cleaning, pile on the heavy-weather clothing until it is hard to recognise the wearer, and then finally a determined foray to the foredeck to set to work on the anchor, which has been well dug into the mud after all the gale-force winds of the last eight days. Meanwhile the woman is diligently tidying up all the seemingly trivial details in the saloon and galley, but which are nevertheless essential before putting to sea, and is also, of course, wishing to visit the heads and get warm clothes on; quite often these aspects were brushed aside impatiently. It used to be like this in the charter boat I worked in in the Windward Islands over forty years earlier, and also in our own boat in the Mediterranean with my late husband, and now to an extent with David Scott Cowper in *Polar Bound*. It is almost as if what has just been thought of should already have been accomplished.

Finally, we were under way once more, having raised the anchor around 9.30am (boat time). David worked on GMT, which was most confusing as I never knew how many hours to add on. Sometimes with extreme fatigue I could equally well deduct them. As we motored out of the bay, David once again called the small schooner *Gitana*, which had entered two days earlier. Apart from their call to us on the first day, we had seen no sign of them, despite the fact that both days had been beautiful and sunny. Their dinghy had not been launched, although they had asked how to access the hut and where the key was hidden. They had failed to answer five attempts to contact them on the VHF, so it was a bit of a mystery. It occurred to me that they might have succumbed to carbon-monoxide poisoning. We heard later that they were changing their propeller, as they had damaged the other one trying to navigate through ice. We never saw them on deck, so had no idea how they could have managed this.

As we slid out of Depot Bay, we turned hard left and started across the Prince Regent Inlet, motoring west to east. We were heading for the far side of it, at which point we would turn and start going directly north up towards the Lancaster Sound. It wasn't long before we encountered our first ice field. We were right on the open stretch between two gigantic ice masses, proceeding through two-tenths ice, becoming three- or four-tenths, with treacherous bergy bits half concealed below the waves, only the tips of their spires and minarets glinting an ugly malevolent grey, so easily missed between the white crests of the waves. The seas had died down and it was calm – this was the benefit of the ice mass, but it did require great concentration and vigilant hand-steering to weave through. Elsewhere there were more of the fluffy meringues, sparkling in the sunshine, and a blue sky overall.

In the afternoon and evening the wind took up again and blew ferociously. The entire contents of the boat's galley came to life – it was a full orchestra tuning up, with rattles, clangs and bangs, and over it all the relentless and faithful chonking of the Gardner 150SHP engine with its eight pistons and unending staccato rhythm. (SHP, for the uninitiated, stands for Shaft Horse Power.) Latched doors flew open as the movable parts of the interior flexed themselves; sauce-pans jumped about like hot popcorn; the fruit bowl shed its contents of a lemon, green pepper, half a tomato, kiwi fruit, Baby Bel and Parmesan cheeses, and they all retreated to hiding places of their own. The dry goods containers, full of rice and sugar and flour, are tall clear Perspex with self-sealing suction lids, and they all rocked forward in unison with relentless deference behind their retaining fiddle, like a reception committee of obsequious mandarins. The spice cupboard proved the hardest to tame as all the jars and drums are different shapes and sizes. The moment one is removed, the rest roll gleefully into the vacated space and the cacophony starts again. I can sometimes trick the fusillade of missiles by opening the door just a crack and putting my hand beneath to fend off the disorderly one that is waiting to spring out and roll across the galley floor towards the heads, shedding a trail of its contents. Above all this demoniacal activity, the wind blew without let-up.

We heard on the radio from Peter Semitouk that Bob Shepton and his four crew in *Dodo's Delight* had reached the shelter of a small bay – Fitzgerald Bay – on the opposite side of the Prince Regent Inlet. They were in a vulnerable position as they needed to go directly north up the inlet to gain the Lancaster Sound at the top – as we also planned to do – and the wind was too strong for their engine so they would have made little headway, and attempting to sail against the wind with clouds of freezing spray would have been suicidal. The danger was that more ice would blow down from the north and trap them in the bay.

TWENTY FIVE

PRINCE REGENT INLET

W E SURFACED THE NEXT MORNING AFTER two or three hours' snatched sleep – not of the best kind, and neither of us felt up to much as *Polar Bound* rolled her scuppers under. Civilised life was put on the back-burner. Ablutions were abandoned, and the cuisine was whatever packet or tin came easiest to hand. David, who had all the responsibility, was particularly petulant and responsive to the first sign of a slammed door, and when I turned off the autopilot switch in the DC distribution box instead of the HF radio, following his call to Peter Semitouk, I was ferociously told, 'Absolutely, by no means, are you allowed to touch *any* switches' – and, warming to his theme, 'I simply can't have you fiddling with these switches; they are the lifeblood of the boat, and it might be absolutely vital.'

He was evidently feeling oppressed and dejected that the ice gods were not to relent. There was now no possibility this year that he would be able to make a challenge on the last transit still unconquered. Quite possibly it would be the same next year too, he said, as there is a cyclical pattern to the weather in the Arctic, with one bad year almost certainly being followed by another.

It was a horrendous day, crawling across then north up the Prince Regent Inlet – equal to the whole length of England. Instead of taking thirty-six hours, it finally took us three days. We plugged into relentless northwesterly gale-force winds and made only 3 knots per hour instead of the normal 6 to 6.5. By this time most of the deck was well and truly iced up and I wished I had made more of an effort to clean the snow residue in Depot Bay, David having done the lion's share one morning. Now it was too late. As we plunged through the sea, freezing waves swept over our super-structure, rapidly turning it to ice. This build-up covered the decks, railings and windows. We both knew that all this weight was likely to destabilise the boat, but the conditions were not conducive to a sortie on deck to clear it.

Once we turned to start heading up north towards Lancaster Sound, we encountered four separate ice fields stretching from horizon to horizon. At the first one, by striking along a section, it was possible to see open sea over the other side. We picked our way with great care, wending between the great rafts of billowing, not-yet-consolidated ice that surged up and down around us, and occasionally having to nudge a whole section aside with considerable rasping and grinding noises, David putting the throttle into neutral when he deemed the propeller was vulnerable.

The next ice field was not so easy. We motored up to a seemingly impenetrable barricade of solid ice, new, one-year and multi-year, with pressure ridges that forced the ice up here and there into frightening fantasy shapes – a jumbled, tortured prairie of chaos, intimidating and ghastly to behold. At this point I felt fear for the first time: at the enormity of the expanse, at the barricade we had to get through to gain our objective. By motoring along its face for a few miles, we finally found a weakness where loose pieces were still heaving up and down on the swell, preparatory to closing ranks with the mass, and we were greatly relieved to be able to pick our way through at last. The temperature had dropped to minus 2 or 3 degrees centigrade, but with the wind-chill factor, David said it was considerably colder, and the sea was beginning to show signs of pancaking, ahead of freezing right over. Pancaking is an extraordinary sight, exactly like it sounds, only the 'cakes' are about three or four feet in diameter like gigantic lilypads.

This sort of ice did not move independently, it was a solid, bonded mass to which new drifters attached themselves like long-lost friends, and the whole then proceeded like a great juggernaut with unstoppable force, moving with the current or driven by the wind, whichever was greater. And if you should be caught in its clutches, with frightening certainty you would either be crushed, or engulfed, or forced upwards and held for an indeterminate time until the forces of nature relented and a series of gales coupled with a strong current broke up the titan and relinquished its prey. *Polar Bound*'s enormously strong hull and keel had been specifically designed for just such conditions, but had not yet been put to the test. Nevertheless, we did not want to find ourselves pushed upwards like a cork out of a bottle. Nor did we wish to spend the whole winter there.

One of Franklin's ships on an earlier voyage had been carried along a thousand miles in just such a manner, to his great inconvenience. It was a possibility that this was the fate of the *Erebus* and *Terror*; they could have been overwhelmed and eventually crushed.

On waking the following morning we gazed out upon *Polar Bound* in winter plumage – an Arctic bride clad in her white winter wedding dress. She was covered with ice, head to foot – an unbelievable sight. Sheet ice over the foredeck and forward coachroof, and every boat-fitting covered with a sheath exactly following its contours, but magnified many times over. The boat was pitching and hobbyhorsing into the gale-force northwest wind and every few moments a great wall of spray would engulf the forward section, favouring the port side, and drenching everything in its path. The anchor began to assume grotesque proportions, the cheeks of the fairlead united as one with the anchor stock, shackle and cable; the air-vent pipe to the fore-peak, the pulpit, the hatch cover and hinges, the naval-type windscreen wipers, foredeck spotlights, and the inner railings surrounding the roof of the forward hold – all magnified in size; the plaited wire-steel safety rail surrounding *Polar Bound* and all the stout aluminium-threaded vertical securing posts – all immersed time after time in clouds of freezing spray. Most dramatic of all was the plaited 8mm steel wire which underwent a transmogrification into a huge rope-twist hawser with a glittering, tessellated fringe, each point bejewelled with a semi-frozen droplet awaiting resolution into another 2mm of sparkling ice. Some of these stalactites were at least 6 inches in length, and as the boat rolled, the frozen fringe faithfully followed suit, swinging to and fro in a stately waltz. The twelve windows of the bridge deck, too, were engulfed so that we could barely see out.

Our third barrier gave us quite a lot of outriders to contend with, and we consulted one another as to where seemed a likely place to pass through. Peering through the frozen windscreen and using binoculars, we finally picked up a hopeful opening with four-tenths ice still on the move. Proceeding, David gently nosed into a raft 2 or 3 feet in thickness, with probably about 9 inches showing above (and no doubt weighing hundreds of tons); he coaxed and cajoled it into a sideways slide, and steering with great coolness in the face of seemingly overwhelming odds gradually gained on it. Relenting, it slid to one side to allow passage to the next obstacle. It was a question of hard to starboard, and then to port, as we slowly gained the far side of the floe.

At one point I spotted that the piece we had been shunting aside, and which was covered in newly fallen snow, had a line of great paw marks marching across its length to a smooth shoulder on the far side, where perhaps a seal had hauled out to rest. The ice was heavily indented with claw marks and it looked as if there could have been a scuffle, but the seal hopefully got away as there was no sign of blood. It couldn't have happened too long before we got there as the marks were very fresh. I felt a great sense of moment and awe at witnessing a natural scene without help of a television presentation; respect for the majesty of the polar bear and its daily struggle for survival, and relief for the seal. I looked all round but there was no bear to be seen. They are strong swimmers and can easily swim a hundred miles. A huge floe of ice would be their favourite hunting ground, but this one appeared to have got away. I still had yet to see a bear, though I did manage to grab the camera and got a parting shot of the imprints.

Soon after this David braved the elements clad in padded suit, boots and gloves, and went out on deck to start chipping away the ice, which was now getting rather critical. Armed with a hammer, and a scoop to shunt the ice chippings over the side, he ventured along the deck. After about twenty minutes or so of keeping an eye on him, and feeling guilty at the same time, I decided that I must make the effort too. Donning all the necessary gear, I went out to join him armed with the plastic dustpan, which proved remarkably effective at prising up the edge of a sheet of ice and shovelling it along until the section broke off. Before long, fingers had no feeling. We retreated inside as we saw another ice barrier in the distance.

We had travelled about twenty miles over this last open stretch of water and surveyed the barrier ahead with some dismay as it seemed to be an impasse. The wind was blowing hard and the sea was black and menacing, with short steep waves and frothy crests. White ripples snaked across the surface of the water and the cold was intense. David rang up Peter Semitouk to ask if he could advise whether we should go west or east, as in both directions the ice appeared like a solid wall as far as the eye could see. We picked an easterly direction, approaching the ice wall with great caution. The sea was dotted with brash ice and bergy bits, and waves flung clouds of spray against the windows. There was a tremendous swell, and the odd rogue wave slammed into the side of the hull, giving us a sickening lurch and then gurgling along the hull with occasional cavitation in the propeller tunnel.

As the evening drew on and darkness fell we finally spotted a lead out into Lancaster Sound. After some hours and with quite a sense of relief, we rounded Cape York, followed by Cape Crawford. Exhausted by the rough weather and the vigilance, we decided to lie a'hull after supper for a few hours to have some sleep. We awoke at 4.30 the following morning to get under way once more.

At this point David decided to make a deviation from our outward voyage in 2012, and so instead of carrying on to exit in Baffin Bay, he cut the corner by turning south down the Navy Board Inlet, a scenic, almost intimate entrance after the vast distances we had covered, and interesting as it was narrow and we could see both sides. However, in the early morning murky light there was no colour whatsoever; we were in a shadowy world of daguerreotype images. We passed a bizarrely shaped iceberg resembling a giant-sized delta-wing aeroplane, frozen in time with its vast tail sitting in the water. On the first bend we came upon the spectacular sight of three glaciers in a row on the starboard hand, and motored over to them. The first one was in a process of retreat, and the flow stopped some hundreds of yards from the shore, but the other two had carved a passage for themselves through the rock and in so doing had thrown up high moraines on their outer curves. They were very much alive and we went up close to look at them. One was dramatic with huge fissures across its surface and showed signs of recent calving. I wanted

David to turn the engine off to hear if the glacier made creaking and groaning noises, but he was reluctant in case by some chance it refused to start again in such a vulnerable spot. The titanic forces of this unstoppable 200-foot-high wall of blue ice flowing from the plateau above was an awesome spectacle.

Then followed a second bend to port, and a long and dreary low peninsula on the port side of about 80 miles, beside which we had to keep station all day, the only relieving features being two fantastic icebergs; the first almost unbelievable in its fine, architectural, fairy-like tracery, sculpted and honed by the wind, reminiscent of Bolton Abbey in Yorkshire. You could see right through its arches, and we took a number of photographs. The second was spectacular only for its immense size: a monolithic slab, perhaps over half a mile in length and a good 200 feet in height. Both these features appeared to have grounded themselves – the depth of the Navy Board Inlet is approximately 1,600 feet, so if indeed they were grounded, and since an iceberg hides nine-tenths of its bulk beneath the water, one wondered where they had originally calved. David thought that they had quite likely calved in Greenland in the Vaigat (behind Disko island) and floated across Baffin Bay into the inlet. They were so large that they may not have grounded at all, and were instead moving so slowly as to be barely discernible. Surely it will be over a thousand years before traces of these monoliths have disappeared.

At the end of a very long day, after dinner, we arrived at Pond Inlet in the dark, where we finally spotted a suitable place to anchor. The name of this settlement is marked out on the hillside using small stones; it is the first sign of human habitation for at least a thousand miles. Looking through the binoculars, we saw its pretty twinkling red, green, yellow and white lights in two rows; one at waterline level and the other on the hill above. It seemed almost like Christmas time and made us feel quite festive.

By the following midday, the wind was blowing with great ferocity parallel with the shore, and *Polar Bound* lifted and plunged on her cable, and for the first time she dragged quite dramatically. We started to drift fast down towards another statuesque iceberg, which we had awoken to find as our neighbour, and we had to contend once again with the struggle of donning thick clothing to work on the foredeck, David hauling the anchor and securing it around the Sampson post while I made huge coils of the rope on deck, like a curled-up cobra ready to snake out again once we had manoeuvred into the right position. When all was ready, I went down into the forward hold to knock away the chocks holding the horizontal drum from spinning, so that more cable could be freed off to compensate for the greater depth of the new position.

There followed a period of enforced rest, when we took stock of the stores buried in the bowels of the ship. A tedious job but quite fun when something in short supply comes to light. This time it was five tins of sliced pineapple and three bottles of single malt whisky, along with several more mundane findings: a pot of Bovril, some tins of anchovies, a tube of toothpaste and half a red cabbage. Items which store quite well in the forward hold are cabbages, potatoes in a thick brown paper bag, folded well down, kiwi fruit, oranges, apples, bananas in a polystyrene foam box with lid, tomatoes, stacked vertically in an egg box, onions, garlic, turnips and parsnips – carrots do not appear to keep well.

The indigenous Inuit in the Northwest Territories are apparently a huge financial drain on the Canadian government. The cost of transporting and building one single house for a family to live in is around $250,000, and of course all the supporting infrastructure needs to be supplied as well. They do not appear to value these modern trappings of 'civilisation' as, if the need presents itself, they are quite likely to tear the door off a house to carry a dead seal – David had seen this done.

Pond Inlet has a school and a hospital for simple procedures, but for anything complicated the patient would have to be flown out. The Inuit are either supplied with, or acquire, guns and skiffs, and we noticed a couple of bulldozers where they were constructing a launching ramp down into the sea. We also noticed a small aeroplane, possibly a Twin Otter, circle around to land on the plateau above the settlement.

The white man has much to answer for with the introduction of guns, thus weakening the Inuit's inherited skills of trapping their food, and for undermining their ability to survive in such an inhospitable wilderness by providing housing to take the place of traditional dwellings. The installation of settlements hindered their nomadic ways of moving to summer hunting pastures following the herds of caribou. Their way of life had been manifest for over four thousand years.

David was still hankering after his thwarted route.

'It's only 150 miles back from here to the Hecla and Fury,' he said, pleadingly. This remark was not really addressed to me, but to his own reason. He must have known that it was much further than that, and in any case Prince Regent Inlet would have been almost completely frozen by now. It was the middle of September, and after much heart-searching and consultation yet again with both Doug Pohl and Peter Semitouk, we made a final decision that we would not be attempting the Hecla and Fury route in view of the early freeze-up, now very much in evidence. Bob Shepton had only just managed to escape the clutches of Prince Regent Inlet, and was now in Admiralty Inlet at Arctic Bay. He had told us by email that he encountered thick pancake ice – known as ice pans in Franklin's day – at the northern exit, which we transited only three days ago. These pancakes are razor-sharp. Bob was lucky to get out.

There was still ice on our decks, despite our taking it in turns to do half-an-hour's chipping away to get rid of some of the weight of it. It was very cold work and my fingers became useless, with no feeling whatsoever. I already had chilblains on my toes, despite the warmth of the Dickinson stove in the saloon.

TWENTY SIX

POND INLET TO FISKENAESSET FJORD, GREENLAND

W E WERE NOW NEARING THE END OF OUR Arctic voyage of uncertainty and going south to warmer climes. We decided to leave Pond Inlet at about five in the evening on 16 September, after a siesta, and by this time the east wind had melted away. We never went ashore – it would have been rather risky as we were anchored a little way off and had no outboard, only the oars. Leaving Pond Inlet in daylight, we could appreciate the magnificence of the mountain scenery surrounding us. Heading east we continued through the Navy Board Inlet and out into Baffin Bay. One spectacular mountain called Herodier was like a minia-ture Matterhorn, with a steep escarpment sliding from the summit straight down to the water thousands of feet below. On the other side of the inlet were several more glaciers.

As we got out into the open sea the waves became quite moun-tainous. It brought home to me just how substantial they were when the boat was carried upwards and then slid down the backside, a frothing crest marching away downwind as *Polar Bound* sank in a deep valley below. Thankfully there was no other navigation around. We had only the occasional iceberg for company – two, on our first night out on the open sea again, spotted on the radar and then identified, then a third, unscheduled one, which must have been too low for the radar. Somehow we could never relax until the iceberg had been located, so it was always an anxious time. We now operated our old system of one and a half or two hours' sleep, using the alarm clock, which lived by my bunk on the saloon table. On the first night there was no need for it to go off at all as we were both up periodically.

Polar Bound surged along between 6 and 7 knots, her stern rising and falling in a comfortable groove with the northeasterly wind on her starboard quarter, weaving her 48 feet between the big breaking seas in a disdainful manner as if to say, 'You needn't think you can stop me now – I'm riding on the Labrador Current and going home to my Scottish fastness.' (The Labrador Current goes anti-clockwise up the west coast of Greenland, around at the top and down the east coast of Baffin Island, and there we had picked it up.)

Periodically David's computer came out of its bag and I was required to type a missive to his office. The typing did not always tally with what was being dictated as, when a large wave surged against the beam, the boat gave a huge roll and I became airborne, rising from my cushion – a curious feeling of weightlessness, although my feet remained anchored to the cabin sole. Nevertheless, it was fun, and it also introduced a minor diversion; in fact, it gave me a feeling of reassurance to type something official on a subject divorced from marine life.

The only wildlife in evidence were beautiful seabirds with snow-white heads and short, fat bodies with stumpy tails, which swooped and wheeled, soaring over the bridge deck and skimming in front of the bow with effortless grace and symmetry. Their huge, powerful, grey scimitar wings with charcoal barring were perfect camouflage, evolved for scouring their element in search of food. It also seemed on occasions that they were performing their ballet for the sheer joy of being alive.

We heard the following evening that once again the wind was due to increase considerably, to about 30 knots, or gale force, and we found ourselves already adopting the stance of a giraffe. If you put a cup of tea down for a second while you turned to do something else, it would go straight over. Reach down into the saucepan cupboard to bring out a pan, and you were likely to lose your balance and lunge forward. For supper we were going to have the last of the Arctic char given to us by our Swedish friends in Port Ross, and in a lull in the afternoon David, clad in a warm padded boiler suit, had heroically gone out on deck to the hold to get me some supplies for the galley. I thought he was feeling a bit 'shrammed', as they say in Norfolk, and probably needed a good sleep.

He had a party trick, and I always knew when he was about to show off as there would be a naughty gleam in his eye. He made sure he caught my attention that way. Once he'd established that, he then grabbed the handhold above the companionway in the saloon, like an orangutan, and, with arms fully extended, pulled himself up, at the same time raising his legs clear of the cabin sole and swinging them out horizontally in front. Turning to see if he still had my attention, he would then draw his knees almost up to his chin in the foetal position. Not bad for a 71-year-old. I tried, but could only just lift my feet off terra firma, and then only for a second.

His other form of entertainment was to get on the high-frequency radio to Peter Semitouk. There then would follow the most banal conversation about nothing very much, constantly interrupted on both sides by *Roger, roger*, and then, when the exchange was particularly difficult owing to a lot of phizzing and squawks but the content was finally understood, an extra *Roger* thrown in for good luck. Or else it was *Affirmative, Peter, affirmative*, if David had understood what Peter had just said. There was a lot of talk about propagation, which was something to do with atmospherics and nothing to do with horticulture, and good or bad reception; it usually seemed to be the latter. A time was then set up for the next exchange, which quite often got forgotten, and the dialogue usually finished with:

'Well – all the seventy-threes.'

'And to you, too,' came the response.

This meant 'Best wishes and all the best'. A variant, 'All the seventy-nines', was shorthand for 'Love and kisses', though I didn't actually hear this one being used. What I did know was that the timing schedule for these noisy exchanges invariably coincided with my supper preparations, which had to be put on hold because I was required to go aloft and take the wheel. The self-steering had to be disconnected when the transmission was under way or it upset the selected course.

The next morning we woke an hour earlier than usual as we were trying to catch up with time zones hitherto overlooked. For once, the wind was in our favour, although still northerly; there had been a big depression to the south of us in the Davis Strait and, although the wind was behind us, we were confronting a big residual swell coming up from the south. This created quite a tumultuous sea, but as the day wore on, the northerly wind took precedence and big seas were building behind us in an endless procession.

The next day it was too rough to venture on deck, even to dispose of the wet rubbish. It was blowing at 30 knots and that evening there was a full moon. The seabirds continued to entertain with their endless and beautiful ballet of dives and turns, darting beneath the bows and skimming past the bridge windows – I was sure they were looking at us through the glass. There were several varieties of birds now: the soft, overall grey one that settled on the water and was most perfectly camouflaged once buoyant, then the white-headed, white-bellied one with the scimitar wings and puffin-like body shape; then there was a dusky coot-type, inconspicuous on the dark grey water. It was a puzzle to know what these birds were catching but there was no doubt that the rougher the water, the more it stimulated the plankton or krill – whatever it was, this bird caught it in full flight, just barely an inch above the water.

We passed two icebergs: lone outriders, as we had seen no others; one looked like a lotus flower and was rather treacherous with a whole lot of discarded bergy bits, the other was a vast frozen flying saucer, far larger than at first glance, resembling that white elephant legacy of one of Tony Blair's extravaganzas, the Millennium Dome. That night the moon cast its ethereal beauty over the turbulent sea. I was quite startled for a moment by what appeared to be a great liner bearing down on us, passing across the windows of the bridge deck – it was a cloud passing over the face of the moon, and as it retreated to the horizon its path stretched from west to east like a thin silver riband. The waves marched on, sailing majestically into the distance as our stern rose to meet them. They lifted *Polar Bound*'s approximately 35 tons as effortlessly as if she were gossamer, and soared forward with frothing tops. During the night three more icebergs were sighted on the radar, one of which resembled the Faraglioni rocks off the Island of Capri in the Mediterranean. The third one was a phantom; it never put in an appearance, unless it was small enough to be concealed by the heaving ocean.

It was now 20 September, the season of equinoctial gales; the wind had increased to 35 knots, and the waves approaching our stern and viewed through the window above the companionway came rearing up and surging forward so that our nose lifted, pointing heavenwards, then *Polar Bound* sank comfortably down into the welter of white froth, twisting around with the momentum of the onslaught, her propeller cavitating in the tunnel beneath, the wave riding on ahead as high or higher than the roof over the bridge deck. I don't think I had ever seen such an angry, dark grey, heaving sea before, with such tumbling water, spume streaking down the face of the waves, and spray and white horses in every direction. At this moment I was glad not to be in a sailing boat – we were snug and warm, and for once going downhill with the wind behind us. And we still managed to get off about seven emails via David's office.

Around about now David announced that we must advance our clocks another two hours. Two days earlier we had advanced them by one hour, so we were now all adrift, eating breakfast at noon, lunch at 5pm and supper at 10pm (boat time). I spent a while baking some bread, which was quite a performance. It was when the entire kitchen counter was monopolised by sticky dough that David chose to do his ham radio act. Propagation was non-existent, so we had the usual symphony of squealing pigs, whistling and squawking, with the faint drone of Peter Semitouk trying to compete but drowned out by a carrier signal – i.e. another user. Of course, on occasion, it can all go very well and you can have a long conversation with no cost – or frustration – involved.

While I was writing up my notes that evening, I was also sampling my nightly tipple of a whisky or two. David, although mostly teetotal, did like the associated nibbles that came with Happy Hour – i.e. nuts and crisps. These are not good if you have to watch your cholesterol, so I had to contrive some means of concealing the main supply of the nibbles, and allocating a small quantity in a dish specifically for him. He didn't take kindly to this and soon became like a rather tiresome dog, begging for more. In the middle of this indulgence, there was an enormous bang against the hull, followed by crunching. In the darkness we had just hit a growler – the only one in ten square miles, it seemed. We leapt up the companionway and David slowed the engine; mercifully no harm appeared to have been done.

The next day we crossed the Arctic Circle at 66 and a half degrees north. I was steering as David had his tracker switched on, which caused the autopilot to go haywire; the tracker gave our position via HF radio to anyone who cared to follow our progress, and so throughout the voyage we had periodically – most days – turned it on for about twenty minutes or so, which logged our position.

Supper that evening met with misadventure. I had viewed with suspicion several items of food David had been storing in the bowels of the ship, but it was so rough that I thought it appropriate to open a packet of dehydrated chicken tikka masala – it was called 'Black Country', from New Zealand: 'fast, nourishing food for adventurers – just add boiling water and let stand for ten minutes'. So boasted the directions. I sat down with considerable relief to have an evening off cooking as *Polar Bound* was in full roll mode. With kettle on and drink in hand, I went up to the bridge deck to admire nature in unbridled mode. Ten minutes later supper was ready, and with much anticipation I dished up a mulch of rice with neat factory-presented cubes of meat and sauce. Instantly my plate sailed over the edge of the saloon table, despite the non-skid mats, tipping half the contents on the velour seat next to David, and the remainder on the carpeted cabin sole. With fish slice in hand, I scooped up what was on the seat and put it on my plate, but stopped short when it came to the floor; that was consigned to the wet rubbish bag.

After the fiasco of supper, I felt the pangs of night starvation in the small hours. I had already been up out of my bunk to check for icebergs at least three times, and had kept resetting my alarm clock accordingly. This next time, with the Gardner engine thumping away, I crept over to the fridge and got the bottle of milk out; then I tried to deal with the maddening rattle across the cabin which I thought might be coming from under the port saloon berth. I lifted out the huge, heavy cushion with infinite care, followed by the plywood lid of the locker – as quiet as a mouse. Instantly there was a pale face leaning over the sofa back from the opposite side of the cabin.

'What are you doing *now*?'

A lot of muttering followed, and the sleeping vigilante subsided rather grumpily. Not many things went unnoticed by the captain.

One morning we had boiled eggs for breakfast, and I discovered that it took about six and quarter minutes in salt water to produce one which still had a soft yolk but a solidified white. When it came to lunch, I racked my brains, and in desperation decided to open a tin of tuna and mix it with other ingredients. Turning my back on David, who was sitting at the saloon table busying himself with the log, I pulled the ring on the top of the tin and peered round to see if he had noticed. He was still engrossed in writing, so I carefully levered off the top of the can and quietly tipped the contents into some rice. Oily fish was deemed very good for David, but unfortunately he had an aversion to sardines, and an even greater dislike of tuna, which had to be concealed with hot horseradish sauce if he was to eat it at all. The next moment, craning forward for a better look, he eyed me accusingly.

'Have you just opened a tin of tuna?' he said, with a frown of disapproval and a petulant set to the mouth.

I thought of the whole pack of sardine tins lying under the bunk still not opened, and wondered how many more circumnavigations they were destined to make.

We learned by email that *Dodo's Delight* was only now leaving Pond Inlet. At this time of year, it was best to press on with your objective. If you sat tight for too long waiting for ideal conditions, you were likely to be beset. Doug Pohl had sent us an email to say that Bellot Strait now had six-tenths ice and Prince Regent Inlet, which had taken us three days to transit, had seven-tenths, so we'd only just made it out in time, and thank goodness we hadn't headed south to the Hecla and Fury Strait. Doug also told us to expect 45 to 50 knots of wind right where we were going in the next twenty-four hours. A storm on the horizon, and this was corroborated by our ice grib, which David downloaded every five days.

We had been heading for the safety of the Fiskenaesset Fjord, which was now about 25 miles off. We crossed paths with our first vessel since leaving Fort Ross – a large red-and-white supply ship called *Royal Arctic Line*, a big powerful vessel carrying stores to the settlements and which also had the benefit of icebreaking capability. Although no icebergs had been seen for the last thirty-six hours, we were not far from the largest breeding ground in the world – the Vaigat, which calves at least 3,000 icebergs per year, roughly equivalent to one every three hours. These bergs are carried out and up north on the west Greenland current; they then circle round and ride down on the Labrador Current to the west of the Davis Strait, some of them drifting into the Lancaster Sound and elsewhere. We were only going to make the haven of Fisken-aesset by a short head as David said the wind was rising rapidly;

45 to 50 knots of wind was not to be trifled with. This was gale force 9/10 on the Beaufort Scale.

With great relief we arrived at the very small and rather delightful settlement in the dusk, right up in a narrow bight of the bay, and only just in time. We passed numerous rocky islands and skerries, reminiscent of Godhavn further to the north, at which we had stopped on our outward voyage. It looked most attractive, with a pretty array of wooden houses nestled at different angles on the hillside – green, indigo, mustard, white, blue and terracotta. We found a high floating steel pontoon with a derrick on it, and numerous large, wheeling gulls. There was a fishing boat ranged alongside, as there nearly always seems to be, but it had an inviting row of coloured pompoms bobbing down one side, and we circled up to it. Grabbing its rail with our boathook, we slowly pulled up to it, and I scrambled aboard and up to its bow, where David threw me a line. Like magic, two Greenlanders arrived: thin, wiry men – one young man with a shock of black hair, and the other a wizened elderly man who appeared to be the owner. Tying up a boat is the same the world over and language was unnecessary. Soon we were secure with some very long lines knotted together, and with grateful thanks – as darkness was imminent – we retreated below. We altered our clocks forward by yet another hour, making it a total of four in the last three days. We had been travelling eastwards for some days and had to advance the clock accordingly. David was not so attentive to this, and we had to play catch-up when he remembered.

At crack of dawn we were disturbed by clomps on deck as the fishermen next door arrived, and there was the sound of an engine starting up. Great boxes were being shovelled full of dry ice while David and I scrambled into our clothes, stumbling about in the dark, rocking on one leg while we pulled our trousers on. As we were lying to the outside of them, of course we had to move to release them. I felt somewhat resentful as the weather had deteriorated considerably and I would have thought it was obvious to anyone that conditions were not suitable, but perhaps these fishermen do not have the facility of a local forecast. David always seemed very calm at these moments, which would faze a lot of people.

'You better get ashore, so you can take the lines when they've gone,' said David.

I climbed over the freezer boxes and fishing tackle and scrambled up a vertical iron ladder to a slimy wooden baulk at the top, which I grabbed and hooked my arm over. There were a couple of pallets on the other side on top of the floating pontoon, and in almost complete darkness I hauled myself up and climbed over the top of them. There were two great cast-iron bollards with double horns and collar and, as I stumbled over to inspect one, I felt my shoes being sucked down into a gluey substance. I put my hand down gingerly to feel what it was, and my glove came up looking like a snowman. I had stood fairly and squarely in a huge lake of white paint that had been thrown out and was now growing a wrinkled skin across its surface, making it extremely glutinous – one does not normally expect to find pitfalls like this on a dockside.

The fishing boat moved away while David motored out into the darkness, leaving me feeling rather anxious and uneasy as my floating home disappeared, just the anchor light twinkling. Proceeding with considerable caution, he then motored back alongside the pontoon and we made ourselves secure. This entire manoeuvre had taken about two hours, but it was still only 7am (or 3am by the old time), so we climbed back into bed to try and catch up on sleep, only to find a little over an hour later, just as we were both sound asleep once more, that the same fishing boat came chuffing back to the jetty, which was no surprise to us. We sat tight and they tied up to the outside of us. The old skipper was quite experienced, and although David, relenting, had gone up to see if they needed a hand, it proved unnecessary. A small skiff then went heading out and the two men exchanged greetings. Our fisherman, who had recently returned to the quayside, gave a shake of his head, and with arm extended, waved it up and down in an undulating way – the gesture unmistakably indicating the 50 knots out in the bay from which they had retreated. Having done their good deed, they then stood around smoking and admiring *Polar Bound*'s sturdy shape, and discussing the finer points between themselves; it would have been interesting to know what they were saying.

TWENTY SEVEN

REFUGE IN THE FJORD

ALL THAT DAY IT RAINED WITHOUT CESSATION. I glanced at the iron ladder up which I had climbed the previous night. Any thought of doing the same today was arrested by the sight of an outlet just below the top rung that was gushing water like a geyser. Our boots would have filled in a moment. Our plans to go ashore thwarted, instead we spent the day cleaning the paint off my shoes, gloves and trousers, sorting stores and finding clean underwear and tea towels. David also lubricated the pump in the heads, which had virtually seized up again, after which it worked like a Rolls-Royce.

As the afternoon wore on, the wind freshened until by evening it was blowing a gale. *Polar Bound* bucked at the restraints we had put on her, and later that night David got up several times to check our lines. He even managed to double up the forward line by making a large bowline in the end of a rope and lassoing, with a whirling swing over his head, cowboy-fashion, the bollard above. I was most impressed that he had managed this feat alone and in the dark. By this time, he told me, it was blowing force 11 (50 knots), and had it not been for a small islet offering a modicum of lee, we could not have

269

remained where we were. The hawsers creaked and groaned under the load, and the large fishing buoy fenders we had acquired in Dutch Harbour squawked and protested as they repeatedly took the strain of *Polar Bound* plus that of the fishing boat secured alongside us.

The fishermen had left one of their windows open and David said he could hear an alarm going off on their bridge. Periodically the great plastic lids from their fish crates became airborne and slammed against our hull, some settling comfortably wedged on *Polar Bound*'s decks. The fishing boat snubbed and chucked at her warps like a race-horse in the starting gates, and tackle was thrown about on shore as polythene coverings were torn off and flapped with frustration. Through the murk thrown up on the windows of the bridge deck we could see the loom of a very large, deep-sea fishing trawler coming in for refuge, ablaze with navigation and floodlights, approaching with great caution up the rock-strewn channel towards us. They had evidently thought to go further past the bight we were in, to the small peninsula up the fjord, but changed their minds and retreated out towards the minimal shelter of the outlying skerries, with the raging seas beyond. All night they plied to and fro –at 300-foot depths in the channel there was nowhere to anchor and visibility at sea was virtually zero, so they had no other option. We had been extremely fortunate to find sanctuary against the small projecting jetty, but there was no more room in our small basin, only space for a few fishermen's skiffs.

The next morning the weather showed a marked improvement. The rain appeared to have stopped and gradually the squalls scudding across the water towards us in savage gusts abated. After break-fast we felt it safe to leave the boat and were just washing up when a small skinny man appeared, banging urgently on our door to ask rather incongruously if we would like to buy some rubies, and that he would be back later to show them to us. Some years ago, back in the hinterland, rose pink fragments had been visible in the rock, and ruby mining had begun. He went on to say that if we looked carefully while we were ashore, we would see rose-pink fragments in the hard rock. This turned out to be the case. However, when he came back at lunchtime, we were rather disappointed at the tiny size and had to turn him down.

After he had gone, we decided to make a reconnaissance of the settlement, and this time clambered ashore fairly easily as the tide was up. There was no need to mount the ladder again and end up in the paint mire, which by now lay under a lake of water.

Among the few sheds near the shore, we learned that there was a small supermarket – though it lacked any signage. It was very much a local affair, and we were surprised to find such a variety of things on offer to the small community of two hundred people. There were limited but varied vegetables and fruit, clothing, stationery, fresh bread, banking facilities, two guns priced at about 3,500 Danish kroner (about £420), and even supermarket trollies. We bought washing-up liquid and a new brush, a Galia melon, four nectarines, apples and pears, and two tomatoes; total cost about £12. We walked on through the settlement with its gaily painted wooden houses, and noticed among them two stone buildings. We visited the church, with Byzantine-ornamented interior and a small electric organ, and walked on over the hill down to the bay on the far side – in the sunshine this would have been quite beautiful. We passed a father with a son of four or so who was wrestling with a pair of caribou horns; they were draped around his shoulders and the still bloodied skull stared out over his back. Many houses we passed had a range of caribou horns nailed to their facades. Some of their washing lines were occupied by drying caribou hides stretched between wire mesh 'presses', as well as drying headless, gutted fish. We met a white-skinned Danish woman who spoke excellent English, and she filled us in with local directions and said that it had been a bad summer, and very windy. She also said that quite soon there would be six foot of snow lying over everything until the arrival of spring, but she added that the sea here did not freeze during the winter.

The far side of the promontory had an old wharf with bollards for the *Royal Arctic Line* icebreaker/supply ship to tie up to, and also a large, adjustable, locally made cradle on railway tracks that curved down into the sea. David thought it capable of lifting 50 tons, but there didn't appear to be a crane. The houses are accessed by small tracks of concrete sets, and many of the inhabitants had all-terrain vehicles which buzzed about carrying varied, and sometimes ambitious, loads; a door went flying past on one. We visited the small library at the back of the school and asked to use the internet; we were instantly connected, but I failed at the last fence, unable to access emails.

That night was quiet and peaceful, but we both found it difficult to sleep after the tumult of the last two days. At about 5.30 the thwarted fishermen from the neighbouring vessel came aboard again, retrieved the lids of their fish boxes from *Polar Bound* and cast off their lines from our Sampson posts before heading off for a few days' fishing. A couple of hours later David, too, decided to get under way, and went ashore to untie all our six warps, braving the water-filled quagmire of cast-out paint which had settled exactly where you needed to get ashore to make fast. He left me with a jumble of rope to sort out and the two huge fishing buoys to bring in, while he navigated *Polar Bound* out of our refuge and past the many rocky islets through the thick sea fog that had now rolled in. Despite our radar, you had to be extremely vigilant, as there were many hazards.

Some of the warps were contaminated with paint, which then transferred itself to the ship's gloves, and my fingers froze into senseless lumps. I was amazed that morning to glance at David's log, which is written on specially printed sheets, and to see that he had made no mention of the ferocious winds we had endured in Fiskenaesset, other than to say under his Observations Section that 'we were glad to have had the sanctuary of the place from the storm that raged outside'. 'Brevity' has to be his middle name, and he was certainly a master of understatement; we might just as well have been to Blackpool for the day.

Following our departure from Fiskenaesset Fjord, we had a calm day with variable winds, through which a gradual swell predominated from the northeast, freshening into a horizon of white breaking caps by supper-time. David called me up to see a huge whale that was ranging alongside *Polar Bound*, but by the time I arrived on the bridge deck, it had melted away into the depths, leaving only a smooth whirlpool to show where it had been; he said it was quite a bit longer than the boat, which is 48 feet.

The moon appeared, and just at bedtime so did the icebergs. It had become something of a spectator sport, and we had pole position with seats in the front row of the balcony. Despite the moon, the horizon dead ahead always appeared as a murky vista, and the icebergs delighted in hiding themselves from view until the eleventh hour.

It was virtually impossible to sleep when there were two yellow blobs on the radar, which we estimated were 7 or 8 miles ahead. Doing 6 knots, you would be upon them just as you were gaining oblivion. So that night I took up station in the captain's seat and waited. The tell-tale blob was large and sat right on the black line of our track. I called David when it finally emerged into the moonlight ahead of us – over 100 feet in height, a shimmering pinnacle, the top 30 feet or so bent over in a tortured spire and defaced with fracture veins, shocking in their bleak finality as the edifice could not hold together much longer. A great angled ramp jutted out and upwards over the sea and appeared to have no association with its mother ship, but beneath the water they were joined at the hip, and on the swell the hideous attachment slowly rose up and then, equally slowly, sank down beneath the water; a third family member like a smooth turret was to be seen clinging on the other side.

The following morning, in what was then an established gale with force 8 winds, we had a new parade of icebergs to port and starboard; all different, and all of interest. Two were completely smooth like alabaster, and David said they would have capsized from the vertical and been polished and honed by the action of the sea. To make matters worse, after a near sleepless night, it wasn't surprising that the stove got inadvertently turned off with an expectant saucepan of porridge, and a kettle for the tea never seemed to reach boiling point. We finally finished breakfast at lunchtime. David was always immensely good-natured on these occasions, though it did cross my mind that perhaps he had replaced the handle for lifting the ring on the hob, which was removed when it rattled irritatingly at night, and in doing so had accidentally hit the knob himself.

David said he had never seen so many icebergs on the southwest corner of Greenland before, and thought they had calved from the east coast and been carried down around Cape Farewell, and were still travelling on the current, remorselessly clawing their way back up the west side, only to circle around at the top and join the Labrador Current coming south again at Baffin Bay on the west of the Davis Strait. We seemed to have been charging down the coast of Greenland for a long time; it is a vast country, 1,500 miles in length, so this was not surprising, as we only averaged about 120 miles in 24 hours.

When evening approached, David decided to drift as the sea was by now quite calm, but there were still many icebergs about and we awaited the dawn to get under way to enter Julianehåb, the largest town in southwest Greenland, otherwise known as Qaqortoq, and easiest to remember as 'Quackertalk'. For once, we had a straightforward, smooth arrival, and went alongside a big, stable, concrete jetty. Here David took on about 440 gallons of diesel. A bright yellow fuel bowser arrived and the driver came on board and filled us up himself, with David dancing attendance with rags for the odd spillage, and diving down numerous times first into the forward hold, then the engine room, to monitor progress into the respective tanks.

We also took on water. At the Texaco building, which we were almost alongside, a man came out and unrolled a huge canvas fire hose. Halfway through filling our water tank, David produced our two spare water canisters. Upon filling the first one up, which was transparent, it was discovered that the water was the colour of lemon juice. We asked the man on the quay if he was putting diesel into our water tank, whereupon two more men emerged from the building, and there was consternation all round. After some fiddling with the hose, they gave it full blast into the sea in a great arc until it had cleared; there must have been some sediment lying in the hose which had caused the problem. The source of the water was a sparkling little burn cascading and tumbling over its rocky bed down through the middle of this small township. It reminded me of the Scottish water in the Highlands. As the 3,500 inhabitants of this locality drank from it, it couldn't be too harmful.

After completion of the bunkering, we decided to take a walk about the place, which we found to be spotless. It reminded me of Denmark with its colourful houses, the small marina of local skiffs, and a large untidy-looking shipyard. By the quayside, under a covered area, was a weekly sale of seal and whale meat, and also lamb from local sheep farming, which I was delighted to see. I had to buy a whole leg of lamb as the stallholder had neither knife nor saw. It looked quite good, with plenty of fat on it, and when we returned to the boat,

275

David produced a small hacksaw and we carved it up into three joints. The man also gave me two plump little chump chops that we ate for supper that night – they proved very good, and the rest went into our small deep-freeze chest.

I was rather upset to see the whale meat with its thick layer of blubber, white with the outer black skin, which had been cut into manageable pieces about 2 or 3 inches thick. The locals called this chewy, oily-looking substance *muktuk*. They ate it raw, and it was very popular. Apparently they live to their eighties and have few diseases – we saw no overweight people. There were two supermarkets and we did a last shop, stocking up with fresh fruit, eggs and local bread, and so finally *Polar Bound* was ready for the final leg, from Cape Farewell across the North Atlantic to Scotland, a distance of 1,500 miles, although we still had quite a way to go to reach the cape and our departure point, and would put in a brief visit to a small settlement in Prins Christian Sund, which I much looked forward to.

TWENTY EIGHT

NANORTALIK AND CAPE FAREWELL TO NORTHERN IRELAND

W E LEFT AT TEATIME THE FOLLOWING DAY. It was late September and we had to be on our way. Motoring away from the coast out to sea, we passed quite a collection of icebergs that had grounded themselves in the shallow water – reminiscent of Monument Valley in Utah/Arizona. There were two small speed boats systematically working their way across an area of sea, facing in opposite directions and then coming together again, scouring the mirror-calm surface; we heard the crack of a rifle from one of the men standing in the bow and were upset to realise they were firing at seals. They cannot be blamed for utilising the weapons to which their forebears were introduced by early explorers and visitors from overseas, but the outcome of it is that they sometimes succeed only in wounding their prey, and if they are unable to reach it in time to recover it, it may well sink in its death throes and be lost to the hunters. This can happen in the case of whales, too, as we have seen. There is no legislation prohibiting this indiscriminate slaughter. Only a few minutes before, we had seen the furry face of a seal popping up

277

out of the water several times to take a look at us – they are inquisitive things and have no idea that a predator may await them with a gun.

As we were washing up after supper in the evening, there was a tremendous bang and crunching sound; we were almost knocked off our feet, and scrambled up the companionway to see what we had hit. It was a growler, now disappearing to our stern – it certainly gave me quite a fright. David has immense confidence in the strength of the construction of his boat, and appeared quite nonchalant. Nevertheless, despite his assertions, I did notice him the following morning on his hands and knees peering over the bows.

The alarm clock, together with the alarm on the autopilot monitor, which squawks if the cursor moves off its target, is very reliable. That night we kept a two-hour vigil and lay a'hull, just drifting – wonderfully peaceful, with only the sound of the water gurgling under the keel. The boat barely moved and, after two hours, I went up and outside on deck to look at the sky – a velvet dark night, with a panoply of stars, glittering like jewels, and the incredible sight of the Milky Way, something I remembered my father pointing out to me as a child, but which in recent years has been hidden from sight by light pollution in the industrialised world.

On the morning of Sunday 29 September we were once again assailed by fog, but still with a mirror-calm sea, which surprised David, who said that normally this is the windiest part of the world. We were headed for Nanortalik, a settlement about 25 miles north of Cape Farewell, and as we closed the bay we were surrounded by icebergs on all sides, together with growlers and brash ice. At a safe distance we circled one very unstable, vast iceberg, from which David had seen a chunk fall into the sea. It had a crack from top to bottom which, even as we watched, appeared to widen significantly, with fracture lines visible in a number of places. I suggested to David that he might try and shoot into one of the cracks in the hope that the implosion would cause the iceberg to sever into two pieces. He agreed to try and so I got out his Browning 270, cocooned by my furry purchases from Alaska, and he loaded it with four huge slugs. The noise was deafening as it ricocheted off the iceberg; I was standing in the airlock between the outer watertight door and inner one, with camera ready to photograph him and the anticipated explosion and tidal wave, but nothing dramatic happened.

We reached Nanortalik later that day. Rather conveniently, just as we arrived, an old green fishing hulk pulled away and we took their place. We spent a quiet day, with a lunchtime siesta to make up for lost sleep, then a walk onshore afterwards. Being a Sunday, few people were around in the settlement. The houses were spread out at random on any low rocks where foundations would sit happily. There was a supermarket, tourist office, fish outlet, hospital, boatyard and slip, with an interesting adapted haul-out for boats up to about 50 tons. David was quite interested in this and took a number of photographs. Apart from the iron wheels to carry the equipage, it also had eight rubber tyres, set lower – two on each side of the iron ones, which made it more versatile, and a mechanism to enable it to swing sideways, with the rubber wheels to lift its load clear of the tracks and place it elsewhere.

The next day, before leaving, we visited the tourist office. The population now seemed more in evidence and the girl in the visitors' centre was most welcoming and spoke excellent English. There was quite a selection of things for sale, but many of them had been imported from Canada – sealskin boots with elegant heels and neat front zips at a cost of £450, or snug furry mittens, slippers trimmed with fur, waistcoats and quite a lot of outerwear, gold jewellery (the goldmine nearby still being worked), bone jewellery and rather poor ivory and bone carvings. We escaped with some lenticular postcards, which David bought, then went to take a look at the old stone buildings from earlier times, one of which had now been converted to a museum housing contemporary artefacts.

There was an old bakery; a tiny building that had served first as a school, then a police station, then a youth club and lastly a hospital – all now long defunct; a shipwright; a building with great vats outside that had been used for processing whale blubber, and a lookout point reached by a flight of incredibly steep wooden steps mounted on top of a rather singular rock. Another rock we passed had a remarkable profile of a hatchet-faced man with heavy eyebrows, large pointed nose and a great chin with a cleft – a freak of geology. Later we found a postcard of this in the supermarket. The wooden church, very Danish in its form, constructed like a huge 'A', was quite attractive with external bracing boards, and dated from 1916.

On 1 October we set off on our final leg to the southern tip of Greenland. Leaving the harbour, we passed some rounded outlying rocks; on the far side of them was a group of about fifteen men in overalls who had arrived there in a number of skiffs. Laid out on the smooth face of the rock was a substantial quantity of butchered whale. They seemed preoccupied and David, curious to see what they were doing, circled *Polar Bound* around to take a closer look and photograph the scene, at which they all turned away to hide their faces from us. I went out on deck to look through my binoculars and take a couple of pictures, and every now and again, after several minutes, one would look round to see if we were still watching them. Clearly they didn't want to be recognised, so possibly it was illegal to have caught a whale. *Polar Bound*, with her smart livery and purposeful appearance, does look quite official, and no doubt they thought David might be some kind of inspector taking an interest in their activities.

A bit further on, when we got clear from Nanortalik, David located our fractured iceberg from the previous day, and we were disappointed to find that it had still not succumbed to his bombardment.

We finally reached Prins Christian Sund later on that day. This sound, approximately 60 miles in length, is spectacular beyond belief and I had longed to see it again. In August 2012 we traversed it east to west, and this time we were entering from the west. It effectively cuts off the tip of Greenland at Cape Farewell, in David's view the roughest cape in the world. The feeling of awe and majesty that is inspired by these towering mountains up to 6,000 feet in height, some near vertical, standing like sentinels with their ice-cap topping, is hard to put into words. If I were religious, this is where I would find my god.

The western entrance to the sound, through which we were now passing, must have seen tumultuous geological upheavals. The skyline is filled with unscaleable razor-sharp pinnacles and minarets. Rising against the azure sky, and with dark grey water gently lapping at their base where they emerge from the depths below, their timeless mighty stature conquered all human pretensions and brought me down to the size of an atom.

Our final port of call, before setting off into the North Atlantic, and which we had visited on our way north the previous August, was Augpilagtoq. This very small, beautiful, natural harbour nestles behind a vast rounded boulder. The entrance, in what is essentially a cleft in the rock, is barely 60 feet wide. From the outside there is no evidence of any kind of habitation. The only concession was a navigation light placed on the top of the rock to mark the entrance, which was a comforting sight when arriving in the dusk. The alternative was to try for one of the few anchorages marked on the chart, but they are mostly very deep and steeply shelving, and there was also the risk of fierce down-draughts from the mountains all around.

In the gathering darkness we motored up to the small projecting wharf. I received the usual stern warnings from David as to how nimble and quick I must be as he would only have one stab at coming alongside the narrow slot adjacent to the high wooden quay. However, on this occasion, it did not seem such a fearful obstacle as it had been before, possibly because it was nearly high water. Not much escapes the locals and almost immediately a small family came wandering down to the jetty to help with our lines, and we were soon secure.

No sooner had I got started on supper preparations than a peremptory command issued from David – 'Jane! Come and help!' I dashed up, and there was the same old green fishing trawler that had been at our berth in Nanortalik. They rafted up next to us and, once secure, disappeared to the shore, possibly to stay with relations who lived in one of the wooden houses. After supper, a third, smaller boat arrived, and tied on to the trawler, and we recollected that we had seen them, too, at Nanortalik, so it seemed that they were all friends and were off on a fishing trip together. We were now three abreast, all hanging on *Polar Bound*'s warps. They too went ashore, and total silence enveloped us except for the gentle splashing of the waterfall nearby. A few twinkling lights lent intimacy to the scene, some reflected in the tiny little bay so well protected by the gigantic boulder we had circumvented.

Morning was heralded by heavy boots on deck as the occupants of the outlying small boat boarded their vessel and manoeuvred themselves around to the free side of the wharf before re-securing her to allow their friends in the green fishing trawler to get under way. After breakfast we went ashore and visited the small supermarket. Considering there are only about 123 inhabitants of this isolated community, it seemed to sell all the essentials, although fresh green vegetables were non-existent. I was surprised by the sophistication of their personal hygiene; when I was a child at school, we were required to draw pictures of igloos, and learned that the women washed their hair in their own urine, which made it gleam. Now the shelves stocked shampoo and personal toiletries such as pant liners, sanitary towels and tampons. There were also fishing nets, a small selection of tools and electrical equipment, clothing, frozen food and, best of all, the most wonderful long loaves of fresh bread, the outside covered in seeds, quite dense and satisfying. On another shelf were guns for sale at 7,000 kroner (about £1,000).

Outside, on a nearby rock, we spotted the owner of the smaller fishing boat, which was still tied up near us. He had a couple of discreet polythene bags at his feet, with whale meat quite clearly in evidence, and a customer was just getting out his wallet to pay. It was evident that the green fishing trawler had brought some of the whale meat that we had seen being butchered at Nanortalik along to this settlement, rafted up to his friends in their small boat and passed some to him to sell locally, rather covertly we thought.

We got under way again soon after this, and as we progressed along the sound, which had one or two gentle bends and junctions with branches forking off in a couple of places, we identified two of the anchorages marked on the chart. In the cold light of day they did look vulnerable to ferocious gusts. We encountered a bank of thin fog as we neared the southern end, and a quantity of brash ice bobbing on the water – even one small, lonely, rogue iceberg, which had drifted in. Just at the exit from the sound, there is a building set back from the foreshore: the Greenlander Weather Station, which monitors conditions. Rumour has it that, being quite lonely work, they are always pleased to see visitors, and will offer a cup of something hot if you take the trouble to secure yourself and go ashore. It wasn't easy to see where you could find any place to tie up, but it must be feasible; so far David has not tried it and on this occasion he was anxious to set off across the North Atlantic as time was creeping on.

For a while now I had been noticing that my corduroy trousers had got loose at the waist and I was forever hitching them up. I couldn't understand it, and thought the elastic must be getting worn out. So when I was stark naked doing my ablutions, I had a good look at myself. I was rather appalled to see that my bosoms had almost disappeared and my ribs and hipbones were projecting like an old nag's – I was quite shocked. With no big mirror to see myself in I had not realised that the virtually fat-free diet I was trying to give David didn't suit me. I showed myself to David and he gallantly said, 'Nonsense – of course you haven't lost weight,' but he did go and rummage in the forward hold and came back with a food supplement. David seems to think of everything. It would never have occurred to me to pack away a large tin of food supplement. Like a lot of the other stores it had seen better days. Nevertheless, I diligently took it every day all the way home until the tin was empty; I didn't notice much difference, though. When we were next able to get on some scales I discovered that I had lost nearly fourteen pounds in weight, while David had actually gained a couple. On his return, the staff in his office said how well he was looking. Normally he comes back from these long trips looking rather emaciated and tired.

As we pulled away from the land and headed out into the North Atlantic I felt quite vulnerable, especially since there were dire weather warnings from Douglas Pohl. He had received word of a storm due in our vicinity in three days, followed by two lows in quick succession. We were heading into a horrible, grey ugly sea almost on the boat's nose, so we could well believe him.

The following day what was forecast came to pass, though rather sooner; the glass had dropped dramatically and the seas were monumental. David says it was blowing force 9 or 10, and also that the seas in high latitudes are always larger than those to the south. I was ensconced in the heads when I felt that split-second's hesitation that comes just before you are struck by a titanic wave, followed instantly by a sickening thud, rather like a crash, as if we had hit a brick wall. When I reappeared, David was standing on the bridge deck. An absolute master of understatement, he called out, 'That was quite an impressive sea that struck us, and it took a time to reorganise itself.'

He ordered me up into the wheelhouse to take a look, and asked me if these were the kind of seas my husband and I had seen in *Golden Harvest*, our Bowman 40-foot sailing boat. I had never seen such big seas – they were like vast blocks of flats with foaming white tops stretching to the horizon, with here and there a particular monster riding way above the rest, marched with towering determination to conquer all in its path.

The satellite compass, which is linked to the autopilot and steers the boat, kept losing orientation and setting all the alarms off so that the boat didn't know which way she was going. When this happens, it necessitates cancelling the autopilot and reminding yourself of the course you should be steering. The trick is to look at David's log if you cannot remember; this will be a true course – you must deduct the variation, or, depending which hemisphere you are in, add it (in this case it was 30 degrees) – then steer using the binnacle. Once the desired course is achieved, you can then quickly reset the satellite compass. If it is not absolutely spot-on, click a switch to add or deduct a degree for accuracy. Matters were not helped by the fact that the wonderful Sestrel magnetic compass has ceased production, and the spare bulb needed to light it at night was no longer available, so it was necessary to use a torch. It is very sad that these household names are folding all over the country. At one time Sestrel were the principal suppliers of compasses and nearly every yachtsman had one on their binnacle.

As quickly as it arrived, so this tremendous gale blew away. The following morning I did not wash and dress, but I did stagger about and make a cup of tea. We also had a couple of rye biscuits with Marmite followed by an apple each. After this, I decided the safest place was bed, but David had got up. I surfaced after lunch when things had quietened down a bit.

What a vast ocean we were in. Nearly 1,000 miles since we left Cape Farewell and we only had schools of dolphins and seabirds for company. At night, with Orion's belt visible in a clear, starry sky, the glass rose from 967 to 1,006 millibars. David chose the next morning, lying back on my bunk like a caliph, to dictate emails to me. Outside it was blowing force 7, but thankfully, for once, from astern. Nevertheless this generated a big roll, and when I looked up from the saloon through the open door by the companionway to the wheelhouse above, the sky described a huge arc overhead with scudding clouds, and every few seconds great waves soared past the saloon portholes. We saw a supertanker coming up behind us, most probably doing about 10 knots. They are vast; something like a fifth of a mile long.

The glass rose to 1,009, but despite this the North Atlantic was in full majesty with mountainous seas and steep walls of angry black water. Her marching soldiers were dressed with gleaming helmets and frothy plumes atop, but their ranks were disorderly. They were in confusion and tumbling in their eagerness to be on their way as they jostled and pushed each other aside for supremacy, their receding backs with spent foam starkly white, and sparkling droplets in the intermittent sunlight, only once more to regroup some distance ahead gathering themselves for the next onslaught. Every once in a while a towering Matterhorn of a sea would rise up, mightier and more menacing than all around it. Surprisingly, the barometer was steady. The sky was full of scudding strands of grey cloud interspersed with thin sunshine, and even a huge arching rainbow to add to the drama, under which the constant tumble of seabirds as they wheeled and fell back again against the savage gusts of wind kept us entertained.

We were nearing the north coast of Ireland and were in differing frames of mind. David was unhappy at the waywardness of one or two members of his staff in his absence, and he had various plans in the offing that were preoccupying him. As we neared our destination, the thought of office work loomed once more, and the realisation dawned that something that had been conveniently languishing on the back-burner might now have to acted upon, and decisions made, the closer we got to land.

For my part, I was filled with ambition to make more of my music; to lay plans for returning to Italy to improve my Italian, and to find two kittens to 'make my house a home' (as we are constantly urged to do in some advertising jingle). We were nearing the end of our voyage and were both disappointed that we had been unable to fulfil David's wish to transit through the Hecla and Fury Strait.

At this point we had to heave to for about four hours as the surges of the following seas became too great and David thought his gearbox and governor would be damaged as *Polar Bound* struggled to correct her course. The seabirds loved the tumult and wheeled low over the waves to land. They banked and drifted and, when nearly at touchdown, their skittering feet just made contact with the water, preparatory to doing a side slip as they settled down. Later we got under way again, but the conditions had barely improved. We were then soon into soundings, and I also found I could get a signal on my mobile telephone, which up to this point had been left lying in my bag.

The last twenty-four hours had been relentless, with the wind blowing at the top end of force 7 and 8 and with a rolling, heaving sea. We were slapped and banged on our topsides by mischievous waves, and had been on high alert for fear of being thrown at the last fence and hurled around. You could not relax for a second; mugs of tea and cups of water were sent flying; missiles from every quarter were imminent. There was a new moon just visible above the swaying skyline and, by day, new, bigger, different seabirds to look at – more overall grey in colour with longer beaks and tails, and altogether more drab. We were tearing along like a helter-skelter downwind towards our destination of Portrush. It was low tide, but the harbour master said we should be all right crossing the bar. I sent both my children a text message to say that we were in the Western Approaches and just into soundings, and my daughter rang within half an hour – it was delightful to hear her chirpy voice again. My son's reaction was something different; his response by text message was: 'R U back? Lots 2 chat about. Pls call me!' Evidently there was an economy drive in force.

Portrush has a straightforward but narrow entrance into a man-made harbour. On approaching with a following sea we had the alarming sensation of surfing along on the wave tops directly into a bay of frothing water breaking on the beach. We were scanning the water for any sign of the two entrance buoys, which were concealed by the backsides of the waves. Just as we were beginning to get apprehensive, two clear red markers appeared at either side of the rocky breakwater, and within lay a welcoming harbour with a few boats on moorings to starboard, and to port the harbour quay with a pontoon lying alongside. David, far from slowing down, put on a big spurt as we approached the entrance in order to maintain steerage for the sharp turn, and in moments we were snugly inside and confronted by the reassuring sight of the United Kingdom offshore lifeboat, a 17-metre class Severn snuggled up between two large, red, iron mooring buoys.

It was 3.30pm on 10 October, and we had arrived at Portrush, nine days after leaving Cape Farewell, having experienced stormy seas and mountainous waves in the North Atlantic, which had lived up to its fearsome reputation.

We tied up to the pontoon then took stock of our peaceful location while we had a cup of tea before walking up the hill into the heart of Portrush, past all its pretty painted Regency houses, to a good vegetable shop and the second-hand bookshop. David suggested dinner ashore and it was a marvellous thought not to have to cook that evening. I even found a hairdresser who would cut and wash my hair the following morning so I could start feeling civilised again.

TWENTY NINE

FROM PORTRUSH, NORTHERN IRELAND TO SCOTLAND

WE SPENT A WONDERFUL EVENING IN PORTRUSH after the previous days of tumultuous conditions. A helpful new harbour master, Robert, a retired Merchant Navy captain, made us welcome, and with the key to the shower we were able to indulge in some lukewarm water, which kept turning itself off if you pushed the dial up. Clean clothes had to be sought out for David, but as my wardrobe was not extensive I made do with clean underwear. We were tied up alongside the floating pontoon, which made life easier because no adjustments were necessary to the warps with the rise and fall of the tide. David took me out to a delicious dinner at the Mermaid down on the harbour, just a few steps away, and we had a very good evening. It was such fun, and so relaxing not to have to think about what to cook, and instead to have a choice from which to select, and someone else to do all the work – and the washing-up afterwards.

The management own the whole building overlooking the harbour. Below is a wine bar, and on the ground floor a pizza house;

so something for everyone, and the procession of cars and taxis down on to the quay from 5pm onwards provided evidence of the place's popularity. Last orders in the restaurant were at 10pm, and we were told that on Saturdays you might have to queue for three hours. We both had roasted crispy duck breast with little medallions of potatoes underneath, and then made the mistake of ordering an additional bowl of Jersey Royals. However, a doggy bag was obligingly provided, and another meal half catered for in advance. The restaurant was absolutely full and with all the chattering voices it sounded like an aviary – any music would have been drowned out.

We had barely finished breakfast the next morning when the harbour master, somewhat excited by our arrival, brought the first of a few visitors to see us. The first was a newspaper reporter, who took lots of photos and quizzed me. David often hides at these moments, saying, '*You* talk to them.' Later came a rather hyperactive, energetic man in his mid-fifties, Robin, who was immensely interested in David's adventures. He had seen the framed photo of *Polar Bound* in the Harbour Office, and enthused at length. He and his wife, Janet, could not have been more kind. He insisted on taking us to look at the Giant's Causeway. We had such a busy day that in the event we did not get away until about 6.30pm, with the result that we arrived at dusk, and so, ignoring the rules, Robin drove us right to this extraordinary freak of nature, and we picked our way around the promontory of the basalt hexagons, which are like sentinels faceted together, one layer upon another, dating from the Tertiary period some 60–65 million years ago. The National Trust have introduced something of an eyesore on the site with fixed red iron posts which can be utilised for throwing lines in case anyone falls into the water.

It was a great privilege to have solitude during our private conducted tour around these geological fantasy formations. Judging from the enormous car park, they must be inundated in the tourist season. The dusky evening, and dramatic cliffs with castle ruins silhouetted by the sinking sun, gave a certain mystical enchantment to our visit. Robin, hopping over the rocks ahead of us, was eager to point out the incised signatures and dates cut into some of the stones. David spotted one dating from the early eighteenth century. A number of people had even driven a coin between the rocks in a few places for good luck, and posterity.

Robin then dropped us back at the boat, and hardly had he driven away than we received a telephone call to say that we were expected for breakfast the following morning, and that he would pick us up at nine. We were duly collected and given a delicious breakfast by Janet. After this feast, their daughter, Kate, who is a beautician, gave me a back massage – a heavenly experience, after all the hauling and heaving about of five-gallon oil cans over past months. Various oils and unguents were worked into my aching muscles, followed by the application of some heated basalt stone. I felt very much relaxed.

This family are deeply committed to helping the local community; Robin works at the Adventure Centre, involving young people in kayaking, canoeing and bicycling, among other things. He also took us some distance to a boatyard to see his boat, the famous *Wild Goose*, originally a ketch, and formerly owned by Wallace Clark, father of the author Miles Clark, who died tragically young after completing a remarkable voyage from the Arctic to the Black Sea through Russia – the first Westerner to do so since the Vikings.

Miles wrote a superb biography of his godfather, Miles Smeeton, entitled *High Endeavours*, a masterpiece of exemplary research and fluent literary style. Beryl and Miles Smeeton made history in their famous yacht *Tzu Hang* when they capsized on two separate voyages, both times rounding Cape Horn, and through their tenacity and Beryl's courage, survived both ordeals and saved the boat. Their well-known book, *Once is Enough*, describes their adventures.

Wild Goose came into Robin's hands when Wallace Clark, in his early eighties, mistook the entrance to Portrush harbour in darkness and ran aground on the beach. It was about 4.30 in the morning. He and his crew stepped ashore, and the lifeboat arrived and attempted to rescue the boat; through mishap, they pulled her under the water and she sank. Robin salvaged her and paid £1 for her. At the boat-yard, we found a ladder, climbed up and unfolded sufficient of the tarpaulin cover to gain access and make an inspection. It gave me a strange feeling to be aboard this boat. I had much admiration for Miles Clark after reading excellent reviews of his book. I had brought both the book and the two postcards I had received from him aboard *Polar Bound* for David to read, and he had been spellbound.

Wild Goose was not a big boat, her displacement only 10 tons, and she appeared distinctly fragile. She would not have stood up to any robust ocean crossings. However, she had been sailed by Miles Clark and that was good enough for me. Compared to modern yachts with their caravan interiors, she retained that damp, oily, boaty atmosphere, with water-stained cushions and mildew clinging to the wardrobe. Her tiny cockpit seemed snug and safe, and had a dark teak sliding hatch on a slant; very traditional. The interior had two little swinging paraffin lamps in gimbals, and the galley, with curtained-off area for the heads, was forward of the saloon, with a tiny fo'csle in the bow, which apparently originally had two pipe cots above the bunks. Robin had done away with the mizzen, but in all other respects he had faithfully adhered to the original colour scheme, and used recycled materials, even down to old nails and screws for authenticity – a most admirable restoration project.

We sat down in the tiny saloon, perched on the edge of some very damp cushions and, with great ceremony, Robin produced a flask of local whiskey – Bushmills with honey, and poured some into a wassail (loving cup) made of pewter, which he drew out of a soft wrapping cloth. We might almost have been receiving Communion. We passed it around, having first offered a toast to the former owners of *Wild Goose*. Later we signed her original, water-stained visitors' book, which Robin had salvaged, and which had some very interesting and famous names in it, a few of which I recognised from my childhood.

The next morning – our last, before leaving on the final home stretch – Robin arrived once more, this time with a trailer-load of kayaks and some suitable clothing and, after kitting us out, launched us individually in these most tipply of craft. We paddled around the harbour in the early morning sunshine on a perfect beginner's day – tranquil sea, little tide or wind and wonderfully flat calm water; all great confidence builders. It was fun, but we had to leave on the tide, and by midday, with a small party of well-wishers on the shore, including a couple of journalists, we were away on our final leg. It was a long, tiring and uncomfortable passage across the North Channel to the Kintyre peninsula in Scotland. Passing up the east coast, we finally arrived at 11.30pm and anchored at Carrodale.

Our last night was spent at the Kyles of Bute, but not without a minor slip. Entering Loch Riddon, which dries out some length from its head, we didn't appear to be making much progress. David consulted the chart anxiously, then, blinking like a puzzled professor, announced, 'I believe we're aground.' Sure enough, our final anchorage shelved so steeply, so suddenly, that we found ourselves lodged on the bottom. *Polar Bound*, wishing to show her independence for once, had to be coaxed and cajoled with the greatest tenderness to release her grip on the seabed. However, all was well, and we spent a beautiful and peaceful evening in this sparsely populated backwater, with minimal lights to intrude in the velvety blackness, and only an occasional call from the Barn Owl searching for a mate.

The next morning, 15 October 2013, we awoke quite early and, hauling up the anchor without further problems, got under way, eating our breakfast as we went. My few visits to Scotland in past years had all been by car, so this gave me a different perspective, as we made our way through myriad islands and islets. It was cold, and the weather a mixture of sunshine and showers. We rounded the point and continued up the Firth of Clyde. Round the next point lay Gourock and Greenock, and consequently a lot of shipping. After the loneliness of the oceans and seas we had voyaged through, it seemed immensely busy and we had to be attentive: ferries scurrying here and there, private sailing boats, some police launches. Plenty of the last, as we were now approaching Rosneath Peninsula on the Gare Loch where the Trident submarine is housed.

David's boatyard is on the opposite side of Rosneath, looking towards Rhu. It has a slipway and a short length of pier with a floating pontoon, to which you can tie up at any stage of the tide. On the shore behind are two huge, high-roofed sheds housing a number of sizeable boats of every description, with a large area of hard-standing for those who prefer to lay up their boats outside. I was looking forward to being shown around, and to seeing the wooden prototype of *Polar Bound*.

It was getting late in the afternoon as we circled rou   Gare Loch to make the final approach. Our reception comm of the yard manager Alan Sadowski, his wife Patrici tant, plus two little white Scottie dogs. They ha telephone of our imminent arrival and were st lot of waving and, as always at such moments right. I had consulted David about how h

295

floating pontoon as there was a stiff wind blowing, and had suggested getting the longer lines out from the after-locker, but he had requested the shorter ones. In the event these had to be changed in a hurry. We were hauled alongside against the wind, which was trying to push us off, and the faithful Gardner engine was finally switched off.

The following day, loads of stores and heavy equipment were lifted out with the aid of the Manitu and its fork-lift capabilities, preparatory to floating *Polar Bound* onto her cradle. This had to be put into the water at low tide so we could slide onto her as the tide rose. After this, with David driving the Manitu in front and Alan behind in his excavator, she was slowly and carefully hauled up the slip into the big shed where she was chocked up to steady her, ready for work to commence on a major refit.

David had navigated us safely through a voyage of 22,000 miles of potentially dangerous waters, always keeping calm, always anticipating the requirements of the route and taking the necessary steps to give us safe passage. How he managed to make these long voyages, and world circumnavigations alone, with minimal supporting equipment in the early years, is truly remarkable. He was only the seventeenth person ever to transit the Northwest Passage, over 30 years ago, when there was considerably more ice around. He is a gentleman adventurer of the old school who has achieved new records for the honour of his country without the rodomontade of many of his peers who have been awarded the highest accolade for many lesser feats. Thank you, David, for a marvellous and unforgettable experience.

There are always mixed emotions at these moments when one chapter over, and the next not yet determined – how, and where, only fate te, and fate very nearly decreed that my life was over.

Before the boat could be emptied of her contents, the containers standing in one of the huge sheds at the boatyard had to be cleared out, swept, and heavy metal shelving put up in them, on which to store everything. This operation, which necessitated erecting vertical metal braces, slotting in supporting cross bars, then finally placing the heavy chipboard shelves on top, took a couple of days to complete.

The shelves were long and it was as much as I could do to carry one on my own, tucked under my arm. Before we started putting any items on them, David thought it would be a good idea to place protective squares of plywood under the sharp metal legs to distribute the weight and prevent the container flooring getting damaged. The manager, Alan, went off and came back a few minutes later with some squares of ply, and I volunteered to push them under the legs while Alan and David lifted each end.

The problem came when the shelving stack across the end of the container had to be lifted; being in the corner, it was awkward, and I grovelled on my stomach underneath to reach in far enough, while David, with his foot on the shelf above my head, grabbed the framework to haul it up. Quite unexpectedly, the great slab of chipboard of the lowest shelf collapsed, and one side of it crashed down on to the back of my head.

My face was screwed round sideways by the impact, and the pain was excruciating, blinding. I thought that my life was over – snuffed out by a piece of chipboard. It seemed an eternity before the weight could be released from my head. Finally, I squirmed out backwards and was helped to my feet. My head felt as if it would burst, the pain was so intense. Tears poured down my face, which was grazed from pressure against the flooring. I felt the back of my head very gingerly, expecting to find a bloody mess, but there wasn't any – not even a haematoma. I subsequently learned that I could have died within twenty minutes from a subdural haematoma, which is when a swelling has no outlet other than to press against the brain which causes death within half an hour or so.

I tried to speak, thinking that I must have lost all brain power, but the yard manager silenced my efforts and said, 'Don't say anything – believe me. It's best if you just stay quiet – I'll get you a chair.' David put his arm around my shoulders with great tenderness and concern. They offered to take me to hospital, but I put on a nonchalant manner and said I was fine. I took three paracetamol and, after an hour or so of sitting quite still, I wandered off down to *Polar Bound* afloat alongside the pontoon, thankful to be able to climb down a ladder and get aboard without incident. I lit the diesel stove for the last time to generate some warmth and comfort aboard, grateful to find that there was still life ahead of me.

THE FINDING OF THE
EREBUS AND THE *TERROR*

B ACK IN MID-NINETEENTH-CENTURY ENGLAND, the Franklin Expedition was a voyage of enormous interest. The hopes of the nation were vested in an expedition which was equipped like no other, and whose purpose was, once and for all, to discover the shortest possible route from the Atlantic to the Pacific, and therefore open up trade to the east without the necessity to undertake the lengthy and perilous voyage around Cape Horn. The expedition set out in 1845 under the command of Sir John Franklin, my four-greats uncle, in the ships *Erebus* and *Terror*, and never returned.

Many search expeditions were sent by England and the United States and by Franklin's wife, Lady Jane herself. In desperation, having already sent out three vessels and used up much of her capital, Lady Jane bought a fourth ship in Aberdeen in 1857 – a screw yacht, the *Fox*, 124 feet in length by 24 feet broad, and bearing a draught of 13 feet and 177 tons burthen. She engaged the services of Captain McClintock (later to be knighted) to search for her husband, together with a complement of twenty-five crew.

The *Fox* overwintered in Port Kennedy, an inlet off the Bellot Strait between Somerset Island and the Boothia Peninsula. From here,

McClintock made several lengthy expeditions by sledge to search for Franklin. His success came in the spring of 1859 when on one of his sledging journeys he and his lieutenant, Hobson, came upon the cairn where a record was found of the Franklin expedition right up to 25 April 1848; Franklin himself died on 11 June 1847, as revealed by a note found under the cairn, stating that Sir John had died on board. McClintock and Hobson learned also that the 110 men who had set out for the Fish River all died on that terrible journey.

Willingham Franklin Rawnsley, Sir John's nephew and godson, wrote *The Life, Diaries and Correspondence of Jane Lady Franklin 1792–1875*, published in the USA in 1923:

> *Two officers and six men had left the ships on Friday, May 24th 1847. They had taken four days to reach Point Victory, and no doubt pushed on to Cape Herschell, where they would sight the American coast, and know that from thence "it was all plain sailing to the westward." After this they would return at once to the ships, and no doubt would reach them a week before Sir John's death, for the record goes on to tell us that "He died on June 11th 1847", and it is pleasant to think that Sir John, before his death, would be made happy in knowing that they had at last solved the question of the North West Passage . . . [And so he died] "a man of great force of character, one of indomitable energy and courage; an ardent geographer; an enthusiastic devotee of science, a good officer and seaman, and above all a sincere and true Christian".*

The *Fox* returned to England in September 1859.

At the time of our journeys, the wreckage of the ships had never been found, although most other vessels that had ventured into these waters and been lost had been located. Then in 2014 John Geiger's expedition, mounted by the Royal Canadian Geographical Society, using solar imaging, located the wreck of the *Erebus* to the west of O'Reilly Island in the Queen Maude Gulf, a treacherous area full of shallows. This finding caused huge excitement.

The location added weight to the belief that those aboard were on course to make the discovery the Franklin Expedition had set out to achieve.

Two years almost to the day, as this book was going to press, the second ship, HMS *Terror*, was discovered in shallow water in the centre of Terror Bay on the southwest corner of King William Island, about sixty miles to the north of HMS *Erebus*, by a survey vessel dragging an underwater camera. The image showed her standing upright with nearly all her windows intact, in virtually pristine condition. This has electrified the world of marine archaeology and has ended the greatest Arctic mystery of all time. In the course of innumerable searches made for Franklin's two ships over the past 166 years, vast tracts of the Arctic were charted for the first time.

The Arctic Medal that Sir John Franklin received posthumously, together with one or two other small items, has been presented by my sister and I to the museum in Stromness from where most sailing expeditions to the Arctic departed.

THE HECLA/FURY STRAIT

Just as this book was about to go to press, David set a new world record by completing a transit of the seventh route through the Northwest Passage. The Labrador Narrows, known popularly as the Hecla/Fury Strait, is a channel 105 miles in length and from 30 miles wide narrowing at one point to only half a mile across. Consequently it is normally blocked with ice from both directions. No private vessel had been through this route since Parry first discovered it back in 1822.

Having transitted the other six routes, David was determined to conquer this last one, but knew that it was not an undertaking for the faint-hearted. It had been planned that I should go with him but at the last minute his son asked to go. They set off from Julianehåb (Quaqortoq) on 17th August 2016. Encountering very rough seas (which David described as 'atrocious') and formidable currents with a huge tidal range in the Hudson Strait, they entered the Foxe Basin, proceeding 350 miles north through fog in poorly charted water, finally reaching the Labrador Narrows, which they exited on 26th August. In doing so, David became the first person to transit all seven routes of the Northwest Passage.

DAVID SCOTT COWPER: LIST OF RECORDS

1974 *Airedale*, 30-foot sloop (owned by DSC)
Participated in and completed the Observer Paired Round Britain Race with Colin Lindsay MacDougall – out of 61 starters and 39 finishers, *Airedale* was eighth, taking 29 days

1976 *Airedale*
Participated in and completed the Observer Single-handed Transatlantic Race (OSTAR)

1978 *Ron Glas*, 50-foot Chinese junk rig, designed by Angus Primrose (owned by Jock McLeod)
Participated in and completed the Observer Paired Round Britain Race with Jock McLeod

1979–80 *Ocean Bound*, 41-foot sloop (owned by DSC)
Became the fastest person to sail solo round the world via the Capes, beating Sir Francis Chichester's time at sea and gaining an entry in *The Guinness Book of Records*

1981–2 *Ocean Bound* (owned by DSC)
Sailed solo around the world against the prevailing winds, and around all five Capes, setting a new record and gaining another entry into *The Guinness Book of Records* as the fastest person to sail single-handedly round the world in both directions, and the first person to have sailed both ways around Cape Horn in a circumnavigation

1984–5 *Mabel E. Holland*, 42-foot ex-RNLI 'Watson' lifeboat (owned by DSC)
First person to circumnavigate the world solo in a motorboat

1986–90 *Mabel E. Holland*
First person to circumnavigate the world solo via the Northwest Passage

Note: There was considerable interest by the media worldwide after the first and second circumnavigations, and much further interest after subsequent 'Firsts'

2001–4 *Polar Bound*, 48-foot custom-built motorboat (owned by DSC)
Undertook his fifth solo circumnavigation down to the Antarctic and back through the Northwest Passage in the High Arctic, west to east

2009-11 *Polar Bound*
Undertook another solo circumnavigation, transiting the Northwest Passage east to west, then on down to the Antarctic, crossing the Antarctic Circle and continuing across the Southern Ocean, taking in South Africa, Australia and New Zealand (in the 40- and 50-degree latitudes), and then up again to the Arctic, transiting the Northwest Passage *for the fourth time*, from west to east

2012 *Polar Bound*, with Jane Maufe
Departing from Whitehaven, Cumbria, UK, transited the Northwest Passage from east to west via the Davis Strait, Lancaster Sound,

Barrow Strait, Viscount Melville Sound, McClure Strait, Beaufort Sea and Bering Strait, thus gaining the record for the first people in a private vessel to transit the entire passage via the most northerly route

2013 *Polar Bound*, with Jane Maufe
Return voyage from Petersburg, Alaska via the Northwest Passage, west to east, to *Polar Bound*'s base in Scotland

Awards from professional bodies, and others

1980
Awarded Chichester Silver Trophy for the fastest solo circumnavigation of the world, presented by HRH The Duke of Edinburgh at the Royal Yacht Squadron in Cowes

Elected by the press as one of the twelve Men of the Year at a luncheon held at the Savoy Hotel and run by RADAR (the Royal Association of Disability and Rehabilitation)

Made an Honorary Life Member of the Royal Northumberland Yacht Club

1982
Awarded The Seamanship Medal by the Royal Cruising Club

Made a Freeman of the City of Newcastle in recognition of two circumnavigations of the world

Made an Honorary Life Member of the Royal Institution of Chartered Surveyors' Sailing Club

1990
Attended a reception at No.10 Downing Street in recognition of his first transit of the Northwest Passage

1991
Elected Yachtsman of the Year by the Press

Made an Honorary Life Member of the Royal Institute of Navigation

Made an Honorary Life Member of the Cruising Association

Presented to Princess Diana aboard the *Mabel E. Holland* in Newcastle following his first Northwest Passage voyage

1993

Northwest Passage Solo by David Scott Cowper published by Seafarer Books

2013

Awarded the Blue Water Medal at the New York Yacht Club by the Cruising Club of America

Awarded the Tilman Medal (for High Latitude sailing) by the Royal Cruising Club